ASPECTS OF BUDDHA-DHAMMA

by Angraj Chaudhary

Pariyatti Press

Pariyatti Press
an imprint of
Pariyatti Publishing
www.pariyatti.org

First Pariyatti Press Edition – 2019
ISBN: 978-1-681723-65-5 (softcover)
ISBN: 978-1-681723-66-2 (ePub)
ISBN: 978-1-681723-67-9 (Mobi)
ISBN: 978-1-681722-44-3 (PDF)
Library of Congress Control Number: 2018966721

Contents

Abbreviations of Pāli Books

A	Aṅguttara Nikāya
AA	Aṅguttara Nikāya Aṭṭhakathā
AT	Aṅguttara Nikāya Ṭikā
ApA	Apadāna Aṭṭhakathā
Aṭṭha	Aṭṭhasālinī
Bu	Buddhavaṃsa
BuA	Buddhavaṃsa Aṭṭhakathā
Cp	Cariyā piṭaka
CpA	Cariyā piṭaka Aṭṭhakathā
Cv	Cūlavagga (Vinaya piṭaka)
D	Dīgha Nikāya
DA	Dīgha Nikāya Aṭṭhakathā
DT	Dīgha Nikāya Ṭikā
Dh	Dhammapada
DhA	Dhammapada Aṭṭhakathā
Dhs	Dhammasaṅgaṇi
DhsA	Dhammasaṅgaṇi Aṭṭhakathā
It	Itivuttaka
ItA	Itivuttaka Aṭṭhakathā
J	Jātaka
Kh	Khuddakapāṭha
KhA	Khuddakapāṭha Aṭṭhakathā
M	Majjhima Nikāya
MA	Majjhima Nikāya Aṭṭhakathā
MT	Majjhima Nikāya Ṭikā
Mv	Mahāvagga (Vinaya piṭaka)
Mil	Milindapañho
Mnid	Mahāniddesa
Pāci	Pācittiya
PāciA	Pācittiya Aṭṭhakathā
Pārā	Pārājika
PārāA	Pārājika Aṭṭhakathā
Ps	Paṭisambhidāmagga
Pv	Petavatthu
PvA	Petavatthu Aṭṭhakathā
S	Saṃyutta Nikāya
SA	Saṃyutta Nikāya Aṭṭhakathā
ST	Saṃyutta Nikāya Ṭikā
Sn	Suttanipāta

SnA	Suttanipāta Aṭṭhakathā
Th	Theragāthā
ThA	Theragāthā Aṭṭhakathā
Thi	Therīgāthā
ThiA	Therīgāthā Aṭṭhakathā
Ud	Udāna
UdA	Udāna Aṭṭhakathā
Vbh	Vibhaṅga
Vin	Vinayapiṭaka
Vism	Visuddhimaggo
Vv	Vimānavatthu
VvA	Vimānavatthu Aṭṭhakathā

Note: Verse numbers, not page numbers, are given from Dhammapada, Suttanipāta, Theragāthā and Therīgāthā. Volume number and page number of books like Dīgha Nikāya and Majjhima Nikāya are given. All references, unless otherwise mentioned, are given from books published by V.R.I., Dhammagiri in 1998.

Abbreviations of English Books

Abh Sts	Nyanaponika Thera, Abhidhamma Studies, BPS, Kandy, 1976 B D (Tr)
Aes.	B. Croce, Aesthetic Noonday Press, 2000
AL	William Hart, The Art of Living, VRI, Dhammagiri
AMIMT	M.W. Steinberg, Arthur Miller and the Idea of Modern Tragedy
ATP&FA	S.A Butcher, Aristotle's Theory of Poetry and Fine Art, Dover Publication, London, 1907
BD	I B Horner, The Book of the Discipline, PTS London
BE	Ven Saddhatissa, Buddhist Ethics, Wisdom Publication, Boston, 1997 p. 22
BGS (Trs)	F.L. Woodward & E.M. Hare, The Book of the Gradual Sayings
BGB	Ananda K. Coomaraswamy, Buddha and the Gospel of Buddhism, New York, Putnam, 1916
B&H	Narada Thera, The Buddha and His Teachings
B&HD	Dr B.R. Ambedkar, The Buddha and His Dhamma
BHL	T.W. Rhys Davids, Buddhism: Its History and Literature, G.P Putnam's Sons, New York & London, 1896
BKS (Trs)	F.L. Woodward & E.M. Hare, The Book of the Kindred Sayings
BL	Coleridge, Biographia Literaria, Oxford The Clarenden Press, 1907
BMM	M.M. Sukumar Dutta, Buddhist Monks and Monasteries, Motilal Banarsidass, Delhi, 1998

Bu Wisd	George Grimm, Buddhist Wisdom, Motilal Banarsidass, Delhi, 2008
CA	Matthew Arnold, Culture and Anarchy, Cambridge Library Collection, 2011
CAEW	A. Chaudhary, Comparative Aesthetics: East and West, EBL, Delhi, 1994
CDB, (Tr)	Bhikkhu Bodhi, The Connected Discourses of the Buddha, Wisdom Publications, Boston, 2000
DB (Tr)	T.W. Rhys Davids, Dialogues of the Buddha, Oxford University Press, London 1910
DBRRM	George Grimm, The Doctrine of the Buddha: The Religion of Reason and Meditation, Pilgrims Publishing, 2002
Dial P, (Tr)	B. Jowett, Dialogues of Plato, Macmillan & Co. London, 1892
EAM	T.S. Eliot, Essays: Ancient and Modern, Houghton Miffin Harcourt, 2014
EBPL	Angraj Chaudhary, Essays on Buddhism and Pali Literature, Eastern Book Linkers, Delhi, 1994 Edu Sys Hin Santosh Kumar, Das, The Education System of the Ancient Hindus
En Br	Encyclopaedia Britanicca, Reprinted 1995
EV The (Tr)	K.R. Norman, The Elders' Verses, Theragāthā, P.T.S, London, Luzac and Company, Ltd., 1969 EV Thi (Tr) K.R. Norman, The Elders' Verses, Therīgāthā, P.T.S, London, Luzac and Company, Ltd., 1971
GOD (Tr)	K.R. Norman, The Group of Discourses, Sutta Nipāta, Volume 1
Gol B	Sir James George Frazer, The Golden Bow, The Macmillan Company, New York, 1951
H Aes	B. Bosanquet, A History of Aesthetic, The McMillan Company, 1904
LCIR	Bernard Weinberg, A History of Literary Criticism in Italian Renaissance, Chicago University Press 1961
LDB, (Tr)	Maurice Walshe, The Long Discourses of the Buddha, Wisdom Publication, Boston, 1995
MANight	Aldous Huxley, Music at Night and Other Essays, Penguin Books, 1957
MAP	I. B Horner, The Major Anthologies of the Pali Canon, PTS London
MLD (Trs)	Bhikkhu Ñāṇamoli & Bhikkhu Bodhi, The Middle Length Discourses of the Buddha, Wisdom Publication, Boston, 1995
MLS	I.B. Horner, The Middle Length Sayings, PTS. London
Nal Uni	H.D. Sankalia, The Nalanda University, Oriental Publishers,

	Delhi, 1972
NDB	The Numerical Discourses of the Buddha, Bhikkhu Bodhi, Wisdom Publications, Boston
NRs	V. Raghavan, The Number of Rasas, Adyar Library and Research Centre, Madras, 1940
OD	The Oxford Dictionary
OPP	T.S. Eliot, On Poetry and Poets, Faber & Faber, London, 1957
ORD	The Oxford Reference Dictionary
PDFA	Edward Bullough, Psychical Distance as a Factor in Art and an Aesthetic Principle in Aesthetics: A Critical Anthology, ed by George Dickie & R.J Sclafani, Boston, 1989
Psalms EB,	(Tr) C.A. F Rhys Davids, Psalms of the Early Buddhists, P.T.S, London, Luzac and Company Ltd, 1964
Ps M (Tr)	Bhikkhu Ñāṇamoli, The Path of Discrimination, English Translation of Paṭisambhidāmagga, Buddhist Publication Society, Kandy, Sri Lanka
PsychoAEB	Lama Anagarika Govind, The Psychological Attitude of the Early Buddhist Philosophy, Shanti Niketan, 1939
Psycho&Zen	Eric Fromm, D.T. Suzuki, Psychoanalysis and Zen Buddhism, 1999
QKM	(Tr) T.W. Rhys Davids, The Questions of King Milinda
S E	T.S. Eliot, Selected Essays, Faber & Faber London, 1993
St Ph	Will Durant, The Story of Philosophy, Garden City Publishing Co. New York, 1927
TAH, (Tr)	S. Beal, Travel Accounts of Hiuen Tsang, London, 1905
TBD (Tr)	Ven Ñaṇamoli, A Treasury of the Buddha's Discourse from the Majjhima Nikāya, The Middle Length Sayings, PTS London
TNA	A.K. Coomaraswamy, The Transformation of Nature in Art, Cambridge Massachusetts, Harvard University Press 1954
WBT	Walpole Rahul, What the Buddha Taught? Reprinted by The Corporate of the Buddha Educational Foundation, Paper Back Edition, 1978
WLCM	Cleanth Brooks, The Waste Land; Critique of the Myth
WL	T.S. Eliot (Eds) C.B. Cox and Arnold, P. Hinchliff, Palgrave 1964
WWR	Schopenhaeur, The World as Will and Representation, Dover Publications Inc, 1966
2500 years	(Ed) P.V. Bapat, 2500 years of Buddhism, Publication Division, Sixth Reprint, 1997

Introduction

This book is a collection of twenty-eight essays written over a period of two decades. Most of these essays are published in different journals and proceedings of seminars, both national and international. The journals and proceedings include Journal of the Department of Buddhist Studies, University of Delhi; Proceedings of the International Buddhist Conference, Indosan Nipponji, (Japanese Temple) Bodh Gaya; Somaiya Publications Pvt Ltd, Mumbai; Indian Institute of Advanced Study, Shimla and Aryan Books International, New Delhi; Nava Nalanda Mahāvihāra, Nalanda Publications and Dr. Gustav Roth Felicitation Volume, Patna.

These essays can be broadly put into ten groups. In the first group comes the essay entitled 'Why Dhammacakkaṃ?' which explains why Dhamma has been compared with a wheel (*cakka*). In the *Rathakāra Sutta* of the *Aṅguttara Nikāya*, the Buddha makes it clear why physical and vocal actions of monks and nuns should be free from all kinds of faults and flaws in order for Dhamma to work as efficiently as the wheel which has no fault and no crookedness. Just as a wheel which is free from faults and flaws moves efficiently and does not fall on the ground, goes on and on, conquers time and distance, so the Dhamma free from faults, if practiced and developed by monks and nuns, will help them much and they will not 'swerve, circle around, go astray and meet their fall'. The Buddha compared his Dhamma with a wheel because the wheel is the greatest invention of mankind to conquer time and distance.

Essays in the second group like 'Nature of Buddha-Dhamma', 'Spiritual Foundation of Buddha-Dhamma', 'Walking on the Noble Eightfold Path', 'Buddhism: Where Philosophy and Religion Converge' and 'Humanism of Early Buddhism' bring out different aspects of Buddha-Dhamma. When I say Buddha-Dhamma I mean the teachings and views of the Buddha as found in the Pāli Tipitaka. These essays explain that the Dhamma taught by the Buddha is based on universal laws that operate in the moral-spiritual world. As it is founded on experience and reason, so it is scientific. There is nothing sectarian about it and it can be practised by all belonging to any race, religion or sect. Some of these essays explain the laws such as the Law of Dependent Origination that the Buddha discovered. This law makes it clear how suffering is caused and how it can be ended. One of the essays in this group shows how observation of precepts helps one get rid of impurities and defilements of mind, the other shows that the Buddha was more concerned with the mind than with the matter. He believed that *cittena nīyati loko. cittena parikassati* i.e. the world is led around by mind and by mind it's dragged here and there. It is true he gave more emphasis on purifying mind, which is the Gaṅgotri of all actions, wholesome or unwholesome but he did not lose sight of the material aspects of life and people's material welfare.

Another essay of this group shows how the philosophy propounded by the Buddha can be lived in life. 'Walking on the Noble Eightfold Path' is the action-plan of his philosophy. This makes it into a religion. How it is true Dhamma has been shown in 'Walking on the Eightfold Path is True Dhamma'.

Essays in the third group deal with Buddha's Social philosophy. 'Buddha's Law of Kamma and Rebirth vis-à-vis Social Order', 'Buddha's Social Philosophy in relation to Equality, Freedom and Justice', 'Buddha's Pragmatic Approach to Social Harmony and Material Prosperity', 'Buddha's Spirit of Tolerance', 'Buddha's Altruism', 'Buddha's Concept of Good Governance', and 'Was the Buddha a Misogynist?' throw light on his view on caste, on good governance, on how problems of law and order can be solved, on human rights, on the duties of a king or Government and on his view of women.

Essays in the fourth group examine whether Buddha's views are relevant to modern issues. 'Buddhism and Modern Issues', 'Bioethics and the Buddha' and 'Ecological Reflections in Pāli Canonical Literature' are important essays in this group.

One very important essay entitled; 'Causes for the Enduring Greatness of the Nalanda Mahāhavihāra' in the fifth group clearly explains the Buddha's view of education.

In the sixth group are essays on the cardinal teachings of the Buddha. 'Four Noble Truths'; 'Brahmavihāra'; 'Buddha's Anattavāda: Why?'; 'Paṭiccasamuppāda', 'Buddha's Theory of Kamma and Rebirth' and 'Ethicization: an Important Constituent Element of the Buddha Dhamma' enunciate them.

'Buddha's Concept of Mind and World Peace', and 'Mechanism of Vipassana' are essays in the seventh group. How one's peace of mind and world peace can be attained by driving out negativities like anger, jealousy, greed, etc. has been shown in the first essay. The second essay 'Mechanism of Vipassana' explains the process to purify mind of different impurities and defilements by practicing Vipassana.

In the eighth group, a very important essay entitled 'Bhāvanāmayā paññā—an Invaluable Contribution to World Culture' highlights that not only knowing 'the best that has been thought and said' as pointed out by Matthew Arnold can be said to be the best element of culture, but its living in life as said by the Buddha that constitutes the best element of culture. Therefore, '*Bhāvanāmayā Paññā*' and not *Sutamayā Paññā* and *Cintāmayā Paññā* is the Buddha's invaluable contribution to world culture.

'Nature of Pāli Literature' is the only essay in the ninth group. It brings out the salient features of Pāli literature and also shows how this literature takes off from where other literatures based on imagination land. It also underlines the importance of Pāli literature by analyzing that this literature delineates *śānta rasa* (quietistic sentiment).

In the tenth group also there is only one essay entitled 'Ethicization of the Concept of Beauty: A Great Contribution by the Buddha'. In this essay it has been shown that the Buddha does not put a premium on physical beauty but says that one whose mind is free from impurities like anger, jealousy, etc. and who is full of love, sympathy, compassion, and sympathetic joy is really beautiful..

It is true that there are repetitions in the essays collected here. One reason is that each essay was written for a different audience. Therefore, the same thing was repeated. The other most important reason is that the Buddha saw the genesis of all problems and their solutions in the mind. An impure mind is the spring of all evils, of all kinds of problems and sufferings. And a pure mind is the panacea for all problems. Therefore the crux of his teaching is how to purify the mind. And the mind can be purified by observing moral precepts (*sīla*), attaining concentration (*samādhi*) and developing insight wisdom (*prajñā*). So the importance of these three cornerstones of the Buddha's teaching has been shown everywhere. Whether it is a spiritual problem or a social or material problem, the role of the mind is great. *Sīla, samādhi and paññā* find place in practically all the essays collected here.

I sincerely thank Pariyatti, particularly Brihas Sarathy, the Executive Director, for showing interest in this collection of different aspects of Buddha-Dhamma and for publishing it from Pariyatti.

Āṣāḍha Pūrṇimā
Angraj Chaudhary

Why Dhammacakkaṃ?

We all know why the Buddha was not inclined to teach the deep, difficult to understand and subtle Dhamma that he had realized, to the people of the world. We also know that at the request of Sahampati Brahmā, he made up his mind to teach. When he saw that the group of five bhikkhus, who were once waiting upon him when he was engaged in practicing austere penances and had left him thinking that he had gone astray, could learn this Dhamma, he decided to go to them and teach the Dhamma. On his way to Kashi he met an Ājīvaka, Upaka by name, who asked him who he was and who was his teacher. Upaka was hesitant to believe his words when the Buddha said that he was an arahant and that he had attained knowledge himself without any teacher[1] but he could not dare contradict him because he could see that his sense faculties were calm and serene and his complexion was very bright and clear-—an irrefutable proof of his spiritual attainment. The Buddha also further said that he was going to Kashi to set in motion the wheel of the Dhamma.[2]

He went there and taught the Dhamma to the group of five bhikkhus. We also know that the first thing he taught them was to avoid the two extremes of indulging in sensual pleasures and practicing austere penances. The first is 'among sense-pleasures, addiction to attractive sense-pleasures, low, of the villager, of the average man, unariyan, not connected with the goal'[3]... and the other is 'addiction to self-torment, ill, unariyan, not connected with the goal.'[4] By teaching them this Dhamma, his first aim was to disabuse their minds of the efficacy of austere practices in realizing the highest good and also to refute the premise that 'pleasure cannot be gained by pleasure but pleasure can be gained by pain'[5]. He learnt it from his own experience that no amount of austere practice can enable one to attain the highest good. Therefore the Dhamma that he taught was the *majjhimā paṭipadā* known as the Noble Eightfold Path, also called the middle path consisting of *sīla, samādhi* and *paññā*. All that he taught them was not based on hearsay or on his intellectual reflection but on his own experience. He

---

1. Mv p. 11 (V.R.I. edition. Unless otherwise mentioned all books referred to here are published from VRI, Dhammagiri in 1998) *Ahañhi arahâ loke, ahaṃ satthâ anuttaro/ Ekomhi Sammâsaṃbuddho, sîtibhûtosmi nibbuto//*
2. ibid., *Dhammacakkaṃ pavattetuṃ, gacchāmi kāsinaṃ puraṃ.*
3. BD p. 15
4. ibid.
5. M2 See *Bodhirājakumāra Sutta.*
Na kho sukhena sukhaṃ adhigantabbaṃ, dukkhena kho sukhaṃ adhigantabban' ti.

was convinced that neither indulgence in sensual pleasures nor practice of austerities could lead one to the attainment of the highest good.

Then he went on to teach them the four noble truths. The first noble truth is a ubiquitous fact of life. All sentient beings suffer from one kind of suffering or another. The Buddha said that suffering is not only physical and mental but also there is a third kind of suffering which is the source of the first two kinds of suffering. It is to be born again and again with five *khandhas* (aggregates). The longer one moves in the cycle of birth and death, the longer he suffers from physical and mental suffering. When he taught the second noble truth, he propounded his philosophy. Craving and aversion are the causes of suffering. This he explained with the help of the Law of Dependent Origination. His practice of Vipassana had enabled him to annihilate the causes of suffering. He says that suffering can be ended. Finally, the fourth noble truth, he says, is the way leading to the cessation of suffering. This is called the Noble Eightfold Path. He had walked on it and had attained a peaceful state of mind. Thus we see that unlike other philosophers, like Heraclites and Leibnitz he comes out with an action-plan to put into practice his philosophy. Philosophy put into practice and lived in life is religion. So the philosophy propounded by the Buddha is not barren like Leibnitz's, for how can his (Leibnitz's) monadology help solve the existential problem of mankind, which is suffering? Compared to the Buddha's philosophy even Heraclites' philosophy is barren because his understanding that things are in a constant state of flux could not enable him to develop *nirveda* (non-attachment).

The Buddha also goes deep into each of the four noble truths so that it can be thoroughly clear at the experiential level. He explains each of them from the view point of *sacca ñāṇa* (the knowledge of truth), *kicca ñāṇa* (the knowledge gained by trying to understand the truth thoroughly) and *kata ñāṇa* (the knowledge gained by thoroughly understanding the truth at the experiential level). All that is suffering has to be completely comprehended (*pariññeyyaṃ*) and when one comprehends it, it is said it has been comprehended (*pariññātaṃ*). The second truth is that suffering has a cause. This cause has to be abandoned (*pahātabbaṃ*) and when one abandons it, it is said it has been abandoned (*pahīṇaṃ*). The third truth—the cessation of suffering is to be realized (*sacchikātabbaṃ*) and when one has realized it, it is said that it has been realized (*sacchikataṃ*). The fourth noble truth must be developed, must be made to become (*bhāvetabbaṃ*) and when it is developed and made to become i.e. when one has walked on the Noble Eightfold Path, it is said is has been developed (*bhāvitaṃ*). Thus each truth has three phases (*tiparivaṭṭaṃ*) and only when all four truths are understood in twelve aspects (*dvādasākāraṃ*) the vision of knowledge (*ñāṇadassana*) is purified.

Only after Samaṇa Gotama had purified his vision of knowledge like this, he became the Buddha, 'thoroughly awakened with the supreme full awakening.'[6] When he thoroughly comprehended each truth, 'vision arose, knowledge arose, wisdom arose, higher knowledge arose, light arose' about something not heard before.[7] This was a sort of 'eureka' for him in the spiritual domain. This was his vision of knowledge–*ñāṇa dassana* not only knowledge but its vision at the experiential level. He came to know at the experiential level that 'Freedom of mind is for me unshakable, this is the last birth, there is not now again-becoming.'[8] While the Buddha was giving this discourse, Dhamma vision—dustless, stainless—arose to the Venerable Koṇḍañña that "whatever is of the nature to uprise, all that is of the nature to stop."[9] In other words, Venerable Koṇḍañña was convinced that suffering could be ended. Suffering has a cause. If its cause is removed, suffering will end. This was the first ever success achieved by the Buddha when he set the Dhamma-wheel in motion.

Now the question is why does he call his Dhamma a wheel? Why is it said that the Dhamma-wheel was set in motion? Is Dhamma compared with a wheel (simile or *upamālaṇkāra*) or is it regarded as a wheel (metaphor or *rūpaka alaṇkāra*) or does the wheel belong to Dhamma (*Dhammassa cakkaṃ*, like the *Buddhassa Dhammaṃ*—an example of case compound or *tappurisa samāsa*)? Or can it be interpreted as *Dhammañca cakkañca* in which case it will be a copulative compound or *dvandva samāsa?*

Before I give my own explanation I would like to take you to the mass of explanations given by the celebrated Pāli commentators. In the *Sīlakkhandhavagga Abhinavaṭīkā* of the *Brahamajāla Sutta*[10] *Dhammacakkaṃ* has been explained as '*Dhammo eva cakkanti Dhammacakkaṃ*' i.e. Dhamma as a wheel or simply Dhamma-wheel. Here Dhamma has been seen as a wheel. It has been said here that this *Dhammacakka* is of two types, *paṭivedha ñāṇa* and *desanā ñāṇa.* The *Khandhavagga Aṭṭhakathā*, besides explaining *Dhammacakkaṃ* in the way it has been explained above has also explained it as what is *paṭivedha ñāṇa* (penetrating knowledge) and what is *desanā ñāṇa* (discoursing knowledge). *Paṭivedha ñāna* is that *ñāṇa* with which Samaṇa Gotama comprehended the four noble truths each in three phases and in all twelve aspects and became the Enlightened One at the Bodhimaṇḍa (under the Bodhi tree) and *desanā ñāṇa* is that *ñāṇa* with

6. BD p. 17

7. Mv, p. 14 '*Pubbe ananussutesu dhammesu cakkhuṃ udapādi, ñāṇaṃ udapādi, paññā udapādi, vijjā udapādi, āloko udapādi.*'

8. The Book of the Discipline, p. 17.

9. ibid.

10. DT p. 65

which he explained the four noble truths each in three phases and in all twelve aspects and set the wheel of Dhamma in motion.[11] In the *Saṃyutta Nikāya Aṭṭhakathā* also *Dhammacakkaṃ* has been explained as *paṭivedha ñāṇa* and *desanā ñāṇa.*[12] In the *Mahāvaggaṭīkā* of the *Saṃyutta Nikāya*[13] it has been given a new explanation. Because *dhammas* like *saddhindriya* (faculty of faith) etc. are set in motion like a wheel so the whole or the multitude is called *Dhammacakkaṃ*. Because *Dhamma* itself is a *cakka*, so setting in motion *Dhamma* is like setting in motion the *cakka* and vice versa. As it is set in motion by *Dhamma* or by *dhammacariyā* so it is called *Dhammacakkaṃ*[14]. In the *Yuganaddha vagga* of this book *Dhammacakkaṃ* has been translated as the wheel of the True Idea and has been defined in the following words[15].

"In what sense Wheel of the True Idea? He sets rolling the True Idea and (that itself is) the Wheel, thus it is the Wheel of the True Idea. He sets rolling the Wheel and the True Idea (as well), thus it is the Wheel of the True Idea. He sets rolling by means of the True Idea, thus...He sets rolling by means of the habit of the True Idea, thus... Standing in the True Idea, he sets rolling, thus Established in the True Idea, he sets rolling, thus... Establishing (others)...Attained to mastery in the True Idea... making (others) attain to mastery in the True Idea... with True Idea dominant, he sets rolling, thus... And that Wheel of the True Idea is not to be stopped by ascetic or brahman or deity or Māra or Brahmā or anyone in the world, thus it is the Wheel of the True Idea."

In the same way the *Paṭisaṃbhidāmagga* goes on to say that 'the faith faculty is a True Idea and he sets rolling that True Idea, thus it is the Wheel of True Idea.[16] In the same manner *viriya* (energy), *sati* (mindfulness), *samādhi* (concentration) and *paññā* (understanding) all faculties in the sense of dominance, all five powers having the same name in the sense of unshakability, all seven *bojjhaṅgas* (enlightenment factors), constituents of the Noble Eightfold Path in the sense of outlet, the path in the sense of cause, the foundations of mindfulness in the sense of establishment, the right endeavours in the sense of endeavouring, the bases for success in the sense of succeeding, the actualities in the sense of suchness are each a True

---

11. SA 2 p. 256 *Yena ñāṇena tiparivaṭṭaṃ dvādasākāraṃ dhammacakkaṃ pavattesi.*
12. ST. 2.3.78 *Dhammacakkan'ti cetaṃ desanāñāṇassāpi nāṇaṃ, paṭived- hañāṇassāpīti.*
13. ST 2.243
14. Ps2 pp. 40-41 *Dhammañca pavatteti cakkañcāti dhammacakkaṃ, cakkañca pavatteti dhammañcāti dhammacakkaṃ. Dhammena pavattetīti dhammacakkaṃ, dhammacariyāya pavattetīti dhammacakkaṃ*
15. Ps, English Translation p. 334
16. (Tr) Bhikkhu Ñāṇamoli See pp. 341-42 of the English translation of the Ps.

Idea and he sets rolling that True Idea, thus it is the Wheel of True Idea.[17] In the same way other dhammas have been pointed out as True Ideas and he sets rolling those True Ideas. Thus they are each the Wheel of True Ideas.

We have seen so far that *Dhammacakkaṃ* has been explained as 'Dhamma -wheel.' It is a *karmadhāraya samāsa* (adjective compound) and not a *tappurisa* (accusative) one as its English translation 'the wheel of Dhamma' seems to denote. However, in the commentary of the *Paṭisaṃbhidāmagga* it has been interpreted as a compound case (*dvandva*) also. It is said here that while teaching Dhamma to the five bhikkhus at Isipatanamigadāya the Buddha rolled it like a wheel in order to kill all the *kilesas* of those who were being taught. It has been taken here as a weapon (*āyudha*). But nowhere else in the commentarial literature has it been interpreted as an accusative compound. It is not the 'wheel of Dhamma' on the analogy of the 'horse of Rama.' But it is a wheel of Dhamma which indicates that the wheel is made of Dhamma just as 'the wheel of gold (*svarṇa cakra*) means the wheel made of gold. Dhamma itself is the wheel. English translators like I.B. Horner understood the difficulty inherent in translating this term. That is why, lest there should be any confusion, they took sophisticated care to translate *Dhammacakkaṃ* as Dhamma-wheel denoting clearly that Dhamma itself is a wheel. Those who translate *Dhammacakkaṃ* as the wheel of Dhamma are also right because they do not interpret 'the wheel of Dhamma on the analogy of 'the horse of Rama.'

Of the various meanings of the preposition 'of' in the English language such as 'expressing the relationship between a part and a whole', 'indicating an association between two entities typically one of belonging', and 'indicating the material constituting something' etc. (See Concise Oxford Dictionary, Tenth Edition) 'of Dhamma' should be interpreted in the third sense and not in the second sense. But one has to admire the sophisticated care taken by translators like I.B. Horner who translated *Dhammacakkaṃ* as 'Dhamma-wheel' lest there should be any confusion if translated as the 'wheel of Dhamma'.

It is clear from most of the commentaries that *Dhammacakkaṃ* is Dhamma-wheel. If at one place it has been explained as a copulative compound (*dvandva samāsa*)-*Dhammañca cakkañca*-it may look ingenious but it was not necessary to explain it this way. For is it not implied that when the Buddha was teaching Dhamma to the five bhikkhus, *kilesas* or *adhammas* were sure to take to their heels for how can darkness remain when there is light or how can *kilesas* continue to be there when Dhamma takes root in their hearts?

---

17. ibid.

We have seen that most of the commentators interpret *Dhammacakkaṃ* as Dhamma-wheel which means, as has been shown above, that Dhamma itself is a wheel or this wheel is made of Dhamma—*Dhammo eva cakkaṃ*. But the million-dollar question is why Dhamma has been compared with a wheel or why Dhamma has been conceived as a wheel? This question remains unanswered in the *Aṭṭhakathās*. Why wheel? Why not something else?

Venerable Narada Thera interprets *'Dhammacakkaṃ'* as the 'Kingdom of Righteousness' or the 'wheel of Truth.' His 'Kingdom of Righteousness' has the same flavour as Christians' 'Kingdom of God' has. But when he interprets it as the wheel of the Dhamma, he does not explain why 'wheel' has been used here and what its exact meaning is.

T.W. Rhys Davids in the introduction to his translation of the *Dhammacakkappavattana Sutta* (Foundation of Kingdom of Righteousness, see The Sacred Books of The East, ed. by F. Max Muller, Motilal Banarsidass Publishers, Delhi, Reprint 2001, pp. 140-14) says that he does not agree with the interpretations given by some scholars that this means 'the turning of the wheel of the law' as it has been usually rendered by scholars like Mr. Alabaster and Mr. Da Cuñha. (See ibid. pp. 140-141) [Mr Alabaster said that the Buddha 'did not attempt to teach the beginning of existence, but assumed it as a rolling circle of causes or effects. This was his circle or wheel of the law.' Mr Da Cuñha thinks "Gotama ignored the beginning, and was uncertain to the end."]

T.W. Rhys Davids thinks that these scholars were wrongly led by 'the praying wheels of Tibet' to misapprehend and mistranslate it. So he says. 'But who would explain a passage in the New Testament by a superstition current, say, in Spain in the twelfth century?'

Then he tries to interpret it in the light of what is said about the *cakkaratana* in the *Mahāsudassana Sutta* and translates *Dhammacakkappavattana Sutta* as 'Foundation of Kingdom of Righteousness'.

But this interpretation also does not come close to the Buddha's intention of choosing *cakka* as the symbol of his Dhamma.

One reason to my mind why Dhamma was called a wheel is that it is the symbol of forward movement, of progress. The wheel is the greatest invention of mankind. It brought about a revolution in the field of transportation. With the help of wheels, very heavy load can be carried a long distance with ease and comfort. Imagine people carrying something like a log of wood by dragging it. This process of carrying it would not only require more labourers but it would also make them sweat because of the quantum of resistance caused by the friction with the earth which they would be required to overcome. Almost the entire length of the log would touch the ground and the resistance they would have to overcome would be tremendous. Thus its transportation from one place to another would not be easy and smooth. But we know that if the log of wood is placed on a carriage with wheels, there would be no great problem carrying it. Why? Because the wheel has been designed in such a way that only a small part of it touches the ground at a point of time and at that time the energy required to overcome the resistance caused by friction with the earth will be minimum. The better the design of the wheel, the easier it is to carry things without encountering much difficulty. With a little pull and push it will go on and on and will not fall. Besides, the wheel also conquers time and space. Therefore, it is the symbol of victory over time and space. The Dhamma that the Buddha discovered was a discovery like this. He perfected this Dhamma for aeons and removed all faults and blemishes from it. It has become so efficient and smooth-going that it conquers time and takes one to *nibbāna* in a short time. Dhamma is called *akāliko* (timeless i.e. it produces results immediately) and *opaneyiko* (leading to goal, to *nibbāna*). The Buddha made it so smooth-going and perfect that once the wheel of the Dhamma is set in motion it is not going to be stopped, nor can it be rolled back by anyone whether he is a recluse, or a brahmin, or a deva or Māra or by Brahmā.

Why does the Buddha call his Dhamma a wheel and why does this symbol (wheel) stand for Dhamma can be understood if we just see what he says in the *Rathakāra Sutta* of the *Aṅguttara Nikāya.* In this *sutta* the Buddha narrates a story. Once upon a time a king named Pacetana asked his *rathakāra* (wheelwright) to make a pair of wheels for there was going to be a battle six months hence. In six months, less six days the wheelwright could finish only one wheel. When the king came to know this, he asked him if he would be able to finish the second wheel in six days. He replied in the affirmative. He finished the second wheel and went to the king with the pair of wheels. The king looked at both the wheels and finding no difference at all between them asked the wheelwright why he took such a long time to finish one and only six days to finish the other. The wheelwright then showed the difference between them by setting them rolling. The wheel which he had finished in six days, when set rolling 'kept rolling so long as the impulse that set it moving lasted. Then it circled round and round and fell to the ground.'[18] But the other wheel which he had taken a long time to finish when set rolling 'kept rolling so long as the impulse that set it going lasted, and then stood still, stuck to the axle.'[19] On being asked why so, the wheelwright explained that the wheel finished in six days was full of faults and flaws, its rim was crooked and so were its spokes and hub, but the wheel he took a long time to finish was faultless. Its rim was not crooked and its spokes and hub were also not so but they were perfect.

18. BGS p. 96.
19. ibid.

The Buddha then said that he himself was the wheelwright on that occasion. As an expert in the crooked ways, the faults and flaws of body, speech and thought he instructs the monks and nuns to abandon them and be as free from faults and crookedness as the wheel finished in six months less six days. If they do not abandon them, they will swerve, circle around, go astray and meet their fall. Each of them should make his/her Dhamma perfect, free from the crookedness of body, speech and thought. In other words, all their actions related to body, speech and mind must be pure otherwise they will fall away from Dhamma-Discipline. Dhamma should be developed, made much of, made pure and free from any kind of fault and flaw as the wheel—a symbol of going forward and conquering time and space.

As the Buddha had taken aeons to perfect his Dhamma in all the small details, so he taught his Dhamma also in great detail.

We have seen how he explained the four noble truths to five bhikkhus each with three phases and in all twelve aspects so that they might know and comprehend them thoroughly. His use of the words *'pariññeyyaṃ'* and *'pariññātaṃ'* are very significant. *'Parijānana'* expresses a higher stage of knowing than *'vijānana'* and *'sañjānana.'* In short, he perfected his knowledge and vision in the same way as the wheelwright had made his wheel, which would go on and on and would not fall to the ground. The Buddha had this efficiency of the wheel in his mind. Therefore, he chose this symbol, called his Dhamma *Dhammacakkaṃ* and set it (Dhamma-wheel) in motion. The Dhamma- wheel set in motion by him proved to be so effective and efficient that Aññāsikoṇdañña immediately understood the universal law that whatever arises passes away. The teaching (*Dhamma*) was very clearly grasped by Koṇdañña. And that is why when the Buddha had set the Dhamma-wheel in motion and Kondañña fully comprehended the Dhamma taught by him, the earth devas, the devas of the Four Great kings, the thirty devas, Yama devas, the happy devas etc. made this announcement that "the supreme Dhamma-wheel rolled thus by the Lord at Benaras in the deer-park at Isipatana cannot be rolled back by a recluse or brahmin or deva or by Māra or by Brahmā or by anyone in the world." It was a wonderful smooth-going and very effective wheel. Not only Aññāsikoṇdañña but his four friends also comprehended the Dhamma and became *arahants*. Then Yasa and his friends tasted *Dhamma rasa* and became *arahants*. And then many realized the Dhamma. The *Dhammacakka* began to move smoothly.

The wheel is a great invention of mankind as it is an efficient and effective means of forward movement. Any wheel could be regarded as effective and efficient, let alone a wheel, which is perfected by the Buddha himself.

People may ask if the wheel in the *Dhammacakkaṃ* stands for efficiency to conquer time and space then what about the wheel in the *bhavacakkaṃ?* What purpose does it serve here? Well, before answering this question let me say that the term *'bhavacakkaṃ'* is not found in the Canonical literature. The Buddha does not use this term. Later, the commentators use this term in order to explain *paṭiccasamuppāda* (the Law of Dependent Origination). *Paṭiccasamuppāda* explains how *'bhava'* is caused and how it can be destroyed. It explains the wheel of birth and death. Here also the wheel stands for efficient and quick movement. One is caught in the wheel of birth and death as quickly by the force of one's *kammas. Kammas* act as efficiently as *dhammas.* Both act as efficiently as a wheel. It is for this reason that the wheel, which is a symbol of conquering time and space is used in both the cases.

In the commentarial literature, *bhavacakkaṃ* is used to denote *Paṭiccasamuppāda* of which there does not seem to be a beginning and an end and *sansāracakkaṃ* is used to denote the beginninglessness of the world. If we try to interpret *Dhammacakkaṃ* in the light of these terms coined later we would be putting the cart before the horse. The wheel in *Dhammacakkaṃ* denotes efficiency in conquering time and space and the wheel in *bhavacakkaṃ* and *saṃsāracakkaṃ* denotes beginninglessness.

Nature of Buddha-Dhamma

Before I explain the nature of Buddha-dhamma and bring out its salient features, I would like to make a distinction between Bauddha-dhamma and Buddha-dhamma. Bauddha-dhamma, like Hindu dharma or Jain dharma seems to have a sectarian connotation. It seems to be meant exclusively for those who call themselves Buddhists and not for Hindus and Jains. Hindu dharma and Jain dharma are also meant respectively for Hindus and Jains, not for Buddhists. Buddha-dhamma, on the contrary, does not have any such narrow and sectarian connotation. It is the dhamma taught by the Buddha. And because the dhamma taught by the Buddha is based on universal laws that operate in the moral-spiritual world, so it is universal. It is also founded on experience and reason, so it is scientific. As it is scientific and based on universal laws, so it is universal in character. All can follow it, are free to follow it and derive benefit from it.

As physical laws operate in the physical world with inexorable regularity, so there are certain laws which operate in the moral-spiritual world. As fire cannot be extinguished by fire, so enmity cannot be appeased by enmity (*na hi verena verāni, sammantīdha kudācanaṃ*). Fire requires water to douse it, to put it out, so enmity can be appeased only by friendliness, non-hatred (*averena sammanti*). This is law eternal (*esa dhammo sanantano*).[20]

There is another law which operates as inexorably. If one develops negative feelings and plans to harm others, before one harms others one is first harmed by his own negative feelings. Anger that arises within him begins to burn him as soon as it arises. It causes harm to others, if at all it does, only later. Similarly cravings keep on consuming one and burning one. As soon as one craving is satisfied, others arise. Things one likes cause pleasant sensations in him. He wants them to continue. But they arise only to pass away. So he has more and more cravings for them and he suffers more and more. Similarly, things one does not like cause unpleasant sensations in him. He does not want them to continue, instead he wants them to stop. But they pass away only to arise again, so he has more and more aversions. Here one finds two laws operating. The Law of Dependent Origination explains that nothing arises without a cause. One's cravings are caused by pleasant or unpleasant sensations (*vedanā paccayā taṇhā*). One wants pleasant sensations to continue and unpleasant ones to pass away and one suffers because pleasant sensations do not last forever.[21]

---

20. Dh 5 *Na hi verena verāni, sammantīdha kudācanaṃ/ Averena ca sammanti, esa dhammo sanantano//*

21. S 1.108, *Yaṃ panāniccaṃ dukkhaṃ vipariṇāmadhammaṃ,*

They are fleeting and impermanent. This is the Law of Impermanence. All conditioned things are impermanent (*sabbe saṅkhārā aniccāti*)[22] and all that are impermanent cause suffering (*sabbe saṅkhārā dukkhāti*).[23]

And what are one's cravings due to? They are due to the nature of one's mind. So long as it lives in the world of desires and works out of ignorance, it is fickle and unsteady and like a monkey keeps on jumping from one object of desire to another. The Buddha made an in-depth study of the psychology of human mind and how it works. He also explains how one's immoral and unwholesome actions have three immoral roots, namely, *lobho* (craving) *doso* (aversion) and *moho* (ignorance) and one's moral and wholesome actions have three moral roots, namely–*alobho*, *adoso* and *amoho*. All these laws he discovered by practicing *Vipassana* meditation and realizing clearly at the level of experience the nature of reality. He also discovered that one's mind is the spring of all actions, good or bad that one performs. If one speaks or acts with an impure mind, misery follows him like the wheel that dogs the hooves of the ox and if he speaks or acts with a pure mind, happiness follows him like a shadow that never leaves.[24] In short, whatever action good or bad one performs in his life, one has to reap their results. It is clear from this that one is responsible for what one does. No god or outside force is responsible for his actions. One can oneself make or mar his fortune, and if one likes, he can fashion it after his heart's desire.

By practicing Vipassana meditation, the Buddha developed his wisdom and knew and saw (*jāna passa*) these laws at the experiential level and not only at the intellectual level. He did not learn about them by only reading about them or contemplating about them or listening to somebody explaining them. Practice of Vipassana meditation enabled him to have the first hand knowledge about them. Ubiquitous suffering that he saw in the world moved him deeply. This urged him to find out its cause and the *brahmacariyavāsa* that he took upon himself i.e. the vow to live a life of good conduct enabled him to discover the path by walking on which the cause of suffering could be eradicated. He propounded the four Noble Truths of suffering, its cause, its cessation and the Noble Eightfold Path leading to its cessation. He explained very lucidly with the help of the Law of Dependent Origination the cause of suffering and propounded confidently that if the cause of suffering was removed, suffering would cease to be. There would be no more suffering. But how to remove the causes of suffering? For

22. Dh 277 *Sabbe saṅkhārā aniccā ti, yadā paññāya passati/*

23. ibid. *Sabbe saṅkhārā dukkhā ti, yadā paññāya passati/*

24. Dh 1 *Manopubbaṃgamā dhammā, manoseṭṭhā manomayā/ Manasā ce paduṭṭhena, bhāsati vā karoti vā/ Tato naṃ dukkhamanveti, cakkaṃ va vahato padaṃ//* Dh 1&2 *Tato naṃ sukhamanveti, chāyāva anapāyinī/*

this, he prescribed the Noble Eightfold Path and said that in order to end one's suffering and to attain *nibbāna*—a state of desirelessness, one should walk on this path, which consists of *sīla* (observation of precepts), *samadhi* (practice of meditation) and *paññā* (development of insight wisdom). It is clear from this that his philosophy is quite different from the speculative philosophies propounded by other philosophers. To *Māluṅkyaputta*, the Buddha had made it clear that the philosophy he propounded about the Four Noble Truths has a direct bearing on man's existential problems of suffering and its cessation.[25] He did not exercise his mind to puzzle out the answers to ten *abyākata* or indeterminate questions.[26] But he explained the root cause of suffering and showed the path to eliminate it. The beauty of the Buddha's philosophy is its convergence into religion.[27] Living a religious life helps one understand Buddha's philosophy better and understanding his philosophy inspires one to live a religious life. In short, philosophy and religion complement each other. This has been rather succinctly shown in the *Mūlapariyāya Sutta.*[28]

By practicing Vipassana meditation, the Buddha observed very minutely what happened within himself. Watching his sensations arise and pass away within the framework of his body, he not only discovered the Law of Impermanence but also discovered the three roots of immoral actions. The Buddha rightly calls them three fires which burn one constantly. Pleasant sensations arise. One enjoys them and wants to have more of them but they arise to pass away leaving him insatiable and miserable. In the famous *Ādittapariyāya Sutta,*[29] the Buddha explains metaphorically the causes of one's burning. He also discovered that craving and aversion

---

25. M2. 101. *Kiñca, mālukyaputta, mayā byākataṃ? 'Idaṃ dukkhan'ti, mālukyaputta, mayā byākataṃ; 'ayaṃ dukkhasamudayo'ti- mayā byākataṃ; 'ayaṃ dukkhanirodho'ti- mayā byākataṃ; 'ayaṃ dukkhanirodhagāminī paṭipadā'ti- mayā byākataṃ. Kasmā cetaṃ, mālukyaputta, mayābyākataṃ? Etañhi, mālukyaputta, atthasaṃhitaṃ etaṃ ādibrahmacariyakaṃ nibbidāya virāgāya nirodhāya upasamāya abhiññāya sambodhāya nibbānāya saṃvattati.*

26. M2. 99. *'sassato loko'ti vā, 'asassato loko'ti vā, 'antavā loko'ti vā, 'anantavā loko'ti vā, 'taṃ jīvaṃ taṃ sarīran'ti vā, 'aññaṃ jīvaṃ aññaṃ sarīran'ti vā, 'hoti tathāgato paraṃ maraṇā'ti vā, 'na hoti tathā-gato paraṃ maraṇā'ti vā, 'hoti ca na ca hoti tathāgato paraṃ maraṇā'ti vā, 'neva hoti na na hoti tathāgato paraṃ maraṇā'ti vā"ti?*

27. ibid., pp. 254-255. See my essay entitled *Buddhism: Where Philosophy and Religion Converge* collected in this book.

28. See my essay entitled *The Mūlapariyāya Sutta—a Treatise of Buddhist Epistemology and Ontology collected in Essays on Buddhism and Pali Literature*. Eastern Book Linkers, Delhi 1994

29. Mv *Ādittapariyāya Sutta*

are born out of ignorance. If one realizes that all things of the world, even beautiful things, are in a constant state of flux, he will not crave for them. He will grow weary of them, develop non-attachment (*nirveda*) and consequently eliminate *rāga* and *dosa*. If he eliminates them, he no longer burns but he feels 'cool and quenched' here and now. Cravings and aversions manifest themselves in one's actions. One steals, commits adultery in order to satisfy one's cravings and one kills somebody because of hatred for him. So it is better for one to eliminate them. For eliminating them, one is required to follow certain moral precepts. If one abstains from stealing, one cuts down his greed; if one abstains from committing adultery, one keeps oneself from sexual desire--a form of craving and if one abstains from killing, one eliminates his hatred and aversion because one commits murder only when there is a great amount of hatred in him.

By observing these precepts, one can purify his physical actions and if he does not tell a lie, does not make a slanderous speech, does not speak harsh words, and does not talk uselessly, he can purify his vocal actions too.

Observation of such precepts forms the basis of the Dhamma taught by the Buddha. It goes a long way in planting peace in human society. Man's social life cannot be happy and peaceful without observing these social ethics. For one who leads an isolated life, on an island and is 'the monarch of all that he surveys', as Alexander Selkirk describes it, it does not matter whether he observes his precepts or not. But man is a social animal. His observance of these precepts is a necessary condition for living harmoniously in the society without disturbing the social fabric. Much of the trouble in society is man made and if members of the society strictly observe the precepts of social ethics, many of the troubles will not arise.

For maintaining peace and order in society, certain laws are made and citizens are asked to obey them so that there is no disturbance and breach of peace in society. They are afraid to break the laws as they fear punishment. But ethical codes of conducts which bring about subtle moral and spiritual change in man are not enforced upon them. They are taught to the members of the society so that they can observe them on their own, thinking them as do's and don'ts prescribed by religion and morality. These codes of conduct if followed rightly cultivate one's heart and ennoble his mind. Therefore it can be said without any hesitation that these social ethics lay the foundation of religion. The function of religion is to enable people to live in peace and harmony. Observance of these social ethics creates a congenial atmosphere for peace and harmony to grow.

But these precepts have a deeper, subtler and nobler role to play in religious life. So long as one's springs of actions are craving, aversion and ignorance, one performs immoral actions and burns in their fire. More and more of craving will arise in him which will bind him to the wheel of existence. He will be born again and again and suffer from old age, disease and death and from sorrow and lamentation. So, one has to extinguish these fires. Unless one replaces greed by non-greed, aversion by friendliness and loving kindness and ignorance by light and knowledge, one cannot put out these fires.

The Buddha has shown us how to go about it and how to extinguish these fires. He has mapped out a path consisting of *sīla, samādhi* and *paññā* by walking on which the three kinds of fire can be put out and positive qualities like desirelessness, friendliness and wisdom can be developed. As one of the three constituents of this Noble Eightfold Path is *sīla,* so it is called the foundation of Buddha-Dhamma. Therefore it can be rightly said that the Buddha ethicized religion (Dhamma).[30] In other words, observing ethical codes of conduct means living a religious life.

Thus, Buddha-Dhamma has a direct bearing on our life here and now. Unlike other religions which promise reward and punishment for good and bad actions respectively in next life after death, it promises them here and now and also says that one's birth in a realm of bliss or in a miserable state in next life is determined by the nature of his action performed in this life. Like many other religious systems, Buddha-Dhamma also believes in rebirth shaped and arbitrated by his actions.

Observance of precepts serves two functions simultaneously. It leads to the purification of one's physical and vocal actions and reduces one's greed and hatred. As one gets rid of these defilements, even as one reduces and dilutes them, one experiences peace and tranquillity. One ceases to burn. With one's cravings and aversions reduced or rooted out one is able to concentrate his mind. Concentration of mind results in the attainment of wisdom which in turn, equips one better to see the nature of reality more clearly. Therefore, observance of precepts by the members of society brings peace and harmony to it and its observance by a member enables him to develop concentration of mind and attainment of wisdom. When he sees with his wisdom that all things, even all attractive and beautiful things are transitory, he develops non-attachment to them. This results in the complete destruction of the roots of immoral actions, which is possible not only by an intellectual understanding of the process but by walking on the Noble Eightfold Path. The path has to be developed repeatedly, developed again and again in order to eradicate the cause of suffering. In this way the highest goal of spiritual life can be achieved.

A glorious aspect of Buddha-Dhamma is that it sees infinite capacity in man. For eradicating the cause of suffering, man is not required to depend upon any other force, not even upon the blessings of any god. He is his own

30. See my essay entitled Ethicization Makes Buddhism a World Religion. Op.cit.

master (*attā hi attano nātho*), he can work out his own salvation by controlling his mind (*attanā hi sudantena nāthaṃ labhati dullabhaṃ*).[31]The Buddha says that as man fashions his own destiny, creates his own sufferings, he can very well eradicate his suffering by annihilating his craving. Unlike some other religions, which recommend their followers to placate supernatural powers which are believed to organize the material universe, or to compose and sing hymns in praise of gods or even to perform rites and rituals and animal sacrifice to appease some powers and gods for their safety, security, prosperity and progeny, Buddha-Dhamma makes man responsible for what he does and what he gets, for what he sows and what he reaps. This may be called the 'humanism' of Buddha-Dhamma.[32]

These two aspects of Buddha-Dhamma--its humanism and its exclusive emphasis on observance of an ethical code of conduct have great appeal to all thinking persons, to all who apply their reason, particularly to atheists. They have the satisfaction of becoming religious without being theists, without believing in the son of God as Christ says of himself or without believing in the last messenger of God as Prophet Mohammad claims to be or even without going to the refuge to God or gods for their deliverance as Lord Krishna says he is[33] but they see and understand that by observing precepts in life they can purify themselves of defilements and work out their salvations themselves. They are not obliged to believe in God to whose refuge they are required to go for their deliverance, for their liberation. The Buddha never arrogates to himself the status of God. He says time and again that he can only show the path by walking on which one can attain *nibbāna*. Once he says to Gaṇakamoggallāna that after his instructions and advice, if somebody attains the supreme goal and someone else does not, what could he do about it?[34] He said that the Tathāgatas only show the way. They cannot stand proxy for others. *Tumhehi kiccamātapaṃ akkhātāro Tathāgatā*[35] (You yourselves must strive. The Tathāgatas are only teachers. They only show the path.)

In short, the Dhamma taught by the Buddha is the action -plan of his philosophy and one who executes the plan is a Dhammic person (a religious person) in the true sense of the term. For putting an end to suffering, its root cause i.e. craving will have to be eradicated and one can do so by

31. Dh 160 *Attā hi attano nātho. ko hi nātho paro siyā/ Attanā hi sudantena, nāthaṃ labhati dullabhaṃ//*

32. See my essay entitled Ācārya Śāntideva's Humanism op. cit.

33. Gītā, *Sarvadharmānparityajya, māmekaṃ śaraṇaṃ vraja/Ahaṃ tvāṃ sarvapāpebhyo, mokṣayiṣyāmi mā śucah//*

34. M3 See *Gaṇakamoggallāna Sutta*, pp. 45-49

35. Dh276 *Tumhehi kiccamātappaṃ, akkhātāro tathāgatā*

walking on the Noble Eightfold Path. If one understands at the intellectual level that walking on the path can do one good, it is not enough but if one actually walks on the path, lives a life of good conduct, observes precepts, practices concentration of mind, attains insight into the real nature of things, comes to understand reality as it is at the experiential level, he develops non -attachment and at the end eradicates cravings that bind him to the wheel of existence and liberates himself. For this, what is absolutely necessary is 'doing', 'striving', 'working hard' and 'developing' *sīla, samādhi* and *paññā*. There is no passivity in the teaching of the Buddha. The central theme of Buddha-Dhamma is 'activity'. In one of my essays,[36] I have listed some of the words which may be called 'action words, active action words' the Buddha uses in his teachings. To the list of words given there some more words like *ātappa* (ardour, zeal, exertion), *anuyoga* (practicing) and *padhāna* (energetic efforts, striving) may be added. It has been said by the Buddha that for living a *brahmacariya* life *thāma* (stamina), *viriya* (vigour) and *parakkama* (endeavor) are most important. In short, Buddha-Dhamma is not only knowing the philosophy propounded by the Buddha but it is to live it in life so that the cause of suffering is eradicated and peace is experienced here and now.

Buddha-Dhamma is the realization of truth, attaining it by finally experiencing it directly. Discovering truth is not enough. It is at best an intellectual exercise. What is most important is finally arriving at truth which is possible by repeating it time and again, developing it over and over again and cultivating it time and time again. Living an ethical life is an indispensable condition for attaining truth. It has been briefly explained in the *Mūlapariyāyasutta*[37] that knowledge and virtue go hand in hand. Only virtuous men whose mind is purged of all impurities and defilements can attain knowledge and attainment of knowledge helps him eliminate roots of immoral actions and live a pure virtuous life. He, who has destroyed craving, aversion and ignorance, is a true *Jñānī* and only a true *Jñānī* who has attained and realized truth can destroy *rāga, dosa* and *moha*. In the *Caṅkī Sutta*[38] the Buddha speaks of preservation of truth (*saccānurakkhaṇa*), discovery of truth (*saccānubodha*) and realizing truth (*saccānuppatti*). The last is the most important of the three. Truth must be known and experienced, knowing and experiencing it are its two indispensable parameters. Preservation of truth is possible without knowing and seeing

36. See my essay entitled Buddhism: Where Philosophy and Religion Converge collected in this book.

37. See *Mūlapariyāya Sutta* M 1.1 and my essay on *The Mūlapariyāya Sutta*—a Treatise of Buddhist Epistemology and Ontology op. cit.

38. M2 *Caṅkī Sutta* pp. 382-394

it i.e. without realizing it at the experiential level. There are five factors responsible for preserving truth. They are faith (*saddhā*), preference (*ruci*), oral traditions (*anussavo*), argument and evidence (*ākāraparivittako*) and pondering a view (*diṭṭhinijjhānakhanti*)[39]. None of these five factors can enable one to know and realize truth because some beliefs 'may well have faith placed in it, and yet it may be hollow, empty and false; and again some (belief) may have no faith placed in it and it may be factual, true and no other than it seems.' The same can be said of other four factors.

So for discovering truth it is absolutely necessary to hear the Dhamma taught by one who lives a pure life, who has destroyed greed, hatred and ignorance, who is a man of honesty and integrity and who says what he knows and sees and does not say what he does not know and does not see.

Thus a person who hears the Dhamma from such a man is impressed by him, develops his faith in him. He very often visits him, pays respect to him, and lends his ear to what he teaches, hears the Dhamma expounded by him attentively, memorizes it and investigates its meaning. Then he likes to ponder the Dhamma, so zeal to do so arises in him, he becomes actively involved. He then evaluates his effort and after evaluating them, controls himself. 'When he is self- controlled, he realizes with his body the ultimate truth and he sees it by penetration of it with understanding'[40]. Thus, he realizes the truth of what the man of honesty and integrity teaches him. This is how he discovers truth.

But this is not enough. For finally arriving at truth, for experiencing it directly, he has to repeat it, develop it. So there are certain factors (*dhammas*) which help him develop it. Control, evaluation of one's efforts, active involvement, zeal, a liking to ponder over, investigation of meaning, memorization, hearing dhamma, lending ear, respect to a teacher, paying visit to him very often and faith in him are such factors.[41] Each following factor is most important for the development of the preceding one, for example control is most important for final arrival at truth, evaluation of one's efforts is most important for control and so on.

It is clear from what has been said above that *saccānupatti* (knowledge of Dhamma by direct experience) is not possible without going through all these stages and all these stages speak of action, endeavor, striving and efforts. The faith (*saddhā*) that has been enumerated here as a factor to help one develop Dhamma is unlike the blind faith found in the preservation of the truth. This is born from fully understanding the honesty and integrity of the teacher of Dhamma. One develops faith in him because he says what

39. ibid., p. 388
40. TBD Vol. ii p. 196
41. ibid., p. 391

he knows and sees, because of certain sterling virtues one finds in him and wants to cultivate them himself. But cultivating these virtues requires a lot of striving, a lot of efforts on one's part. Striving for developing such virtues, making a lot of efforts for cultivating them, living a life of good conduct is Dhamma. This is real Dhamma in practice, a real living Dhamma. *Sīla, samādhi* and *paññā* which are respectively beautiful in the beginning, in the middle and in the end have to be developed with zeal and ardour, with effort and exertion. The three make the Dhamma taught by the Buddha complete (*paripuṇṇaṃ*) and pure (*parisuddhaṃ*). There is nothing to add to it and subtract from it.

There are religions which consider spiritual development as the be-all and end-all of leading a religious life, so much so that a life of poverty embraced deliberately is glorified and regarded as characteristic of religion, because poverty is wrongly identified or equated with renunciation. Buddha-Dhamma does not do so. Its emphasis is on an all round development. The Buddha, in fact, regarded poverty as a degrading factor. What he wanted his disciples to renounce is not wealth but the greed for it. He taught a dhamma which takes care of all aspects of our life, not only moral and spiritual aspects but social and material aspects as well. This is clear from what he says in the *Kūṭadantasutta* - [42] it is true that the Buddha did show a great concern for the spiritual well-being of man but he did not lose sight of other aspects which he thought are inextricably related to spiritual development. Any religion which does not speak of planting peace and order in social life, does not at least care to secure the minimum material prosperity for people following it, how can it expect them to practice it in life? A hungry man is not only an angry man, but also a man who would care least to try to know the meaning and purpose of life in this world which is the goal of religion. Hunger hardly inclines a man to live by the higher values of the human life. It is recorded in the *Dhammapada aṭṭhakathā* that the Buddha began to teach the Dhamma to a group of people only when the farmer who was to be the chief beneficiary that day of his Dhamma teaching came and was fed. Buddha-Dhamma seems to me to be a full blooded religion, if I may use this phrase in the context of religion. He did not neglect man's economic aspect. He did not glorify poverty but what he wanted was to give up the greed for wealth. He also wanted people to earn wealth by honest means. He never said like Christ that 'it is possible for a camel to enter into the eye of a needle, but not possible for a rich man to enter heaven'. It is well known that some of the great *seṭṭhīs* (merchants) of that time were his great disciples. Of course he wanted rich persons to set apart a portion of their wealth to give it to the

42. D1 *Kūṭadanta Sutta*, p. 120

needy and deserving and also to those samaṇas and Brahmaṇas who live on alms. The Pāli words *saṃvibhajati* (to share), *saṃvibhāga* (distribution, sharing out), *saṃvibhāgī* (open, generous), *saṃvibhaāga-dāna* (distribution of gifts) bring out the Buddha's idea of using wealth properly.

A large percentage of people are poor in the world. They have suffered so much from poverty that they feel repelled by a religion which glorifies poverty. As Dr. B.R. Ambedkar says, "to declare poverty to be a blessed state is to pervert religion, to perpetuate vice and crime, to consent to make earth a living hell"[43]. As Buddha-Dhamma does not glorify poverty, it holds out great hopes for the poor and the downtrodden. Buddha-Dhamma in fact wants all activities of man to be inspired by his ethical code of conduct, to stem from a mind purged and cleansed of impurities and defilements and also wants that all his activities should be transparent and should manifest his purity and virtue. This is the real goal of religion.

43. See my essay entitled Buddha's View of Harmony. Published in Essays on Buddhism and Pāli Literature (Eastern Book Linkers, New Delhi, 1994)

Spiritual Foundation of Buddha-Dhamma

If one looks at the Buddha's concern it will be immediately clear that he is concerned more with the mind than with the matter; more with the spiritual world than with the material world. The tone and tenor of Buddha's preoccupation is set by the first two *gāthās* of the Dhammapada where it is said that mind is most important in so far as it is the source of all physical and vocal actions, wholesome or unwholesome. Mind precedes all phenomena. Mind matters most. Everything is mind made. If with an impure mind one performs any action or utters speech, then suffering will follow that person as the cart wheel follows the foot of the draught animal. If with a pure mind one does physical or vocal action, the happiness will follow that person as a shadow that never departs.[44]

In the *Saṃyutta Nikāya*[45] the Buddha says that it is mind, which guides the world; it is mind, which drags it about. *Cittena nīyati loko, cittena parikassati.* If *loka* means *papañca* and *papañca* as we know is created by mind in collusion with the five sense organs, so *loka* is created by mind.

The Buddha's preoccupation with the mind is also clear from what he says regarding volition. *Cetanā*[46], monks, determines the nature of action. It also becomes very clear from what he says in respect of actions performed by man. Man is the inheritor of action (*kammadāyādā*), *kamma* is his own property (*kammassakā*), has *kamma* as his relative (*kammabandhu*), has his *kamma* as his refuge or as a protector (*kammapaṭisaraṇā*), has *kamma* as the cause of rebirth (*kammayoni*).[47] All of these make it clear that the Buddha is preoccupied with the mind and mental world more than with the material world and the various kinds of wealth and objects of desire that it has. But this should not be taken to mean that he looks down upon the material world, rejects it altogether and gives it no importance at all. On the other hand, it is clear from his teachings that this material world has its importance in so far as it acts as a stepping stone for many to climb higher and higher on the spiritual path. Even practitioners of Vipassana meditation purify their minds by equanimously observing various sensations that arise on their bodies. All that happens in the mind is signalled by sensations on

---

44. Dh 1&2
45. S.1.45
46. A2.120 *Cetanāhaṃ, bhikkhave, kammaṃ vadāmi.*
47. M.3 *Cūlakammavibhaṅga Sutta*

the body. *Vedanā samosaraṇā sabbe dhammā.*[48] They observe them without reacting to them and thus purify their minds. It is clear from this that body (as opposed to mind) is not neglected.

Man is a social animal. He lives in society. It is human society, which plays a great role in shaping his life. If there is poverty in society, man will find it hard to eke out a living. So how can he aspire after attaining higher spiritual values of life? If there is unrest in society, if the atmosphere is not congenial for peace and harmony, how can he make spiritual progress? If there is not even bare minimum to support his life, then all or most of his energy will be spent in procuring a living. Thus his concern for making spiritual progress will be jeopardized.

It is true that the Buddha did not work for the green revolution or the white revolution. It is also true that material gains and prosperity did not have any ultimate value for him. If they had, he would not have given them up and renounced the world in the prime of his life. Instead, he would have been a Cakravartti king endowed with great pelf and power. He would have all kinds of sensual pleasures. But he saw in this world more misery than happiness, more unrest than peace. Even victory and success bring in their wake enmity and misery, let alone defeat. So he gave up all and went out in search of the deathless.[49]

The Buddha knew it well that poverty is a great curse. It stands in one's way of making spiritual progress. It makes him 'cribbed, cabined and confined'. If there is widespread poverty in society, there will be unrest in it. People will be discontented and discontent causes many other social ailments. Thieves and robbers will disturb the peace of society, which will not provide one with a congenial atmosphere for making spiritual progress. Even monks who have renounced the world need a happy, harmonious and tolerably wealthy society to be free from material worries to peacefully perform their religious duties and walk on the Noble Eightfold Path. How and why society loses peace and harmony has been graphically described in the *Kūṭadanta Sutta*[50]. The Buddha does not only analyze the cause of unrest in society and the law and order problem that arises from it, but also suggests ways and means to remove the cause and achieve peace and harmony. "Give capital to the businessmen," says the priest of king Mahāvijita, "so that they can set up their business, earn their livelihood and keep themselves engaged. Give seeds and other necessaries to the farmers so that they can plough their fields, grow crops, have enough to give to the

48. A.3.159

49. S1.101. *Jayaṃ veraṃ pasavati, dukkhaṃ seti parājito/ Upasantaṃ sukhaṃ seti, hitvā jayaparājayan'ti//*

50. D1 *Kūṭadanta Sutta*

king and also have enough to fend for themselves so that they do not feel the pinch of poverty. Lastly, give employment to the unemployed young men and women so that their minds are occupied and do not remain idle to become the devil's workshop."[51] These are sound measures to take to remove poverty, unemployment, unrest and other social evils.

This proves that the Buddha did not neglect the material world. In fact, he wanted it to be free from poverty and unrest. That he did not neglect this world is also proved by the fact that he did not interfere with it. He did not intervene in the social set up that obtained during his time. The soldiers were useful for the king. He needed them to defend the borders of his kingdom and put down riots that broke in society. Therefore the Buddha neither ordained soldiers himself nor allowed other monks to ordain them.[52]

One has necessarily to live in this material world. The Buddha also lived in it. So, he took care that there should be peace in it. He lived in this material world so he wanted to maintain ecological balance so that he might get fresh air to breathe in and did on no account want it to be full of pollution. He said so many things on so many occasions in connection with maintaining ecological balance in this world and keeping it free from pollution.[53]

He also gave wise counsel so that people following it could live in peace and harmony and do away with class and caste wars. Division of human society into different castes, high and low, is not natural, but this sort of division is based on vested interests. The Buddha showed, like a true scientist, that people do not have characteristics like insects, birds and beasts to classify them into different castes. All people have more or less the same characteristics and are equal. Man is great or small by virtue of his wholesome or unwholesome actions.[54] In spite of such obvious concerns with the material world, his overriding concern was the spiritual world. Why? Because the material world, in common parlance, goes hand in hand with the world of desires. Whenever one's sense organs come in contact with their respective objects, cravings arise in him. The moment he satisfies one craving, the other arises. The more he tries to fulfill his desires, the more he has them. So there is no end to the chain of cravings

51. ibid.

52. See the rules in the Vinaya Piṭaka who should be ordained and who should not be ordained.

53. See my essay entitled 'Ecological Reflections in Pāli Canonical Literature' in this collection.

54. Sn *Vāseṭṭha Sutta*

which pollute his mind. It is said in the Dhammapada[55] that more harm can be done by an impure mind than can be done by one's enemies. An impure mind is uncontrolled as it is unsteady. On the other hand, a pure mind which is controlled, as it is free from cravings can do more good than one's parents and relatives do.[56]

Cravings pollute one's mind. They are at the root of his sufferings. So, an impure mind is his greatest enemy whereas a pure mind is his best friend. The Buddha saw with his three kinds of *pariññā*[57] that so long as man has cravings, he can't have peace of mind. He will only multiply his miseries. He will go on suffering not only in this life but will be born again and again to suffer. In short, he will be bound to the wheel of birth and death. That is why the Buddha epigrammatically says that not only birth, old age and death; not only separation from loved ones is suffering but the five *khandhas* (aggregates) that one is born with are suffering. Cravings according to him are endless. Man cannot fulfill all his desires and cravings. As aptly said in the Dhammapada [58] even if there is a heavy shower of gold coins, the thirst for enjoying multiple pleasures in the world cannot be quenched.

Cravings go a long way in creating the world. The Buddha anticipated Schopenhauer when he explained the role of craving. Schopenhauer[59] says that the will (of imperious desire) gives rise to the world of suffering. So long as there are cravings in man, this world exists for him and time exists for him. The moment he becomes free from craving, this world of suffering and the time through which he suffers cease to be. For him time and space are annihilated. They no longer exist for him.

Because cravings cause suffering - so it is a natural corollary that the lesser the cravings, the lesser the suffering. But how is one to minimize cravings or completely root them out is the million-dollar question. The Buddha showed the path by walking on which one can reduce one's cravings if not completely annihilate them. As mind is the spring of all our actions, wholesome or unwholesome as said above, and as the unwholesome actions spring from an impure mind, so the most important step to take on the spiritual path is to purify our mind. A mind freed from greed and hatred and other negativities like pride is a pure mind but a mind with all such negativities is impure.

55. Dh 42

56. ibid 43

57. See my essay entitled '*The Mūlapariyāya Sutta*—a Treatise of Buddhist Epistemology and Ontology' in 'Essays on Buddhism and Pali Literature', Eastern Book Linkers, Delhi 1994

58. Dh 186

59. WWR

In order to be able to walk on the spiritual path it is absolutely necessary to purify one's mind. But how to go about doing this is the most important question. In order that the mind is not polluted by cravings and aversion, it is necessary to control it. It should not be allowed to go berserk. It should be tamed by practising *ānāpāna sati* (awareness of respiration) and Vipassana meditation, which is walking on the Noble Eightfold Path and observe sensations that arise on one's body. This path consists of morality, meditation and insight wisdom. All three help one another to grow and develop. Observing moral precepts helps one concentrate his mind and practice meditation because it goes a long way in reducing his cravings and aversions—the greatest enemy of his mind. When his mind is concentrated he can see the true nature of all things of the world and develop wisdom. He can know at the experiential level that there is nothing in this world which he can regard as permanent. If nothing is permanent, why hanker after it. The insight wisdom that he develops by realizing the true nature of things at the experiential level while practising Vipassana meditation makes the scales of his eyes fall and he begins to see things clearly. He develops non-attachment to things i.e. develops *nirveda*, eradicates cravings and the knowledge that dawns upon him after all his cravings are annihilated gives him supreme peace and happiness.

Buddha's concern with the mind and mental spiritual world is clear from what he says about the mind in the *Cittavaggo*[60] of the *Dhammapada.* Mind is difficult to control (*dunniggaho*), it is very light and fickle (*lahuno*), goes anywhere in a trice (*yathākāmanipātino*), it is very difficult to understand (*sududdasaṃ*), it is very clever (*sunipuṇaṃ*), it goes far (*dūraṅgaṃ*), is in the habit of roaming lonely (*ekacaraṃ*) and it is formless (*nirākāra*). Such a mind has got to be tamed, has got to be protected. When tamed and protected it brings great benefit, does great good and ensures one's well-being, both material and spiritual. One who controls his mind is freed of the fetters of Māra, who is the symbol of all sorts of cravings. Māra causes cravings in one, makes his mind unsteady and binds him to the wheel of birth and death. An uncontrolled and untamed mind is far from attaining *paññā* (wisdom) and also far away from knowing the noble *Dhamma* of the Buddha.

In the Abhidhamma philosophy propounded by the Buddha, he describes different planes of consciousness - the consciousness that roams in the world of desires (*kāmāvacara citta*), the consciousness that concentrates on an object which has a form (*rūpāvacara citta*), the consciousness that concentrates on the formless (*arūpāvacara citta*) and finally the consciousness that transcends the world of desires and both the worlds of form and

60. Dh *Cittavaggo*

formlessness and enters into the supramundane (*lokottara*). The qualitative change that takes place in consciousness from one plane to another is tremendous and it is because it is in the process of attaining purity. Similarly, the four or five stages of *rūpāvacara jhāna* also differ among themselves qualitatively. It is most impure when it is in the world of desires. It purifies and sublimates itself as it passes from the world of desires through the two worlds of the form and the formless to the world where it undergoes a qualitative change i.e. to the supramundane world where all desires are annihilated. It is here that man's goal of peace is attained. The *Visuddhimaggo*, written by the great commentator Ācariya Buddhaghosa describes in detail all stages of the purification of mind and all the steps one is required to take to attain purity. In short, it describes the journey of consciousness, which passes through different stages of purification till it is purified, till it becomes like a piece of gold with all its impurities and dross blown and burnt away. The Buddha further analyzed the basic pollutants of mind, which are *lobho* (greed), *doso* (hatred) and *moho* (ignorance) inasmuch as all unwholesome actions are done under their influence. Killing, stealing, committing adultery, telling lies, making slanderous speech, speaking harshly and gossiping are physical and vocal actions committed under the influence of these roots of action. They pollute the mind. *Lobho* (greed) is one of the greatest pollutants. It is most basic, because *doso* (hatred) arises in him who does not get what he wants and is consequently frustrated. Frustration causes anger in him and he wants to take revenge on him who puts a spoke in his wheel of fulfilling his desires. Greed gives rise to misfortune, it makes one angry. One who is greedy neither sees the *Dhamma* nor knows what is good for him. There is no fire greater than craving.[61] It burns constantly.

The Buddha regards it as one of the greatest pollutants of mind, which brings in its wake several negativities like anger, frustration, revenge and so on. That is why he says to the monks to give up greed. He asks them to give up one *dhamma* namely *lobho* and says that he stands surety for their becoming *anāgāmī* (non -returners),[62] i.e. they will be reborn in one of the highest heavens and attain arhatship there. Similarly he asks them to give up *doso* (aversion) and *moho* (ignorance). An angry and deluded man neither sees *dhamma* i.e. what is good for him nor sees what is bad for him. The other two *dhammas* the Buddha refers to here are anger and ill-feeling. Both make one's mind dirty and impure. He sees them as great dangers. It is impossible to lead a pure spiritual life with all these negativities lodged in one's mind. The Buddha says that if such negativities of mind are given up and if positive qualities like love, compassion, sympathetic joy and

61. Dh 202.

62. It p. 2

equanimity in all circumstances, congenial or not congenial are cultivated, then one will be able to lead a *brahmacariya* life. He will observe moral precepts, will not indulge in unwholesome physical and vocal actions, practise meditation and attain insight. He will walk on the Noble Eightfold Path, cultivate the four sublime states of *mettā* (loving kindness), *karuṇā* (compassion for those in trouble), *muditā* (sympathetic joy), and *upekkhā* (equanimity) that is he is neither elated nor becomes sad when he gains or loses, respectively.

The practice of *Brahmavihāras* goes a long way in resolving a discordant note in society inasmuch as people practising them think not only of their own good but also of others' good. All the teachings of the Buddha have one great message. The message is to purify the mind by driving out negativities and cultivating positive qualities. Walking on the Noble Eightfold Path is the Buddha's action - plan of achieving the purity of mind. Vipassana meditation enables one to see the real nature of things i.e. the transitory nature of all worldly things. The experiential knowledge thus attained enables him to develop non-attachment (*nirveda*) to the objects of the world he craves for. He sees the futility of his attachment to them and drives out cravings and aversions. Thus, he makes his mind pure.

Modern humanism with its emphasis on material prosperity and creature comforts of man differs from the humanism that is found in the teachings of the Buddha. Whereas modern humanism takes into consideration man's material prosperity and progress only, Buddha's humanism takes into consideration the inner development of man, which is not possible without the purification of his mind. From purification of the mind will follow all sorts of good, even material prosperity. As mind is the cause of bondage, as it binds man to the wheel of birth and death, so it is also the cause of freedom from bondage as it cuts all fetters that bind him to the wheel of birth and death.

Walking on the Noble Eightfold Path is True Dhamma

The word 'religion' does not convey the meaning which the word '*dhamma*' does. The Concise Oxford Dictionary defines religion as (I) 'The belief in a superhuman controlling power especially in a personal God or gods entitled to obedience and worship'; (II) expression of this in worship; (III) a particular system of faith and worship; and (IV) life under monastic vows'. All these are descriptive definitions. The first three definitions do not define the *dhamma* taught by the Buddha. However, it comes very close to the fourth definition because Buddhist monks follow certain *Vinaya* rules and observe certain vows while living a monastic life. Based on the teachings of the Buddha one can define religion as walking on the Noble Eightfold Path.

Buddha-dhamma does not believe in a superhuman controlling power especially in a personal God or gods. As it does not believe in God, it is atheistic and as it does not believe in the existence of various gods, they are not 'entitled to obedience and worship', honour and veneration. The Buddha has made it clear that gods may enjoy long life of plenty and happiness for innumerable aeons, but they are also subject to fall when the results of their past moral actions are exhausted. Besides, gods cannot, the Buddha holds, do what man can do; they cannot attain *nibbāna*, they cannot achieve arahanthood which man alone can do. To be in human existence is one of the eight essential conditions of becoming a Buddha.[63] Gods cannot become a Buddha. If these are their limitations, why should they command man's worship and obedience?

Buddha-dhamma, on the other hand, exalts man, sees immense potentiality in him, so much potentiality that if he likes and exerts, he can fashion his own destiny and become a Buddha. The Buddha says in clear words that man is his own lord and master. No other power is greater than he.[64] Once addressing some monks he asked them to become their own refuge and island and not to seek other refuge[65]. It is clear from these pronouncements of the Buddha that he saw infinite capacity in man to rise higher and higher in the spiritual field. It is for this reason he did not feel the necessity of believing in superhuman power for man to depend

---

63. Bu p. 309 *Manussattaṃ liṅgasampatti, hetu satthāradassanaṃ/ Pabbajjā guṇasampatti, adhikāro ca chandatā/Aṭṭhadhammā samodhanā, abhinīhāro samijjhatī ti//*
64. Dh 160
65. D I. *Mahāparinibbāna Sutta*.Attadīpā viharatha, attasaraṇā, anaññasaranā.

on for ameliorating his conditions. Superhuman power means a power which is higher than man's, a power beyond normal human capacity. But the Buddha proved that man is the highest and most powerful of all beings.

It is his glorification of man that makes his philosophy humanitarian. His philosophy may rightly be called the philosophy of humanism. Siddhārtha Gautam--the son of Māyā Devī and Suddhodana (he was not an incarnation of God as the Purāṇas make him out to be[66]) attained Buddhahood by dint of his *sādhanā* and exalted himself to the position of a Buddha by virtue of his efforts, exertions, endeavours, ardour and zeal. The Dhamma he realized was so deep, profound and subtle that Sahampati Brahmā came to him and requested him to teach it to the world so that people could benefit from it[67]. It is on record in the Tipiṭaka that Indra and other gods waited upon him to listen to his teaching[68]. Once Mahābrahmā (the highest of the Brahmās) asked one of the monks to go back to the Buddha to get the answer of his question and confessed that his knowledge fell far short of the Buddha's[69]. All of these instances prove man's superiority. He can, by walking on the Noble Eightfold Path, attain qualities which even gods aspire after.

As Buddha-dhamma does not enjoin upon man to worship gods, so it is not a dhamma (religion) as the OED has defined it, nor is it 'a particular system of faith and worship'. It is true, however, that later on the Buddha was deified and Buddha-dhamma, particularly the Mahāyāna branch of it became a religion in the sense the OED has defined it. People began to visit the Buddha temple, offer lighted candles to him and burn incenses to please him and seek his blessings. The prayer and worship became elaborate with many rites and rituals which are regarded as part and parcel of religion. But the Buddha did not enjoin upon people to do so. This is clear from the Pāli Tipiṭaka. He simply asked people to walk on the Noble Eightfold Path.

The dhamma that he taught is not concerned with appeasing any god or any supernatural power to grant favour to worshippers in terms of security, wealth and progeny. The composers of the hymns to Indra[70] and Agni in the Vedic times, in fact, wanted to appease them and seek their blessings. They even prescribed sacrifices to be performed by worshippers to keep them in good humour. But the Buddha did not have any such thing in his mind. He did not prescribe sacrifices in which innocent and meek animals are slaughtered. Instead, he prescribed an altogether different

---

66. See *Viṣṇu Purāṇa*, *Agni Purāṇa* and other *Purāṇas*
67. Mv, See *Brahmayācana kathā*.
68. D2. See the *Sakka Pañha Sutta*.
69. D1 the *Kevaṭṭa Sutta*, pp. 189-90. (Nalanda Edition)
70. See the *Ṛgveda*

sacrifice involving no violence and no killing, but a sacrifice in which craving, aversion and ignorance are to be offered as oblations. They were to be rooted out by developing *sīla, samādhi* and *paññā*. The *Kūṭadanta Sutta*[71] gives a description of many such sacrifices which are pure and sublime, less expensive and more beneficial.

Nor was the dhamma he taught based on some kind of blind belief. In the *Caṅki Sutta*[72], he has analysed how truth is preserved. It is preserved either out of faith or on account of oral tradition or personal preference. So those who preserve truth in these ways regard themselves as *dhammic* or religious. But the dhamma taught by the Buddha arose from his own experience of leading a pure ethical life in which he practiced honesty and integrity and eliminated craving (*rāga*), aversion (*dosa*) and ignorance (*moha*): The elimination of these three is the yardstick of a man whose physical and vocal actions are pure. The Buddha was such a pure person who taught only that which he knew and saw (experienced). He did not teach anything he did not know and see. Knowing and seeing (*ñāṇa* and *dassana*) are the two words which qualify a Buddha. These two are also the hallmarks of truth (Dhamma). How can a man teach dhamma whose actions proceed from his craving, aversion and ignorance? Dhamma or the truth is the domain of one who has purged himself of all impurities and defilements. From the *Mūlapariyāya Sutta*[73] it is clear that only he, who annihilates *rāga, dosa* and *moha*, is capable of realizing the truth--the dhamma. Attainment of knowledge of the truth goes hand in hand with living a virtuous life, that is living a life of *sīla, samādhi* and *paññā*. Knowledge dawns upon a virtuous man and only a virtuous man is capable of attaining knowledge.

So what does the dhamma the Buddha taught consist of? It consists chiefly of annihilating suffering which is a ubiquitous phenomenon of human life. Like a pragmatic philosopher of a very high order, the Buddha was concerned with knowing the cause of suffering and the way to put an end to it. So like other philosophers, he did not exercise his mind in solving speculative questions like whether the world is eternal or not. These questions he called *abyākata* and said they are not relevant to the main problem of mankind[74]. He said man would not be happier by trying to solve such questions. So he applied himself assiduously to find out the cause of suffering and the way to eradicate it. He saw that not only physical

71. D1 See the *Kūṭadanta Sutta.*

72. M2 See the *Caṅkī Sutta.*

73. M1 See the *Mūlapariyāya Sutta.* See also my essay entitled '*The Mūlapariyāya Sutta*–a Treatise of Buddhist Epistemology and Ontology'. Collected in Essays on Buddhism and Pali literature EBL, Delhi, 1994.

74. M2 the *Cūlamāluṅkya Sutta.*

and mental sufferings made man's life miserable, but what made him more miserable was his craving to be born again and again and suffer in life after life. He suffers so long as he is bound to the wheel of existence.

By practising Vipassana meditation the Buddha found out the cause of suffering, and also the way out of it. It became clear to him that all phenomena or formations (*sabbe saṅkhārā*) are impermanent[75] and as they are impermanent they cannot give lasting happiness. If happiness does not last, there is more craving for it. Pleasant sensations–the source of pleasure, are fleeting, so naturally there is more craving for pleasant sensations. And unpleasant sensations, which one wants to avoid, pass away to arise again. So they also cause unhappiness. Both craving for enjoying pleasant sensations and craving for avoiding unpleasant ones cause suffering. In the Dhammapada it is said 'from endearment, affection, attachment, lust and craving springs grief and so from endearment etc. springs fear'[76]. Therefore, as long as one experiences grief and fear, how can one be happy and peaceful and fearless? The natural conclusion, therefore, is that endearment, lust etc. ought to be destroyed to eliminate grief and fear.

Vipassana meditation practised by the Buddha made it clear to him that nothing arises without a cause. There is no effect without a cause. In short, he discovered what is called the Law of Dependent Origination which explains that the effect ceases to be if the cause is removed. This was nothing short of a 'eureka' for him. 'Remove craving and suffering will be removed'.

The philosophy of the Four Noble Truths that he propounded succinctly sums up all that a man is required to do to understand the meaning and purpose of life, to quench his endless burning from his hydra- headed desires, to annihilate suffering and to attain *nibbāna*--a state of no craving and no fear which is the most important end of life.

The understanding of suffering leads a man to live a virtuous (*dhammic*) life, that is, to observe moral precepts, to practice concentration of mind and to attain insight into the real nature of things at the level of his own experience, that is, to realize the Law of Impermanence as well as the Law of Dependent Origination at the experiential level. This realization makes him grow weary of the things he craves for in ignorance and makes him detached.

Many kinds of trouble arise in society because one performs such physical and vocal actions which do harm to others. These he does in ignorance. Theft, murder, adultery, lying, slandering and speaking harsh words are such actions. A thief commits theft. It is a loss to the person whose articles are stolen. Besides, some sort of disturbance in the placid

75. Dh 277.

76. ibid., 212 to 216.

atmosphere of society is created. In the same way when a murder is committed, there is greater disturbance in society. The members of the family of the murdered begin to hatch a plot for taking revenge on the murderer. The murderer fears attack on him. In this way, a chain reaction of violence, revenge and fear is set in. How can there be peace in society when such people are there? Lying, slandering and speaking harsh words also create unpleasant situations and on account of them the problems of law and order arise and the peace of society is disturbed. All such troubles which are man made can be reduced to the minimum, if not altogether removed, if people observe moral precepts which will go a long way in making physical and vocal actions ethically pure.

Purity of these actions has a big role to play in driving out greed, lust and craving from one's minds. It is a common knowledge that one commits all sorts of crimes and other immoral actions because he is goaded by craving and sensual desire. If he acts without being egged on by these evils, human society will experience that peace and harmony which is impossible to describe in words. Thus the moral precepts prescribed by the Buddha, if observed, go a long way in establishing peace and harmony in society.

The second great advantage of observing moral precepts is to be able to control and quieten one's mind. Mind, the Buddha says, is very fickle and unsteady. As it roams in the world of desires, it keeps on jumping like a monkey from one object of craving to another. If cravings can be reduced or eradicated by observing moral precepts, mind can be steadied and controlled.

But how are cravings to be eliminated? So long as one is ignorant of the real nature of things he craves for, so long as he thinks that the pleasant sensations he craves for will last forever, he will not be able to get rid of cravings. But once he understands the Law of Impermanence operating in the world, he will be disillusioned, he will understand that all that glitters is not gold. He will grow a little wiser, become weary of things he longs for, develop non-attachment to them and attain real knowledge (wisdom). Only a concentrated mind can attain real knowledge as it develops power to go deep into things and realize their impermanent nature. When he understands at the experiential level that all things are in a constant state of flux, he makes a big leap forward. He stops craving for things which he now knows will not last for long and will not give him lasting happiness. He now begins to understand that craving is a defilement which pollutes one's mind.

Concentration of mind brings into effect a great change in one's thought pattern. One is now not helplessly carried by his mind. As he has realized the law of impermanence, so instead of developing cravings for things, he begins to see them in a detached manner.

Cravings, in fact, burn one. They arise at the sense-doors. So long as one is enveloped by darkness of *avijjā* (ignorance) he craves for pleasant sensations to continue, but as they are impermanent, they arise to pass away and cause more burning in one. With one's mind concentrated, one deeply penetrates into the real nature of things, does not crave for them. With the attainment of wisdom (*paññā*) he becomes 'cool and quenched'. Either there is a great reduction in the quantum of craving or there is complete extinction of it.

The Buddha saw the functions of *sīla*, *samādhi* and *paññā*. Vipassana meditation enabled him to eliminate defilements, understand the Law of Impermanence, develop non-attachment and equanimity and attain *nibbāna*. This is what he taught.

So if instead of generating craving one develops equanimity and watch his sensations without reacting to them, he does not create more cravings and is not caught in their net. Gradually he becomes free from them. He becomes able to understand the meaning and purpose of life and achieve his spiritual goal.

The question is how to go about it? The compassionate Buddha showed the path. But even if one knows all about the path he mapped out for one and knows all about the different milestones on it and understands all about *sīla*, *samādhi* and *paññā*, it is not going to help him much. The real advantage will come to him if he walks on this path. Merely knowing about the path is not enough. It is walking on the path that will benefit one and do him good. Therefore, walking on the path is Buddha-dhamma. The dhamma taught by the Buddha purifies one's mind of all defilements. Cravings--the seeds of another life are fried by observance of moral precepts, practice of meditation and development of wisdom, and become incapable of further germination. Buddha's philosophy of the Four Noble Truths is not like Leibnitz's speculative 'nomad', but it is born out of his deeper realization at the level of his experience. He saw sufferings of all kinds in the world. He saw that all worldly and divine pleasures are subject to change. Even Brahmās and gods and their worlds are impermanent. One craves for pleasant sensations, but as they arise to pass away, they cause burning in one and he suffers as a consequence. He also saw the Law of Dependent Origination, a kind of *ṛta*, and came to the conclusion that one's suffering is caused by craving. So, the natural corollary he came out with was as said above 'remove craving - the cause of suffering and annihilate it'. And he did it by walking on the Noble Eightfold Path with eight constituents such as right view, right thought, right speech, right action, right livelihood, right mindfulness, right effort and right concentration.

If one develops each of these constituents, that is, if he observes *sīla* (morality), practices *samādhi* (concentration) and attains *paññā* (wisdom), he is sure to end his suffering and enter the land of light and liberation, the land where peace and tranquillity reign supreme.

If one cultivates each of the constituents that come under *sīla*, he curtails his craving, concentrates his mind, purges his mind of all defilements, attains purity and establishes peace and harmony within himself as well as in society. Right speech means abstention from lying, from back-biting, from speaking harsh words and from speaking frivolously. With his vocal actions pure and wholesome, he puts an end to a lot of troubles that he creates in society. Some people may ask why is lying a sin, an unwholesome act and not a wholesome one? Because it is not good for oneself (*attahitāya*) nor good for others (*parahitāya*). If one applies these two criteria to judge what one does, it will become clear to him whether it is good or bad, *kusala* or *akusala*. Lying is prompted by greed and fear and both are pollutants. They do not do one any good. Lying is indulged in causing financial loss or any other loss to others. So it does not do good to others. One also tells a lie out of fear. Similarly back-biting is prompted by one's being jealous of others as also by one's greed to be friendly to one of the persons between whom discord is caused. One uses harsh words out of anger and one talks frivolously and wastes others' time because he wants to show off his skill and knowledge and also because he is jealous of others' progress. So all these activities pollute his mind. One knows that volitions determine the nature of action[77]. It is for these reasons that lying, back-biting etc. are called unwholesome actions (*akusala kammas*).

One pollutes his mind with hatred, animosity and aversion when he indulges in killing, he pollutes his mind with greed and craving when he indulges in stealing and he pollutes his mind with sexual desire when he commits adultery. One calls these activities *adhamma* (unwholesome and immoral) because they generate defilements mentioned above.

All these activities, it is clear, do not do any good to one, nor do they do any good to others as they give rise to defilements in others' minds also besides causing perceptible losses to them.

When one earns his livelihood by adopting pure and right mode, it is right livelihood. The Buddha has forbidden to carry on five trades for earning livelihood. They are trade in weapons (*sattha vaṇijjā*), trade in living beings (*satta vaṇijjā*), trade in meat (*mansa vaṇijjā*), trade in intoxicants (*majja vaṇijjā*) and trade in poisons (*visa vaṇijjā*). Many evils and troubles in our society and in the world arise because people carry on these trades. I think if people of a nation and nations of the world assiduously and religiously make it a point not to carry on these trades, most of the troubles and evils in our society and the world will disappear and our mind will also

77. A2.118. *Cetanāhaṃ, bhikkhave, kammaṃ vadāmi.*

be purged of a host of defilements. If the heads of nations take a decision not to carry on these trades, particularly the trade of selling and buying arms and ammunitions, the world will become a veritable heaven with lots of fighting gone and lots of tensions eased.

Under *samādhi* come three constituents of the Noble Eightfold Path namely, right mindfulness, right effort and right concentration. Development of mindfulness fulfils all. It removes ignorance (*moha*) and helps one get all that he desires. Therefore it has been rightly said that right mindfulness is a very effective tool of accomplishing all (*sati sabbattha sādhikā*). Right effort consists in making four types of exertions (*samappadhānas*), namely (I) not to allow unwholesome or *akusala dhammas* to arise and (II) if they have arisen, to root them out, (III) preparing the ground for wholesome *dhammas* to arise and (IV) develop them with great care and attention if they have arisen. Right concentration is the one-pointedness of a wholesome mind—of a mind free from *lobha* (covetousness), *dosa* (aversion) and *moha* (ignorance).

Paññā includes *sammā ditthi* (right view) and *sammā saṅkappa* (right thought). Right view consists in the knowledge of four noble truths, knowledge of what is wholesome (*kusala*) and unwholesome (*akusala*) and what the wholesome roots (*kusala mūlāni*) and unwholesome roots (*akusala mūlāni*), are, knowledge of the Law of Dependent Origination and knowledge of the *āsavas*, their cause, their cessation and the way to annihilate them. Right thought (*sammā saṅkappa*) means doing things thoroughly knowing all about them. The first that comes under it is *nekkhamma saṅkappa* which means renouncing all craving for objects of one's senses knowing full well that they are not lasting objects, they cause suffering and do not have any permanent substance in them (*aniccato, dukkhato, anattato*). The second is *abyāpāda saṅkappa. Abyāpāda* means love and sympathy. One develops love and sympathy for those whom he hated earlier but knowing full well that aversion also does not last forever, he grows wiser and replaces that negative feeling by positive feelings like amity, friendliness and love. The third that comes under it is *avihinsā saṅkappa. Avihinsā* means absence of cruelty. It means friendliness. One develops compassion for all suffering beings. So right thought fills one's minds with qualities like love, friendliness and compassion and removes negative *dhammas* like hatred and cruelty. He develops all of these qualities by realizing at the level of his experience that there is nothing in the world which is eternal and permanent. Knowledge of the things as they are enables him to develop non-attachment, makes him renounce cravings and inspires him to cultivate positive humane qualities like love, friendliness, compassion and kindness.

By practising Vipassana meditation the Buddha discovered the path, by walking on which he could annihilate craving and aversion and attain *nibbāna*. He taught this path to the world, mapped it out in a very detailed manner. He said that anyone who walks on this path will reap a number of advantages. He will not attain peace within himself only, but he will also plant peace in society. By observing moral precepts he will get rid of much of his burning as he will gradually remove unwholesome *dhammas* like craving and aversion, anger, animosity and ignorance. He will also develop positive qualities like *mettā* (love), *karuṇā* (compassion), *muditā* (sympathetic joy) and *upekkhā* (equanimity), he will rise above his petty personal interests and act altruistically, develop his wisdom by concentrating his mind, know the impermanent nature of all things of the world he craves for, develop non-attachment to them by growing actually weary of them, root out all cravings and aversions and finally attain *nibbāna.*

The philosophy of the Four Noble Truths propounded by the Buddha is pragmatic inasmuch as his main concern was to annihilate suffering by walking on a path which enables one to root out its cause. Walking on the path also enables one to purify oneself of all defilements that cause one's suffering. Walking on the path is called *brahmacariya vāsa* (living a pure and holy life); this is called Buddha-dhamma.

For this, not only knowledge of the four Noble Truths in general but also knowledge of the two phases of each in particular have to be attained. Besides, the third phase of each has to be realized at the experiential level. Only then the philosophy of the Four Noble Truths can be said to be comprehensively understood and realized.

The fact of the first Noble Truth of suffering is not only to be accepted, but is to be comprehended at the intellectual level (*pariññeyaṃ*) and experiential level (*pariññātaṃ*). Similarly, the fact of the second Noble Truth of the cause of suffering is not only to be accepted, but it is to be understood at the intellectual level that its cause has to be rooted out (*pahātabbaṃ*) and finally it has to be realized at the level of experience that the cause is rooted out (*pahīṇaṃ*). The fact of the third Noble Truth of the cessation of suffering should be accepted and at the same time it should be understood at the intellectual level that this truth has to be realized by oneself for oneself (*sacchikātabbaṃ*) and finally that this truth has been realized at the experiential level (*saachikataṃ*). Lastly the fact of the fourth Noble Truth that the Noble Eightfold Path leads to cessation and cure of suffering is not only to be accepted, but should be understood at the intellectual level that it should be developed (*bhāvetabbaṃ*) and finally to realize at the experiential level that *sīla*, *samādhi* and *paññā* have been developed and the path has been walked (*bhāvitaṃ*).

If one accepts these truths out of faith, because the Buddha propounded them or even if one comprehends at the intellectual level that the philosophy is sound and will benefit one, they are not going to help him greatly in coming out of the net of *dukkha* (suffering). What he is required to do is to know them and realize them at the level of experience. This one can do by walking on the Noble Eightfold Path oneself. Walking on the path, that is, observing moral precepts that are ethical codes of conduct, practising meditation and attaining wisdom is real *dhamma*--not 'religion' as the OED defines it, but as the Buddha endowed with his deep and profound wisdom explained it and taught it.

But to walk on the path is an uphill task. One cannot walk on it with a passive knowledge and contemplation at the intellectual level, but he can do so by exerting himself, striving and developing *sīla, samādhi* and *paññā* time and again, over and over again, keeping himself alert and mindful, active and vigilant. The teachings of the Buddha are full of active action-words. His message is unmistakable "Exert, strive, make endeavour and work out your own salvation with diligence".[78] If religion is to make one pure, if it is to end his suffering and bring him peace, then walking on the Noble Eightfold Path is true religion.

78. See my essay entitled 'Buddhism: Where Philosophy and Religion Converge' published in Buddhism in India and Abroad (Somaiya Publications Mumbai, 1996)

Buddhism: Where Philosophy and Religion Converge

Before I show in this essay how philosophy and religion converge in Buddhism, it would be better to briefly define each. Philosophy has been defined in the Oxford Dictionary as "the use of reason and argument in the search for truth and the knowledge of reality especially of causes and nature of things and principles governing existence, perception, human behaviour and material universe."[79]

It has also been defined as 'a system of conduct in life.'[80]

Religion, as we understand it, is philosophy and ethics put into practice in life. In other words, when philosophy becomes our 'conduct in life, it is religion'. Religion is not practicing rites and rituals but it is inculcating those higher values of life that people live by. In short, that philosophy by living which our life becomes spiritually richer and more sublime, is religion. Philosophy has more of reason and argument but religion is behaviour and conduct. Thus, religion may be called the execution of the action-plan of philosophy.

Not all philosophies of the world can have an action-plan. Only they can have it, which are spiritually inclined. What action-plan can a philosophy which moves in the domain of intellect have?

The Buddha's philosophy and for that matter practically all systems of Indian philosophy excluding Cārvāk differ qualitatively from Western philosophy. Whereas the latter is mostly characterized by intellectual quest of the truth, the former is intensely spiritual. It (Indian philosophy) has always emphasized the need of practical realization of truth. In India, philosophy is called *darśana* and rightly so, because *darśana* means vision. *Darśana* stands for the direct vision of Reality or seeing Reality intuitively. It is for this reason that practically all schools of Indian Philosophy have action-plans and the two go hand in hand. Religion is the executed action-plan of a philosophical system.

The aim of all systems of Indian philosophy is to annihilate three kinds of pain, viz. *daihika* (physical suffering), *daivika* (suffering caused by gods) and *bhautika* (suffering caused by circumstances around one), become free from bondage and experience supreme happiness. In other words, to be liberated and attain *mokṣa* or *nirvāṇa*—one of the ends (*puruṣārthas*) of life—is the ultimate goal. For this, practically all systems of Indian philosophy

79. OD p. 628.

80. ibid.

regard *śravaṇa* (hearing the truth) *manana* (intellectual conviction after critical analysis) and *nididhyāsana* (practical realization) as the means of realizing the supreme bliss. It will be shown below why the Buddha prefers *bhāvanāmayī prajñā,* the counterpart of *nididhyāsana* to *sutamayā prajñā* and *cintāmayā prajñā*, or *śravaṇa* and *manana* respectively.

In comparison with the aims of Indian philosophy, those of western philosophy fall short. Let us, for example, take the philosophy of Leibnitz. It is at best an intellectual quest. It does not have any direct bearing on one's spiritual well-being. His monadology cannot help one in annihilating his suffering and cannot take him nearer to *nirvāṇa*—the *summum bonum* of life. There have been other philosophers in the west who have gone very near the truth as if they have realized it. But even they are not stirred to the depth of their souls and do not go beyond the world of reason and intellect. Heraclites said, 'you cannot bathe twice in the same river." The water of the river in which you take a dip flows down and is replaced by another mass of water. Thus he propounded the philosophy that everything is incessantly changing. Hume says, "I never can catch 'myself'. Whenever I try, I stumble on this or that perception." These philosophers have experienced or perhaps realized only intellectually the fleeting nature of things, but they stop here. They do not go beyond this and do not develop what is called non-attachment (*nirveda*) to things of the world. This realization of the fleeting nature of things is not at the experiential level, so they do not lead to spirituality.

Indian philosophers' experience of impermanence and fleeting nature of things arouses them from a slumber caused by *avidyā* (ignorance) and enables them to develop non-attachment (*vairāgya) to* things of the world that seem to give them happiness. They make sincere and religious attempt to cut the bondage that binds them to the world. So, taking off from the limited domain of intellect and reason they soar in spiritual skies where their endeavour to live a religious life makes them resplendent with the radiance and lustre of the sun, the moon and the stars.

Although practically all systems of Indian philosophy are religious in character, the quantum of emphasis laid on spirituality and on putting into practice the good and the higher values of life differs from one system to another. It seems to me that the quantum of emphasis laid by the Buddha on executing the action-plan of his philosophy and his concern to see his disciples inculcate higher values of life for ennobling it, enriching it and making it better spiritually is greater than the quantum of emphasis laid by the propounder of any other philosophical system and religious person.

The Buddha was a pragmatic philosopher. Pragmatic philosophers today concern themselves with the immediate problems of life which stem largely from social, economic and political situations and do not concern themselves at all with speculations regarding 'the first principle'. The Buddha also thinks it a waste of time to speculate on problems which have no direct bearing on man's immediate problem of annihilating suffering which is so ubiquitous. Man is subject to physical suffering like old age, disease and death, to mental suffering caused by frustration in not getting what he desires and in getting what he does not like. Besides these two, man is also subject to such suffering which means being born again and again and undergoing physical and mental sufferings. How to get rid of these sufferings was the immediate problem that the Buddha grappled with and found its solution. He had absolutely no interest in speculative philosophy.

The tone and tenor of the Buddha's attitude to speculative philosophy is clear from what he said to Mālunkyaputta[81] who wanted the Buddha to explain such views as: 'the world is eternal, the world is not eternal; the world is an ending thing, the world is not an ending thing; the life-principle is the same as the body, the life-principle and the body are different; the Tathāgata is after dying, the Tathāgata is not after dying, the Tathāgata is and is not after dying and the Tathāgata neither is nor is not after dying'.

The Buddha called them indeterminate (*avyākata*) and explained to Māluṅkyaputta that living a *brahmacariya* life to put an end to suffering is not at all dependent on any of these views. People can dispute whether the world is eternal or not eternal but nobody can dispute suffering as an immediate problem of life as also nobody can deny the importance of walking on the Path to put an end to it. He brought this point home to Māluṅkyaputta by giving the illustration of a foolish man pierced by an arrow who suffers excruciating pain but refuses to be treated by a surgeon unless he knows all about the man who pierced him and all about the arrow by which he was pierced. The Buddha showed it very clearly that man's immediate problem is to get rid of suffering. Therefore, the best thing for him is to find out the cause of suffering and the way to annihilate it. All other questions regarding the eternality or otherwise of the world are irrelevant.

All the four noble truths that he propounded are concerned with suffering, its cause, its cessation and the way leading to its cessation. While explaining the cause of suffering, the Buddha reveals his sound understanding of the psychology of human mind. All one's actions stem from his mind and all of them good or bad have their roots in it. *Lobha* (greed), *dosa* (ill-will) and *moha* (ignorance) are the roots of *akusala kammas* (unwholesome or bad actions) and *alobha, adosa* and *amoha* are the roots of *kusala kammas* (wholesome actions). These six *hetus* (roots) are inherent in

81. M.2.96, *Cūlamāluṅkya Sutta*

one, but the unwholesome ones are found in great measure in most of the people. One has greed for the objects he likes and ill-will towards those he does not like. His greed and aversion arise from his ignorance, from his not knowing that all things and all objects he craves for are subject to change. They are in a constant state of flux. As they keep on changing, they are impermanent (*anicca*) and how can impermanent objects give him lasting happiness? One is attached towards them none the less, because of their 'sparking' nature, even though they do not last forever. In the words of Shelley:

> *"Worlds on worlds are rolling ever,*
> *From creation to decay,*
> *Like the bubbles on a river*
> *Sparkling, bursting, borne away."*

One is deluded by the pleasures that seem 'sparkling' and 'guilded', and does not go deep to see through their 'bursting' nature, because they are nothing but 'bubbles' being 'borne away' by the river in a constant state of flux and in which he cannot bathe twice. If things are so transitory, where is the lasting happiness?

The Buddha saw through the impermanence of things very clearly. He felt it and realized it at the experiential level. It did not take him long, therefore, to conclude that one's craving is at the root of all his sufferings. As pleasures and their sources are transitory, one craves for more and more of them and consequently suffers more and more. With the habit-pattern of his mind, he is not likely to see through the transitory nature of things and as his mind is like a monkey jumping from one branch to another, he keeps on craving for this or that object endlessly. When his sense organs come in contact with their respective objects, sensations arise and enter within through all the six doors, which act as fuel to keep going the in-built generator which produces cravings. Thus craving (*taṇhā*) is produced, craving to get the things he likes and craving to avoid the things or persons he does not like. And these cravings stem from his greed which, of course, rises in ignorance. When the veil of ignorance is rent through *bodhi* or enlightenment, the cravings cease to be.

The Buddha explains through the Law of Dependent Origination (*paṭic-casamuppāda*) the cause of suffering. He explains in detail all the twelve links of this Law. "Conditioned by ignorance are the habitual tendencies;[82] conditioned by habitual tendencies is consciousness;[83] conditioned by feel-

82. *Avijjā paccayā saṅkhārā*

83. *Saṅkhārā paccayā viññāṇaṃ*

ing is craving;[84]... conditioned by becoming is birth[85] and conditioned by birth, old age, dying, grief, sorrow and lamentation, suffering, dejection and despair come into being.[86] He discovered this law through Vipassana meditation. When he found out the cause of suffering, he confidently propounded the third Noble Truth that suffering can be ended by annihilating cravings.

How to annihilate cravings? How to get rid of sufferings? How to achieve this goal in life? These are very important questions to answer. For annihilating cravings and sufferings, for achieving lasting peace and happiness in life - the Buddha prescribed an ethical moral path for one to walk. This path known as the Noble Eightfold Path (*aṭṭhaṅgiko maggo*) consists of *sīla* (morality), *samādhi* (concentration of mind) and *paññā* (insight wisdom). Observing morality goes a long way in reducing one's cravings, practicing meditation helps greatly in controlling his unsteady mind and developing wisdom means seeing through the real nature of things and developing what is called the right view. These three strengthen one another.[87]

Practicing meditation helps one in developing mindfulness which in turn enables him to keep a watch on his sense-doors through which sensations enter the generator which produces cravings, sensations which arise when an object impinges on its sense-organ. What does keeping a watch on one's sense-doors or guarding one's sense-doors mean? It means attaining mastery over sense-faculties i.e. when one sees, hears, smells, tastes, touches and cognizes a phenomenon, he is "not entranced in the general appearance or the details of their objects."[88] He is thus able to restrain that which might give occasion for evil states, covetousness and dejection.

The Buddha's philosophy clearly points out the cause of suffering and his prescription of living a *brahmacariya* life i.e. walking on the Noble Eightfold Path is a sure guarantee of annihilating suffering.

The Buddha applied his extensive reason and great analyzing capacity to show how all steps on the path of purification are interdependent. Walking on the Noble Eightfold Path is going along the path of purification and one can purify oneself from various defilements like greed, aversion, craving etc. by living an ethical-moral life. And when he becomes pure, he attains *nibbāna*--release by knowledge (*paññā vimutti*).

---

84. *Vedanā paccayā taṇhā*

85. *Bhava paccayā jāti*

86. *Jāti paccayā jarā, maraṇa, soka, parideva, dukkha, domanassa, upāyāsāti*

87. BD Book IV .1

88. M3. 51 M3. 51 *Mā nimittaggāhī hohi, mānubyañjanaggāhī*

Release by knowledge is possible by practicing seven limbs of wisdom (*bojjhaṅga*) which are *sati* (mindfulness), *dhammavicaya* (investigation of the law), *viriya* (energy), *pīti* (rapture), *passaddhi* (repose), *samādhi* (concentration) and *upekkhā* (equanimity). Seven limbs of wisdom depend for their perfection on the four arisings of mindfulness (*satipaṭṭhāna*) which in turn depend on the three right ways of practice (*kāya vacī* and *mano sucarita*). For these actions to be good and wholesome, a perfect control of the sense faculties is needed which is developed by mindfulness and self-possession.[89] These are completed and perfected by a thorough working mind (*yonisomanasikāra*) which is possible only when there is faith. Faith grows from listening to true *Dhamma* and this is possible by "following after the worthy man (*sappurisa sevana*)."

In the *Satisampajañña Sutta* of the *Aṅguttara Nikāya* (*Aṭṭhaka nipāta*) the Buddha has shown the importance of *sati* and *sampajañña*. In order to live an ethical-moral life, it is very necessary to cultivate mindfulness and self-possession. If these lack in a person, he cannot attain emancipated knowledge and vision (*paññāvimuttidassana*).

"When mindfulness and self possession are lacking, conscientiousness and fear of blame are perforce destroyed... when conscientiousness and fear of blame are lacking, the control of the senses is perforce destroyed... when the control of the senses is lacking, moral practice is perforce destroyed... when moral practice is lacking, right concentration is perforce destroyed... when right concentration is lacking, true knowledge and vision are perforce destroyed... when true knowledge and vision are lacking, disgust and dispassion are perforce destroyed... and when disgust and dispassion are lacking, emancipated knowledge and vision are perforce destroyed."[90]

The Buddha did not say anything of which there is no base, no cause. The *Tipiṭaka* is replete with passages where the Buddha has shown that conditioned by this (*imasmiṃ sati*) this happens (*idaṃ hoti*), from the arising of this (*imassupādā*) that arises (*idaṃ uppajjati*), this not becoming (*imasmiṃ asati*) that does not become (*idaṃ na hoti*), from the ceasing of this (*imassa nirodhā*) that ceases (*idaṃ nirujjhati*). In the *Avijjā Sutta* of the *Aṅguttara Nikāya*,[91] he explains the origin of ignorance through the Law of Dependent Origination. *Avijjā* (ignorance) is conditioned by five hindrances viz., *kāmacchanda* (sensuality), *vyāpāda* (ill-will), *thīnamiddha* (torpor of mind and body) *uddhaccakukucca* (flurry and worry) and *vicikicchā* (doubt). They, in turn, are conditioned by three immoral practices which are performed

89. The correct English translation of 'sampajañña' is 'understanding the impermanent nature of things and consequently understanding dukkha and anatta.

90. BKS Vol. IV p. 219

91. A.4, p. 189

when the sense faculties are not restrained. They are not restrained because of lack of mindfulness and self possession and this is conditioned by lack of thorough work and so on.[92]

All these explanations are based on sound reason, and on sound reason is based the analysis of one's mind which is fickle[93] and has the roots of *kusala* and *akusala kammas.*

During the time of the Buddha, philosophy, religion, ethics and psychology were all mixed up. All were dealt with simultaneously and all were brought to bear upon man's immediate problem of getting rid of suffering. There was no dichotomy between philosophy and religion, ethics and psychology. The Buddha's *Dhamma* comprehends all. His four noble truths beautifully harmonize all these four subjects. The Noble Eightfold Path concisely sums up the Buddha's *Dhamma* in so far as it consists of *sīla, samādhi* and *paññā.* When a god asks the Buddha, how one can get rid of all tangles of craving:

Anto jaṭā, bahi jaṭā, jaṭāya jaṭitā pajā/
Taṃ taṃ gotama pucchāmi, ko imaṃ vijaṭaye jaṭan'ti//[94]

the Buddha replied that the Noble Eightfold Path is the only path by walking on which one can cut asunder the tangles of craving with the sickle of wisdom.

Sīle patiṭṭhāya naro sapañño, cittaṃ paññaṃ ca bhāvayaṃ/
Ātāpī nipako bhikkhu, so imaṃ vijaṭaye jaṭan'ti//[95]

This is a sure path leading to freedom from craving, from suffering and leading to *nibbāna*—the *summum bonum* of life.

But merely an intellectual grasp of the four noble truths and particularly of the Noble Eightfold Path is of no help at all to lead a *brahmacariya* life. The Buddha has said again and again that *sīla, samādhi* and *paññā* have got to be cultivated. They are to be developed. They are to be made to grow. So of the three kinds of wisdom (*paññā*) viz. *sutamayā paññā* (wisdom gained by listening), *cintāmayā paññā* (wisdom gained through thinking and reflection) and *bhāvanāmayā paññā* (wisdom gained by doing, by experience) the last is the best and most helpful in living a religious life. The Buddha admonished his disciples to work hard and to work out their salvation by diligence. His last words were:

Vayadhammā saṅkhārā, appamādena sampādetha. (D. 2. p. 92)

92. BGS Vol. V, pp. 78-79
93. Dh 33
94. Vism Vol. 1 (Nalanda Edition) p. 14
95. ibid., p. 14

'Decay is inherent in all conditioned things. Work out your salvation with diligence.' He exhorted his disciples to be vigilant and earnest. Indolence, according to him, is the greatest enemy to living a *brahmacariya* life. The Buddha's teaching, therefore, is connected with doing, exerting, striving and working hard. He put a premium on incessant hard work and on cultivating *bhāvanāmayā paññā* so that one can realize the nature of reality at the experiential level.

Therefore, the Buddha's philosophy is not merely intellectual; it has an action-plan that makes it meaningful. To some *paribbājakas* (wanderers) who charged the Buddha with the philosophy of inaction, he replied that his philosophy is the philosophy of inaction in a way. A Brahman also asked the Buddha if he propounded the philosophy of inaction; the latter replied, when he wants his disciples to refrain from killing, stealing and keeping themselves from all ignoble and unwholesome actions, what he teaches is the philosophy of inaction. But is this really a philosophy of inaction? To refrain from *akusala kammas* is a tremendous task, demanding constant vigilance, mindfulness and deliberate effort. It is easy to go down a slope, but to stop going down and try to change the course is really an uphill task. Living a *brahmacariya* life means observing *sīla,* practicing *samādhi* and attaining *paññā* and each one of them requires constant vigil and great effort to perfect it. The observance of *sīla* immediately makes one contented, enables him to become a man of good conduct; the practice of *samādhi* helps him to concentrate his mind and consequently keeps him from burning with the fires of passion and hatred and attainment of insight and wisdom enables him to develop disgust and dispassion—the two vital factors turning him away from the world of desires and leading him to *nibbāna*—a state free from cravings and the goal of *brahmacariya* life.[96]

It is clear from the verse given below that the Buddha wanted his disciples to work hard and walk on the Noble Eightfold Path observing morality and practicing meditation.

Tumhehi kiccaṃattapaṃ akkhātāro tathāgatā[97]

The Tathāgatas only explain and reveal the path but one has oneself to walk on it alone if he wants to reap the fruits. The Buddha made it very clear when he said that even if he were to give directions to go to a place, unless one undertakes his journey and sets his foot on the path, he cannot reach there. How can he reap the fruits of living a *brahmacariya* life unless he lives it?[98]

---

96. A1 pp. 59-60 (Nalanda Edition)
97. Dh 176
98. M3 *Gaṇakamoggalāna Sutta*

If one looks at the list of words used again and again by the Buddha in his teachings, it will be at once clear that the central theme of his dhamma is 'doing', 'striving', 'working hard' and 'experiencing'. *Āsevati* (to practice, to pursue, to indulge), *bhāveti* (to produce, to beget, to increase), *brūheti* (to increase, to cause, to grow), *bahulīkaroti* (to take up seriously) and *vaḍḍheti* (to increase) have been used in the context of *sīla, samādhi* and *paññā*. They are to be practiced time and again, again and again and continuously. *Chandaṃ janeti* (to put forth extra desire), *ghaṭati* (to exert oneself), *vāyamati* (to make endeavourer to struggle), *uṭṭhahati* (to arise to exert onself) have beeen used in the context of keeping *akusala dhamma* away. *Aṭṭhiṃ karoti* (to apply one's own mind), *manasi karoti* (to give full attention) had been used in the context of listening to *dhammas. Pajahati* (to cast out), *vinodeti* (to repress), *vyanti karoti* (to end) and *anabhāvaṃ gameti* (to bring to nothing) have been used in the context of getting rid of *nīvaraṇas* and *āsavas*. If one is to cut the tangles of craving, he is to be ardent (*ātāpī*), earnest (*appamatto*) and strenuous (*pahitatto*). Most important for living a *brahmacariya* life are *thāma* (stamina), *viriya* (vigour), and *parakkama* (endeavour).

All these words are action words, 'active' action words in fact, if I may be permitted to use such a phrase. There is no connotation of passivity in them. "Exert, strive, make endeavour, put forth extra desire and work out your salvation with diligence" is the message of the Buddha.

He also lays emphasis on self-examination, constant self-examination, in order to know one's weaknesses and shortcomings so that efforts can be made to establish profitable states and destroy one's *āsavas* (taints).

"Monks, if on self-examination a monk finds thus; I generally live covetous, malevolent in heart, possessed by sloth and torpor, excited in mind, doubtful and wavering, untruthful with soiled thoughts, with body passionate, sluggish and uncontrolled - then that monk must put forth extra desire, efforts, endeavor, exertion, impulse, mindfulness and attention for the abandoning of those wicked unprofitable states."[99]

Those who walk on the Noble Eightfold Path, determined to live a *brahmacariya* (religious) life have to undertake the arduous journey and train themselves in the training of precepts, have to fulfill virtues, endure the inclemency of weather, hunger and thirst, have to overcome likes and dislikes, fear and dread, achieve the states of *jhāna* (concentration) and finally destroy their taints. In the Vipassana form of meditation, which is the Buddha's unique contribution to world culture, one comes across a method by which he can purify his mind, cut down his cravings which burn him, achieve a comparatively calm state of mind i.e. equanimity, which is

99. BGS Vol. V p. 67

the goal of religion. But not merely an intellectual grasp of Vipassana but a dip into its stream flowing towards *nibbāna* can deliver one's good.

In conclusion, one can say that the Buddha's explanation of the causes of suffering through the Law of Dependent Origination is philosophy. His extensive use of reason and argument to show dependence of one dhamma (used in a wider sense) upon another is also philosophy. But his exhortation to walk on the Noble Eightfold Path and live a *brahmacariya* life to annihilate the cause of suffering and experience *nibbānic* bliss is religion. In Buddhism, philosophy and religion converge.

Humanism of Early Buddhism

Before we talk about the nature of humanism in early Buddhism, let us see how it has been defined as a philosophy. It has been defined as 'any system of thought or action which is concerned with human (not divine or religious) interest, or with man as a responsible intellectual being.'[100] It has also been defined as 'a system of thought which emphasizes that man can comprehend and investigate only with the resources of the human mind and discounts abstract theorizing.'[101]

It is clear from the definition that humanism is primarily concerned with man and his immediate problems, mainly material but not religious and spiritual. Secondly, it is a system of thought or action but not both i.e. it is not a happy blending of thought and action. In other words, the action-plan to execute the thought is not embedded in this philosophy. The thought is concerned with man's immediate problems of life connected chiefly with material progress, security and survival. Thirdly, it puts a premium on the capacity of the human mind with which man can 'comprehend and investigate'. Fourthly, it regards man 'as a responsible intellectual being' so much so that he himself and no outside agency, not even a divine one, is responsible for his misery and happiness, for his weal and woe. And lastly, it discounts abstract theorizing that has occupied the minds of a great number of philosophers who try to puzzle out the answer of questions like who created this universe and what is the ultimate reality. Such questions, in fact, have no bearing on the immediate material problems of man, less so on his spiritual and religious ones.

Lord Buddha also is primarily concerned with man and his problems, but of the two kinds of problems - material and spiritual, he is concerned more with the latter than with the former. He elaborated on the spiritual problems of man i.e. suffering and the cause of suffering. He also showed the path leading to the annihilation of cravings that cause suffering and also showed the way to attain *nibbāna*—the *summum bonum* of life. But this is also true that he did not lose sight of the material problems of man i.e. he did not ignore them. His incidental remarks on some of the material problems are seminal in character and make a deep probe into their causes and their cures. How our society can achieve harmony and live in peace and happiness, how corruptions and crimes like theft, dacoity and murder can be rooted out, how all unemployed persons can get employment and become useful citizens and how farmers, businessmen and cattle rearers

100. ORD
101. ibid.

can help in the economic prosperity of society and overall welfare of people – these have been set forth in the *Kūṭadanta Sutta.*[102] How punishment and fine cannot eradicate corruptions and crimes has also been explained here.[103] What are the strengths of a democracy and how can it strike deep roots and grow into a strong tree full of flowers and fruits and stand firm without being intimidated by storms and gales have been explained in the *Mahāparinibbāna Sutta* in the context of the seven *aparihāniya dhammas* (conditions leading to growth and prosperity) of the Vajjīs. How should a king behave or for that matter how should our leaders behave has been nicely explained with the help of an apt simile. If the bull goes in a crooked way, all cows and heifers that follow him will go the same crooked way. Similarly if the leaders of mankind live an unrighteous life, all others do so. If the king is unrighteous, the entire nation experiences troubles and sufferings.[104] This illustration of the Buddha is very relevant in all times and in all societies, more so in our times and society. What dangerous diseases can be caused by the virus of caste system had been anticipated by the Buddha who raised his voice against it and made a healthy and reasonable pronouncement that it is not birth which should determine somebody's caste, but it should be his thoughts and actions.[105]. In the *Ambaṭṭha Sutta* Lord Buddha makes it amply clear that one who observes *sīla* (precepts), pratices *samādhi* (concentration) and attains *paññā* (insight wisdom) is superior to all people and gods.[106] His exhortation to observe certain precepts provides a sound foundation for achieving peace and harmony in society. If the members of a society keep themselves away from killing, stealing, committing adultery, lying and making slanderous speech etc. much of the man-made troubles in society will disappear. And if they practice the four *Brahmavihāras* (sublime states) the society will become a veritable heaven.

There are many such remarkable thoughts which if put into practice, can ensure peace and prosperity in society as also its material development and progress.

The thought of Marxist philosophers remains confined mostly to economic prosperity of society; that of scientific humanists to survival of mankind from dangerous and deadly nuclear weapons by putting nuclear

---

102. See my article entitled 'Buddha's View of Harmony' in Essays on Buddhism and Pali Literature, EBL, Delhi, 1994.

103. ibid.

104. A.2.80. *Adhammika Sutta* (Nalanda Edition)

105. Sn 136 *Na jaccā vasalo hoti, na jaccā hoti brahmaṇo/Kammunā vasalo hoti, kammunā hoti brāhmaṇo//*

106. D 1.85 *Vijjācaraṇasampanno, so seṭṭho devamānuseti.*

energy at the service of mankind; that of humanist philosophers to all round material development of mankind but their thoughts do not seem to go beyond material problems of man to his spiritual problems and to his spiritual developments. Lord Buddha grapples with man's spiritual problems squarely. His enunciation of the four noble truths does not only spell out man's ubiquitous problem of suffering, but also explains its psycho-ethical cause and maps out the path walking on which suffering is ended root and branch.

Lord Buddha, like a true humanist philosopher makes man responsible for all that he does. Man cannot pass the buck on to anyone else, even if it is a divine agency, for his suffering and happiness. In fact, in the Buddha's scheme of things, there is no God. Man makes himself what he is by his own actions. It is in virtue of his actions that he can raise himself or lower himself. Both wholesome and unwholesome actions make him what he is. His self is nothing but a product of his actions.[107]

But at the same time he sings the praise of man's immense potentiality to rise high and perform wholesome actions. Man is not a weakling but he is his master.[108] This belief in man's immense capacity is corroborated by Buddha's own personal experience. He walked on the difficult Noble Eightfold Path with indefatigable zeal and burnt himself in the fire of *sādhanā* assiduously till he was purged of all the dross and shone like pure gold. He does not talk of God's grace as the Christians do, but he says time and again that one will have to work out one's own salvation. The Tathāgatas only show the path[109] that leads to extinction of cravings and attainment of *nibbāna*, but they do not stand proxy for others. By making man responsible for his welfare and woe, the Buddha does not only hold man responsible for what he does, but he also holds him in high dignity. He has great respect for the dignity of man so much so that he wants him to become his own refuge and does not want him to go to anybody else's refuge except to the refuge of Dhamma.[110]

All theistic systems of philosophy believe in God and his grace. The Buddha's philosophy, on the contrary, is antitheistic, but it is highly ethical. It can be said that man who lives a strictly ethical life has replaced God here. Emphasis on moral actions with a view to earning merit is the hall mark

---

107. S 1.89 *Ubho puññaṃ ca pāpaṃ ca, yaṃ macco kurute idha/*
Taṃ hi tassa sakaṃ hoti, taṃ ca ādāya gacchati/
Taṃ tassa anugaṃ hoti, chāyāva anapāyini//

108. Dh 124 *Attā hi attano nātho, ko hi nātho paro siyā/*

109. Dh 204 *Tumhehi kiccamātappaṃ, akkhātāro tathāgatā/*

110. D2.78 *Attadīpā viharatha, attasaraṇā anaññasaraṇā dhammadīpā viharatha, dhammasaraṇā anaññasaraṇā.*

of all theistic systems of philosophy, but to develop non-attachment with developed intuitive wisdom is the hall mark of the Buddha's philosophy. One should not have craving even for developing non-attachment, not even for attaining *nibbāna*. The path the Buddha showed for annihilating cravings consists of *sīla, samādhi* and *paññā*. The three constituents are so inter- linked that one cannot be developed without the help of the other two. It is not possible to know the real nature of things without attaining concentration of mind and concentration of mind is not possible without observing moral precepts (*sīla*) and only a real knowledge of things enables one to develop non-attachment (*vairāgya*) which goes a long way in making one take up a *brahmacariya* life.

Only man can live a *brahmacariya* life. Thus man stands higher than all, higher even than gods, because it is man who can attain *nibbāna*. *Nibbāna* is beyond the reach of gods and Brahmās except for a few exceptions. It is true that they live for many aeons and enjoy pleasures of all kinds, but it is man who understands the transient nature of all things of the world and as a result develops non-attachment—the pre-requisite for leading a *brahmacariya* life. Human existence is, therefore, one of the inevitable conditions of becoming a Buddha.[111] "Human existence, attainment of the (male) sex, condition, seeing a teacher, going forth, attainment of the special qualities, an act of merit and will-power--by combining these eight things the resolve succeeds."[112]

It is in human existence and no other existence, not even in divine existence is it possible to make one's resolve succeed. As man can observe moral precepts and give charity, so his resolve of becoming a Buddha can come to fruition.[113] The Buddha has spoken exaltingly about human existence. There are many such passages in the Tipiṭaka where human existence is praised. Yama--the king of Death says to a god that it was well if he attained human existence.[114] In the *Itivuttaka* it is said that to be in the company of man is a rare bliss.[115] It has also been said in this book that it is really very happy for a god to be born a man or to acquire human existence.[116]

---

111. Bu p. 309 *Manussattaṃ liṅgasaṃpatti, hetu satthāradassanaṃ/Pabbajjā guṇa saṃpatti, adhikāro ca chandatā/Aṭṭhadhammā samodhānā, abhinihāro samijjhatīti*

112. MAP. p. 15

113. Sn A 1.40 *Aññatra hi manussajātiyā avasesajātīsu devajātiyampi ṭhitassa paṇidhi na ijjhati. Ettha ṭhitena pana buddhattaṃ patthantena dānādīni puññakammāni katvā manussatta eva patthetabbaṃ.*

114. A 1. 166 *Aho vatāhaṃ manussattaṃ labheyya*

115. It 56 *Ito bho sugatiṃ gaccha, manussānaṃ sahabyataṃ*

116. ibid. *Manussataṃ kho, bhikkhave, devānaṃ sugati gamana saṅkhātaṃ*

All these passages bring out the importance of man in the universe and show his dignity. Gods look small in their eyes in comparison to man. Many a time Sakka—the king of gods has been shown saluting and paying tributes to the Buddha. When Mātali—his charioteer asks him why he who is saluted by man salutes the Buddha who is a human being, Sakka's answer is revealing. One who attains Buddhahood, he says, far excels all gods and his glory transcends the glories of all gods. But only a man can become a Buddha. Thus man can achieve such heights that are not attainable even by gods. Therefore, gods seem to envy his lot.

The glory of man has been sung in all religious literatures. 'It is a rare fortune to get human existence. Gods rarely get it. This is what the scriptures say.'[117] Lord Buddha says unequivocally that man is the crown of all creatures in this universe and it is he who is the measure of all things, as rightly said by Protagoras later.

Man can make great achievements even in the spiritual field, but the achievements he makes are not only for himself, they are also for others. After the Buddha set the wheel of Dhamma in motion and after he ordained some persons like the *Pañcavaggiya bhikkhus* and Yasa and his companions, he exhorted them to go from one place to another and teach the Dhamma to the people for their welfare and happiness. Had he been selfish, he would have kept to himself what he had achieved with great efforts and hard strivings but his concern for other human beings was uppermost in his mind and inspired by his altruistic attitude he showed the path to others also—the path which had taken him to *nibbāna*- a state where all cravings come to an end. He does not only talk about the path but also explains in minute detail how one can go along the path without faltering and without missing even a single step.

His concern for man's happiness is so great that the philosophy he propounds is not speculative. It is not an intellectual exercise ending in futility but his is a pragmatic and realistic philosophy concerned directly with man's immediate problems and their solution. To try to find out the answers of the indeterminate questions (*abyākata pañhas*), according to him, is useless because the questions are not relevant and do not have any bearing on living a life according to the Dhamma i.e. a life free from lusts, a life of quietude and tranquillity.[118]

One point, which has been underlined in the definition of humanism, is that it discounts abstract theorizing. Lord Buddha too discounts it. Therefore, his philosophy comes close to humanism. He asserts that

117. Tulasīdāsa, Rāmacaritamānasa—*Baḍe bhāga mānusa tana pāvā/ Suradurlabha sadgranthana gāvā//.*

118. M.2 101. See *Cūlamālunkya Sutta*

whatever man can 'comprehend and investigate' with his pure mind, will be for his good. He does not need to try to know more about this world but his own immediate problem. And by 'pure mind' he means a steady human mind free from greed (*lobha*), aversion (*dosa*) and ignorance (*moha*). Knowledge gained by listening to others and reading books and even knowledge gained with the help of reason and intellect is not of much consequence to the Buddha. Real knowledge gained at the experiential level is of great consequence. Pure intuitive wisdom i.e, pure *paññā* can be attained by a pure mind.

The aspects of humanism that one finds in early Buddhism[119] are the following: (1) Man's dignity has been acknowledged and upheld; (2) he is held responsible for all that he does; (3) his interest and value are predominantly taken care of; (4) his mind is regarded as the ultimate resource with which he can 'comprehend and investigate' things in the universe and lastly (5) abstract theorization or speculative thinking is discounted, if not looked down upon. But apart from these, the most important aspect of humanism of early Buddhism that stands out clearly is its religious or *dhammic* character. I have shown in one of my essays[120] that the philosophy that is lived in life for achieving the highest good becomes religion. A philosophy is lived in life, because ultimately it is good for life, it conduces to one's spiritual development and well-being. One tries to inculcate such moral and ethical values in life which can purify him, enrich him spiritually, make him nobler and better and which can take care not only of the problems of the world but also of the problems of the world beyond. Early Buddhism is not only a system of thought propounded by the Buddha, but also embedded lies in it the action-plan very carefully and meticulously drawn by him, to execute the thought so that it can be lived and practiced in day to day life. Thus, there is a happy blending of thought and action, teaching and practice and *pariyatti* (theory) and *paṭipatti* (practice). What is taught here is meant for practicing in life. It is the practice that enables one to realize the truth of what is taught. Teaching and practice complement each other.

Thus, the humanism of early Buddhism is religious or *dhammic* in character. It is religious without being theistic i.e. without believing in God. It holds that man, by annihilating *rāga, dosa* and *moha* (which he can do by walking on the Noble Eightfold Path) can elevate himself to such a

119. For Aspects of Humanism in Later Buddhism, see my article entitled 'Ācārya Śāntideva's Humanism in Essays on Buddhism and Pali Literature', E.B. L. Delhi pp. 47-54.

120. See my essay entitled 'Buddhism: Where Philosophy and Religion Converge' collected in this book for what I mean by action words.

high position that he can himself become God by cultivating virtues and qualities, which one sees in or associates with God. It is on account of these virtues and qualities that the Buddha was deified in later Buddhist literature.

Another very interesting aspect of this Buddhism is that the Buddha did not only say that the philosophy he propounded must be lived, but he explained in detail how to live it, how to grow with it, how to practice it and how to enjoy its fruits in this very life. One of the characteristics of his Dhamma is 'come and see' (*ehipassiko*). There is no passivity in this philosophy, no idle speculation and nothing that is not useful. Its literature is full of action words. The message of the Buddha is 'exert, strive, make endeavour, put forth extra desire and work out your own salvation with diligence.' The action-plan the Buddha prepared to execute his thought and philosophy is nothing but the art of living. The technique of Vipassana meditation teaches one to be aware and mindful and to constantly self-examine his weaknesses and shortcomings so that he can get rid of them.

In the *Dvedhāvitakka Sutta* of the *Majjhima Nikāya,* the Buddha has explained how to drive out harmful *dhammas* like sensual pleasures and malevolence and cultivate non-harmful *dhammas* like renunciation and non-malevolence. As soon as one sees sensual pleasure arising in oneself which is conducive to hurt oneself and hurt others and conducive also to hurt both, he becomes aware that 'it is destructive of insight wisdom associated with distress, not conducive to *nibbāna.*' He reflects on this harmful aspect and keeps on driving it out and making an end of it. He also does the same with respect to other harmful *dhammas* that arise in him. If he does not reflect the way the Buddha has taught, harmful *dhammas* like sensual pleasures and malevolence will get the better of him. As a result, they will overpower him. But if he is ardent, diligent and self-resolute, aware and mindful, evil *dhammas* cannot sneak into him. The importance of right effort (*sammā vāyāmo*) becomes clear in this context.

In the *Vitakkasanṭhāna Sutta* the Buddha lucidly sets forth the steps that one should take to get rid of *akusala dhammas* and develop higher thought.

"Monks, if a monk is intent on higher thought, from time to time he should attend to five characteristics. What five?'

"Herein, monks, whatever may be the characteristic which a monk attends to, if there arise evil unskilled thought associated with desire and associated with aversion and associated with confusion, that monk should attend instead to another characteristic which is associated with what is skilled. By attending to this other characteristic which is associated with what is skilled instead of to that characteristic, those evil, unskilled thoughts associated with desire and associated with aversion and associated with confusion are got rid of, they come to an end. From getting rid of these, his mind subjectively steadies, calms, is one-pointed, concentrated."[121]

He further says that if attending to characteristics associated with what is skilled, evil unskilled thoughts still arise, the peril of these thoughts should be scrutinized by him. This scrutiny will enable him to get rid of these evil thoughts. If scrutinizing the peril of these thoughts, there still arise evil unskilled thoughts associated with desire, aversion and confusion, he should try to forget them and try not to attend to them. In this way he will be able to get rid of such evil thoughts. If even after forgetting those thoughts and paying no attention to them, there still arise in him evil unskilled thoughts associated with craving (*rāga*) aversion (*dosa*) and ignorance (*moha*), he should attend to the thought function and form of those thoughts, By so doing such evil thoughts are got rid of. Abandoning hard posture one takes to an easy one and succeeds. If even after attending to the thought function and form of those thoughts, there still arise in him evil unskilled thoughts, he 'with his teeth clenched and tongue pressed against his palate' should by his mind subdued, restrain and dominate the mind. Thus, such thoughts will be driven out and his mind will be calm, steady and concentrated.[122]

The *Tipiṭaka* is full of such passages where the Buddha has explained in minute detail how to go about cultivating virtues by ridding oneself of *akusala dhammas*. He has explained all the steps that one should take to get rid of *akusala dhammnas* with great caution and clarity. When he comes to a particular stage in the course of his explanation, he also goes on to explain where we should go from there and how we should go there.

Thus, the Buddha teaches man to cultivate higher virtues by living a religious and ethical life and achieve that dignity which even gods envy. The Humanism of early Buddhism is clearly religious in nature.

121. MLS Vol. 1, p. 153

122. ibid., see for detail pp. 153-156

Buddha's Law of Kamma and Rebirth vis-à-vis Social Order

The Buddha believes in *kamma* and its result. But instead of saying that a man must reap what he sows, he says that what a man reaps accords with his deeds. So, instead of propounding fatalism he propounds man's freedom to act.

The Buddha refutes the wrong view that "whatsoever weal or woe or neutral feeling is experienced is all due to previous action[123]" and says "so then owing to a previous action people will become murderers, thieves, unchaste, liars, slanderers, abusive, babblers, covetous, malicious and perverse in view. Thus, for those who fall back on the former deeds as the essential reasons, there is neither a necessity to do this deed or abstain from that deed[124]."

The Buddha says, "If any one says that a man must reap according to his deeds, in that case there is no religious life nor is an opportunity afforded for the entire extinction of sorrow. But if any one says that what a man reaps accords with his deeds, in that case there is a religious life and an opportunity afforded for the entire extinction of sorrow.[125]

This law is not inexorable. The law of *kamma* does operate, but it does not operate in the way the brahmins interpret it. They use it as a double-edged weapon to exalt themselves and to condemn the sūdras. They say that they are born in brahmin caste because of wholesome actions in the past lives whereas the śūdras are born in low castes because of their unwholesome actions performed in past lives. They thus see a cause to

---

123. A. I 202 *Santi, bhikkhave, eke samaṇabrāhmaṇā evaṃvādino evaṃdiṭṭhino-'yaṃ kiñcāyaṃ purisapuggalo paṭisaṃvedeti sukhaṃ vā dukkhaṃ vā adukkhamasukhaṃ vā sabbaṃ taṃ pubbekatahetū'ti.* A 1.202

124. *'tenahāyasmanto pāṇātipātino bhavissanti pubbekatahetu, adinnādāyino bhavissanti pubbekatahetu, abrahmacārino bhavissanti pubbekatahetu, musāvādino bhavissanti pubbekatahetu, pisuṇavācā bhavissanti pubbekatahetu, pharusavācā bhavissanti pubbekatahetu, samphappalāpino bhavissanti pubbekatahetu, abhijjhāluno bhavissanti pubbekatahetu, byāpannacittā bhavissanti pubbekatahetu, micchādiṭṭhikā bhavi-ssanti pubbekatahetu'.*;

125. A. I. 282 *"Yo, ca kho bhikkhave, evaṃ vadeyya- 'yathā yathāyaṃ puriso kammaṃ karoti tathā tathā taṃ paṭisaṃvediyatī'ti, evaṃ santaṃ, bhikkhave, brahmacariyavāso na hoti, okāso na paññāyati sammā dukkhassa antakiriyāya. Yo ca kho, bhikkhave, evaṃ vadeyya-'yathā yathā vedanīyaṃ ayaṃ puriso kammaṃ karoti tathā tathāssa vipākaṃ paṭisaṃvediyatī'ti, evaṃ santaṃ, bhikkhave, brahmacariyavāso hoti, okāso paññāyati sammā dukkhassa antakiriyāya."*

look down upon śūdras. Had the brahmins interpreted this law in the right manner, they would have accepted that the so called brahmins would also cease to be brahmins if they do unwholesome actions and the sūdras would be born as brahmins if they do wholesome actions. Instead of interpreting it like this, they interpret it wrongly in order to perpetuate their privileges of birth in the brahmin caste.

The Buddha raised his voice against this interpretation of the law of *kamma*. He came out with several arguments based on science and common sense to prove that there is no difference between one man and another even if they belonged to two different castes. Both of them could take a bath in the river and purify themselves, both of them can rub two pieces of wood and produce the same kind of heat and fire, both of them can walk on the Noble Eightfold Path, observe *sīla*, practice *samādhi* and attain *paññā* and both of them can practice loving kindness (*mettā bhāvanā*). If the male member of one caste cohabits with the female member of another caste the child born will not be different - it will be a human being. He showed by giving scientific arguments that as far as the different limbs are concerned one man belonging to one caste will have the same kind of limbs as the other belonging to other caste. There will be no difference between them. Besides, it is not the exclusive privilege of the brahmins to be washed clean by the river water and bath powder and it is not exclusively their power to produce fire by rubbing two sticks. The members of so called other castes also have the same privilege. All these arguments are given in the *Assalāyana Sutta*[126] and the *Vāseṭṭha Sutta.*[127]

By analysing the function of *kammas*, the Buddha proves that out of the four types of *kammas* such as *Janaka kamma* (reproductive), *Upatthambhaka kamma* (supportive), *Upapīḍaka kamma* (counteractive) and *Upaghātaka kamma*[128] (destructive) the last two can counteract and destroy other *kammas* which are likely to produce serious *vipākas* (results). *Upapīḍaka kamma* destroys the results (*vipāka*) of other *kammas* and *upaghātaka kamma* destroys weak results and produces its own results. How can the result of a *kamma* be destroyed is proved by a beautiful example. A pinch of salt added to a cup of water can make it salty and undrinkable but if it is thrown in a river, the river water will still be drinkable. What it means is this - the unwholesome effects of *kamma* can be more than made good by doing wholesome actions in the present life. We get the cards from the past life but how we play them is in our hands. The message is that we are free to ameliorate our conditions by acting freely in the present life. For the

126. M 2 361
127. Sn 173
128. AṬ 2.96

Buddha, the law of *kamma* does not bind one's hands but keeps him free to do whatever he can.

It is clear from what is said above that *kamma* can be counteracted and destroyed. When it is accepted that an *akusala kamma* can be counteracted and destroyed then religious life is possible. It is possible to not only better and improve one's spiritual and moral life but also improve and better one's social and material life.

The law of *kamma* operates in a very complex manner. It is a subject of the Buddha (*Buddha Viṣaya*) to explain how this law operates; ordinary people cannot understand it. But operate this law does.

We can understand the working of *kamma* if we understand how seeds grow and bear fruit. What applies to the vegetable world applies *mutatis mutandis* to the moral world.

As all seeds sown in the soil do not grow and bear fruits, some *kammas* become unproductive and ineffective. But if the seeds germinate and bear fruits, the fruits are like the seeds. Bitter seeds will produce bitter fruits and sweet ones will produce sweet fruits.

"Why is it, Nagasena, that all people are not alike, but some are short-lived and some long-lived, some sickly and some healthy, some ugly and some beautiful, some without influence and some of great power, some poor and some wealthy, some low-born and some high-born, some stupid and some wise?"[129]

The qualities or otherwise which people are shown here to possess are universal. The paradigms given here are universal. They apply to all human beings of all countries. The Buddha never says that certain qualities are responsible for one's birth in brahmin caste and certain bad qualities are responsible for his birth in a śūdra caste. The paradigm of caste is not universally applicable. It is India made.

All paradigms such as long-lived, short-lived, ugly, beautiful, poor, wealthy, stupid and wise are universal. Even low-born and high-born do not refer to birth in a śūdra caste or brahmin caste. People are called low-born and high-born when they are judged ethically. Low-born people will not be inclined to observe the five precepts whereas high-born people will naturally be inclined to observe them. It is their dispositions which characterize them as low-born and high-born. Just as vegetables are not alike, so people also are not alike. They are different because of the different actions they perform.

In the *Cūlakammavibhaṅga Sutta*[130] the Buddha says: "Beings, O Brahmin, have each their own *kamma* (*kammassakā*), are inheritors of

129. QKM, p. 200

130. M 3.250 "*Ko nu kho, bho gotama, hetu ko paccayo yena manussānaṃyeva sataṃ*

kamma (*kammadāyādā*), belong to the tribe of their *kammas* (*kammayoni*) and relatives by their *kammas* (*kammabandhu*), have each their *kamma* as their protecting lord (*kammapaṭisaraṇā*).

It is action that distinguishes beings as inferior and superior (*kammaṃ satte vibhajati yadidaṃ hīnappaṇītāyāti*).

In the *Mallikā Devī Sutta*, Queen Mallika asks the same type of question- "Pray, lord, what is the reason, what is the cause, why in this world some women are ill-favoured, deformed, of a mean appearance and are poor having little of their own, of small possession and are of small account?"

"Again, lord, pray what is the reason, what is the cause why in this world some women are ill-favoured...but yet wealthy, of great riches, of great possession and of great account?

"Again, lord, pray what is the reason, what is the cause why in this world some women are well-favoured, well-formed, lovely to look upon, amiable, possessed of the great beauty of complexion, and yet are poor, having little of their own, of small possessions and are of small account?

"And yet again, lord, pray what is the reason, what is the cause why in this world some women are well-favoured, well-formed, lovely to look upon, amiable, possessed of the greatest beauty of complexion, and are moreover wealthy, of great riches, of great possessions and of great account?"[131]

---

manussabhūtānaṃ dissanti hīnappaṇītatā? Dissanti hi, bho gotama, manussā appāyukā, dissanti dīghāyukā; dissanti bavhābādhā „ dissanti appābādhā; dissanti dubbaṇṇā, dissanti vaṇṇavanto; dissanti appesakkhā, dissanti mahesakkhā; dissanti appabhogā, dissanti mahābhogā; dissanti nīcakulīnā, dissanti uccākulīnā; dissanti duppaññā, dissanti paññavanto Ko nu kho, bho gotama, hetu ko paccayo yena manussānaṃyeva sataṃ manussabhūtānaṃ dissanti hīnappaṇītatā"ti?

"Kammassakā, māṇava, sattā kammadāyādā kammayonī kammabandhū kammappaṭisaraṇā. Kammaṃ satte vibhajati yadidaṃ-hīnappaṇītatāyāti.

131. Gradual Sayings, p. 215

A1.233 *"Ko nu kho, bhante, hetu ko paccayo, yena midhekacco mātugāmo dubbaṇṇā ca hoti durūpā supāpikā dassanāya; daliddā ca hoti appassakā appabhogā appesakkhā ca?*

"Ko pana, bhante, hetu ko paccayo, yena midhekacco mātugāmo dubbaṇṇā ca hoti durūpā supāpikā dassanāya; aḍḍhā ca hoti mahaddhanā mahābhogā mahesakkhā ca?

"Ko nu kho, bhante, hetu ko paccayo, yena midhekacco mātugāmo abhirūpā ca hoti dassanīyā pāsādikā paramāya vaṇṇapokkharatāya samannāgatā; daliddā ca hoti appassakā appabhogā appesakkhā ca? "Ko pana, bhante, hetu ko paccayo, yena midhekacco mātugāmo abhirūpā ca hoti dassanīyā pāsādikā paramāya vaṇṇapokkharatāya samannāgatā, aḍḍhā ca hoti mahaddhanā mahābhogā mahesakkhā cā"ti?

"Idha, pana mallike, ekacco mātugāmo kodhanā hoti upāyāsabahulā. Appampi vuttā samānā abhisajjati kuppati byāpajjati patitthīyati, kopañca dosañca appaccayañca pātukaroti.Sā... na dātā hoti samaṇassa vā brāhmaṇassa vā annaṃ... seyyavasathapadīpeyyaṃ

In reply to these questions, the Buddha says that if a woman is ill-tempered, cross and agitated, stubborn, has temper and ill-will and displeasure, does not give charity, is jealous of others, is revengeful then if she is born in this world, after death she is ill-favoured, ill-formed, of a mean appearance and poor...[132]

In this way he explains why a woman is poor or rich, happy or unhappy and beautiful or ugly.

Nowhere does the Buddha say that one is born a brahmin because of his *kusala kamma* and born a śūdra because of his *akusala kamma*. Caste, as has been said above, is not a universal concept. It is a social organization confined only to India and a few countries such as Nepal and Sri Lanka. What the Buddha says applies universally to the moral world, to the spiritual world. He says that one is either born in a state of deprivation (*duggati*) because of *akusala kamma* or in a happy state (*sugati*) because of *kusala kamma;* one is wise because he has seen the real nature of things and having seen it he develops non-attachment and one is stupid because he remains engrossed in sensual pleasures and wants them more and more and multiplies his misery.

So the law of *kamma* holds good in the moral realm and not in the social and temporal realm. It explains moral order, it explains *sukha, dukkha, sugati, duggati* but it is not responsible for one's birth in a particular caste and does not apply to social order if by social order it is meant a division of human beings into different castes. Persons belonging to any caste will attain good destinations (*sugati*) if they do wholesome actions and go to hell (*niraya*) if they do unwholesome actions. The Buddha does accept other orders in society, say for example an order based on intelligence, an order based on disposition, an order based on one's efficiency but it does not accept order based on caste.

This is clear from what he says in the *Saṃyutta Nikāya*. He talks of four kinds of *puggala*. One heading from darkness to darkness (*tamotamaparāyaṇo puggalo*), one heading from darkness to light (*tamojotiparāyaṇo puggalo*), one heading from light to darkness (*jotitamoparāyaṇo puggalo*) and one heading from light to light (*joti jotiparāyaṇo puggalo*).[133] Light and darkness,

---

132. ibid.

133. "*Kathañca, mahārāja puggalo tamotamaparāyano hoti? idha, mahārāja, ekacco puggalo nīce kule paccājāto hoti, caṇḍālakule vā venakule vā nesādakule vā rathakārakule vā pukkusakule vā dalidde appannapānabhojane kasiravuttike, yattha kasirena ghāsacchādo labbhati. So ca hoti dubbaṇṇo duddasiko okoṭimako bavhābādho kāṇo vā kuṇī vā khañjo vā pakkhahato vā, na lābhī annassa pānassa vatthassa yānassa mālāgandhavilepanassa seyyāvasathapadīpeyyassa. So kāyena duccaritaṃ carati, vācāya duccaritaṃ carati, manasā duccaritaṃ carati. So kāyena duccaritaṃ*

respectively stand for ethically good and bad dispositions. He explains one's lowness and highness by giving examples of different castes that were there in society. This should not be confused with *his* view of the four castes as obtained in India at that time. If one says that the Buddha also believed in peoples' birth in different castes because of past actions then he would be putting the cart before the horse.

How then can one reconcile this view of the Buddha with what he said about the unscientific basis of the caste system in several *suttas*? What can one say to the many common sense arguments that he put forward to demolish this system, which divides man from man and creates social, political and other problems? I think it is for the sake of explaining peoples' dispositions that he talks of castes. He never says that if a brahmin does *akusala kamma* he is born a śūdra or vice versa. What he says is that after death, he is born in a state of deprivation.

He does not talk of caste here but talks of *kula*, which can be said to be a universal concept applicable to all the people of the world. It has ethical connotations rather than secular. *Kuladhītā* and *kulaputtā* refer to girls and boys from families that are good from the ethical point of view.

Kamma is the instrument of moral order. It is a *niyāma* like *ṛtu, bīja, citta* and *dhamma.*[134] There is an order in the physical world. Starry bodies move smoothly without colliding with one another, seasons change, seeds grow into trees and plants and they yield fruits and fruits again give seeds and seeds give bitter or sweet fruits according to their nature. One

---

caritvā vācāya duccaritaṃ caritvā manasā duccaritaṃ caritvā, kāyassa bhedā paraṃ maraṇā apāyaṃ duggatiṃ vinipātaṃ nirayaṃ upapajjati. "Seyyathāpi, mahārāja, puriso andhakārā vā andhakāraṃ gaccheyya, tamā vā tamaṃ gaccheyya, lohitamalā vā lohitamalaṃ gaccheyya. Tathūpamāhaṃ, mahārāja, imaṃ puggalaṃ vadāmi. Evaṃ kho, mahārāja, puggalo tamotama-parāyano hoti. "Kathañca, mahārāja, puggalo tamojotiparāyano hoti? ......"Kathañca, mahārāja, puggalo jotitamaparāyano hoti? idha, mahārāja, ekacco puggalo ucce kule paccājāto hoti,... so kāyena duccaritaṃ caritvā vācāya duccaritaṃ caritvā manasā duccaritaṃ caritvā, kāyassa bhedā paraṃ maraṇā apāyaṃ duggatiṃ vinipātaṃ nirayaṃ upapajjati ... "Kathañca, mahārāja, puggalo jotijotiparāyano hoti? idha, mahārāja, ekacco puggalo ucce kule paccājāto hoti, khattiyamahāsālakule vā brāhmaṇamahāsālakule vā gahapatimahāsālakule vā, aḍḍhe mahaddhane mahābhoge pahūtajātarūparajate pahūtavittūpakaraṇe pahūtadhanadhaññe. so ca hoti abhirūpo dassanīyo pāsādiko, paramāya vaṇṇapokkha ratāya samannāgato, lābhī annassa pānassa vatthassa yānassa mālāgandhavilepanassa seyyāvasathapadīpeyyassa. so kāyena sucaritaṃ carati, vācāya sucaritaṃ carati, manasā sucaritaṃ carati. so kāyena sucaritaṃ caritvā vācāya sucaritaṃ caritvā manasā sucaritaṃ caritvā, kāyassa bhedā paraṃ maraṇā sugatiṃ saggaṃ lokaṃ upapajjati.... S.I 112-114...

134. DhsA p. 309

consciousness gives rise to another. As these *niyāmas* work without fail so does the law of *kamma*, but it operates to make one inferior or superior, ugly or beautiful, stupid or wise but not to make one a member of the artficially and unscientifically organized brahmin caste or śūdra caste. The Buddha does not believe in this. Buddha's world view is quite different from the brahmins' world view.

The law of *kamma* applies in the moral world. Dr. Ambedkar says, "The law of *kamma* has to do only with the question of general moral order. It has got nothing to do with the fortunes or misfortunes of an individual."[135] He further says, "that the effect of the *kamma* recoils on the doer is not always true."[136] Sometimes the actions of one affect others. The wrongs done by a king do harm to his subjects. His sins visit upon his subjects just as the sins of parents visit upon their children.

In the Brahman *weltanschauungen* (world view) the ideal society has four classes, which were based on graded inequality, and each class engages in an occupation. It is binding on them that no class is to transgress. The essence of this theory is inequality. What was once based on division of labour according to one's capacity and ability became one's occupation by virtue of his being born in a particular caste. One's father's occupation began to determine the caste of one's children. Even though the sons of a brahmin were not educated and were not able to recite and teach the Vedas, they began to call themselves brahmins and others who were able to do that were not allowed to call themselves brahmins and were condemned to remain at the station where their fathers were. With the passage of time, brahmins propounded the theory of their origin from the mouth of Brahmā and began to wield the weapon of superiority over others. The law of *kamma* was used as a very effective weapon to condemn those who were looked down upon. They were inferior because of their unwholesome actions and the brahmins were superior because of their wholesome actions. The result was that 'ability' and 'capacity' were neglected by the brahmins and they became the first casualties. What was a changing concept in the beginning became frozen and society was cursed to be divided into castes and sub-castes, which have no scientific basis. The law of *kamma*, which operates in the moral realm, was made to operate in the social realm and birth in a particular caste was made to depend upon one's action.

The Buddha put forward several scientific, biological, commonsense arguments to prove that all people have the same characteristics and are equally capable of attaining spiritual heights.[137] The difference found in

135. B&HD

136. ibid.

137. See my essay entitled 'Buddha's Social Philosophy in relation to Equality,

them is caused by his wholesome or unwholesome actions. Birth in the brahmin caste does not make one superior and birth in śūdra caste does not make one inferior. It is one's *kamma* that makes the difference. The concept of caste is not universal but it is India made and made particularly by the brahmins in their own interest. When Esukari speaks of the four kinds of services and the four classifications of income the Buddha asks him—"Is the whole world in accord with this brahmin classification of income and service?"[138]

By giving very suitable arguments, the Buddha silenced the brahmins. He explained to Aggika Bhāradvāja who an outcaste (*vasala*) is.[139] From this point of view, many brahmins were *vasalas* and many so-called *śūdras* were brahmins.

Dr. Ambedkar says, "Men are born unequal. Some are robust and others are weaklings... some are well to do and others are poor. All have to enter into what is called the struggle for existence. If inequality is recognized as the rule of game, the weakest will always go to the wall. The rule of inequality results in the survival of the fittest."[140]

But are the fittest the best from the point of view of society? The answer is 'no' because if the fittest are regarded as the best then there will be lawlessness.

It is for this reason that religion teaches equality, for equality may help the best to survive even though the best may not be the fittest.

The Buddha taught equality and proved beyond any doubt that all people are equal. The Law of *Kamma* has got nothing to do with one's birth in a particular caste. There are many evils of society that can be got rid of by good governance. Even wealth can be, if not equally, equitably distributed. One's poverty is not caused by one's unwholesome actions but they cause one's happiness and unhappiness. The influential and selfish section of society has been using the law of *kamma* as a weapon to exploit a large section of society. It is time we did away with it.

Freedom and Justice' collected in this book

138. M2.394.(See *Esukārī Sutta*)

139. Sn 102 (See *Vasala Sutta*)

140. B&H p. 308.

Buddha's Social Philosophy in Relation to Equality, Freedom and Justice

If one just ponders over these terms a little it will be clear that they are mutually related. One cannot think of freedom and justice where there is no equality. Freedom and justice are possible in a society where all are regarded as equal. But in a society divided into castes and sub-castes and sub-sub-castes freedom and justice are the first casualties. Equality, freedom and justice are human rights. As far as the Buddha is concerned, he regarded all human beings as equal. A man who considers himself superior will always have the tendency to exploit others. Brahmins who showed their origins from the mouth of Brahmā considered themselves superior. All others were regarded as inferior because of their origins from Brahmā's different limbs. What was perhaps an extended metaphor in order to show the different kinds of people based on division of labour because one cannot be a priest, a farmer, a cobbler and a warrior at the same time--was taken literally and because brahmins were educated, they employed their education as an effective means to exploit other people in society. They propounded and perpetuated this theory in order to serve their vested interests. They kept on giving arguments one after another in order to prove their origin from the mouth of Brahmā. How could they exploit others unless they proved their exalted origin?

The Buddha did not give importance to the yardstick that was applied to make a distinction between man and man in society by brahmins and he made several seminal remarks to prove that man is not great or small because of his birth in a so called brahmin or śūdra caste. Although the Buddha was primarily concerned with the existential problem of suffering and how to get rid of it, he did not lose sight of other social and political problems which cause trouble in society and do not let men live in peace and harmony. He saw that some people are deprived of the right to live on equal terms and on equal footing with other fellow beings because of the prevalent caste system. The society has been so divided by people having vested interests, that some are high and superior because they are born in the brahmin caste while others are low and inferior because they are born in the śūdra caste. If people are not equal, how can they have equal rights to live in peace and harmony? How can they enjoy the things of society equally? Their very division into high and low caste creates situations in which there are bound to be the exploiters and the exploited. Some will be masters and others will be slaves and yet others will be bonded labourers. The children of bonded labourers will also be bonded labourers and such a situation will continue till a kind of revolution takes place and people in bondage break themselves free. In such a social situation, how can the so called high and superior persons allow persons who are low and inferior in their eyes to have equal social, political and economic rights? They will not have the same social status, they will not have the same political right to vote and as far as their economic condition is concerned, they are bound to remain poor.

In the early days, the architects of human society in India divided society into four divisions for practical purposes. Division of labour, as said above, was the chief criterion to divide it into four divisions but all four divisions were equal. They had equal importance in the working of society just as every nut and bolt of a machine has a role to play in its effective working. It is common knowledge that a big and very complicated computer cannot work for want of a very small part. Why? Because that part, though small has tremendous importance.

However, people with vested interests interpreted this division wrongly. Four divisions of society based on occupation began to be called *varṇas* and the brahmins propounded the theory of their exalted origin and their white complexion. All people were not given equal rights. During the time of the Buddha 'human rights' as a concept had not originated. But the Buddha was far ahead of his times. He saw how people's right to equality, fraternity and liberty were violated because the society was divided into castes and sub-castes and sub-sub-castes. Therefore, he raised his voice against the caste system where all people are not treated as equal. He dismissed the theory that brahmins are superior because they are born from the mouth of Brahmā as unscientific and unbiological. Just as any other women have their periods, become pregnant, give birth to their children and give them suck, so do the brahmin women do. How can there be difference between children born to brahmin women and children born to women of other castess as shown in the *Asalāyana Sutta*?[141]

In the same *sutta* the Buddha gives several unassailable arguments to prove that all four castes are equal. There is no fundamental difference among them. He said that when people of different castes rub sticks and produce fire there is no difference between the flames, colours, radiance and heat produced by people belonging to one caste and people belonging to another caste.

"What do you think, Assalāyana? Suppose a head anointed noble king were to assemble here a hundred men of different birth and say to them: 'Come, sirs, let any who have been born into a noble clan or a brahmin clan or a royal clan take an upper fire-stick of sāla wood, salala wood, sandal

141. M.2 (see *Assalāyana Sutta*)

wood, or padumaka wood and light a fire and produce heat. And also let any who have been born into an outcaste clan, a trapper clan, a wicker worker's clan, a cartwright's clan, or a scavenger's clan take an upper fire-stick made from a dog's drinking trough, from a pig's trough, from a dustbin, or from castor-oil wood and light a fire and produce heat'.

"What do you think, Assalāyana? When a fire is lit and heat is produced by some one in the first group, would that fire have a flame, a colour, and a radiance and would it be possible to use it for the purpose of fire, while when a fire is lit and heat is produced by some one of the second group, that fire would have no flame, no colour, and no radiance and it would not be possible to use it for the purpose of fire?"

At another place in the same *sutta* the Buddha says that the water of the river and bath powder do not make any difference between a brahmin and a *śūdra*, they are both equally cleaned by them, so how can they be different? It is not the privilege of the brahmin alone to be washed clean by river water and bath powder.

Besides giving biological and common sense arguments the Buddha gave another argument which relates to human beings' capacity to progress on the path of spirituality. Both so-called brahmins and *śūdras* are capable of developing a mind of loving kindness towards a certain region without hostility and ill-will, so where is the difference between them? Moreover, after death happy destination is not reserved for the brahmins alone, it is reserved for all belonging to any caste if they live a virtuous life. Assalāyna admits that 'whether it be a noble, or a brahmin, or a merchant, or a worker—those of all four castes who abstain from killing living beings... and hold right view, on the dissolution of the body, after death are likely to reappear in a happy destination, even in the heavenly world," [142]

In the *Kaṇṇakatthala Sutta*[143] where King Pasenadi wants to know from the Buddha if there is any distinction or difference among the four castes, the Buddha answers unequivocally that there is no diifference among them. If there is difference among them that difference will be due to the fact that either they have or do not have five factors of striving. The five factors of striving are faith, freedom from illness and affliction, honesty and sincerity, energy and wisdom. If persons belonging to any caste have these factors of striving the deliverance achieved by them will be the same. There will be no difference between the deliverance of one and the deliverance of the others.

The apt similes given by the Buddha to prove that all people are equal were appreciated by Assalāyana and he could find no argument to

142. MLD pp. 765-766

143. M2.333

controvert what the Buddha said but in order to show how the brahmins were insistent on proving their superiority he kept on saying, "Master Gotama, the brahmins say thus: 'Brahmins are the highest caste, those of any other caste are inferior; brahmins are the fairest caste, those of any other caste are dark; only brahmins are purified, not non-brahmins; brahmins alone are the sons of Brahmā, the offspring of Brahmā, heirs of Brahmā, created by Brahmā. What does Master Gotama say about that?"[144]

On behalf of the Brahmins Assalāyana is giving almost the same argument as given by the pigs in George Orwell's *Animal Farm* where they say that 'All animals are equal. But some are more equal than others.'

Besides trying to prove the invalidity of caste system by apt examples the Buddha gave scientific arguments to prove that all homo sapiens are the same. There is no fundamental difference between one man and another although they were from different castes. He said that scientifically speaking there are no distinguishing marks among people as are found in different species of living creatures and in different kinds of plants. Beetles, moths, ants and termites are different because each species is distinguished by different marks. Quadrupeds, both small and large, snakes, fish and birds are different from one another because of different distinguishing marks found in them. But where are such distinguishing marks in men? White men or black men or yellow men all have the same distinguishing marks. 'Not by hair, nor head, nor ears, nor eyes, nor mouth, nor nose, nor lips, nor eye brows, nor neck, nor shoulder, nor belly, nor back, nor buttock, nor chest...nor fingers, nor nails, nor calves, nor thighs, nor colour, nor voice is there a distinguishing mark arising from their species as in other species.'[145] All homo sapiens constitute one species. They may be of different colour living in different geographical regions with different climates but basically there is no difference between them. If a Negro marries an English girl the child born to them will be a human being and will not be different as it is in the case of an offspring which is born when a donkey and a mare mate. Had a brahmin been basically different from a khattiya girl or a śūdra girl the child born to them would be different. But this is not the case. So, there is no difference between a brahmin and a khattiya and a śūdra as there is a difference between horse and donkey.

If there is no difference between them as it is proved by the arguments given above so people of all castes are capable of making spiritual achievement. Making spiritual achievement is not the monopoly of brahmins only. As there is no difference between the fire produced from a sāla wood or a fire produced from a stick taken from a dog's drinking

144. MLD p. 764.

145. GOD, p. 104.

trough so people of all castes are capable of purifying themselve. He thus talked of purification of all castes (*cāturvarṇī śuddhi*).

The Buddha gave another argument to prove that had the division of society into four castes been universal then there would not have been only two castes in Yona and Kamboja. And the two castes which are there are masters and slaves. They are so because of the difference in their economic condition not because of any basic difference between them. They exchange their status with the passage of time unlike India where a śūdra cannot become a brahmin.[146]

In the *Madhurā Sutta*[147] Venerable Kaccāna says to King Avantiputta that had brahmins been superior they would not be employed as servants by a wealthy person of any other caste. But this is not the case. A wealthy person belonging to any caste could employ as his servant a member of any class or caste. A so-called brahmin who is vicious is sure to be born in a woeful state and a virtuous person belonging to any caste is sure to be born in a blissful state. A criminal irrespective of his caste is bound to be punished for his crime but those who join the order receive equal honour and reverence without any discrimination.

In the *Aggañña Sutta*[148] it has been shown that since both the dark and bright qualities, which are blamed and praised by the wise, are scattered indiscriminately among the four castes, the wise do not recognize the claim about the brahmin caste being the highest. Why? Because any one from the four castes who becomes a monk, an Arahant who has destroyed the corruptions has attained the *summum bonum* is proclaimed supreme by virtue of Dhamma. It is the ethical qualities that make one great. All other characteristics of greatness are spurious, the only genuine characteristic is Dhamma. So it is the worth and not the birth as Dr. Ambedkar says that makes a difference between man and man.

What the Buddha proved was that biologically people of all castes are the same. If there is any difference then that is due to their actions. A man is high or low not by virtue of his birth in a particular caste but by virtue of his actions. If his actions are wholesome he is a brahmin (who is a brahmin has been defined in the Brāhmana vaggo of the Dhammapada where all his ethical qualities are brought out) and if his actions are unwholesome he is a *śūdra*.

146. M.2.361 *Assalāyana Sutta*
147. ibid., 2.279
148. D3.58

Na jaccā vasalo hoti, na jaccā hoti brāhmano/
Kammunā vasalo hoti, kammunā hoti brāhmano//[149]

The Buddha proves that what ultimately makes one great is his good character. Even scriptural learning and birth in a brahmin caste do not matter very much, for of the two brahmin brothers one who is studious and acute but immoral will not be preferred to one who is neither studious nor acute but who is virtuous.[150] He quotes Sanatkumāra with approval who says that one who is endowed with conduct and wisdom is great among people and gods.

Vijjācaraṇasampanno, so seṭṭho devamānuse'ti.[151]

Not only ethical qualities make a difference between one man and another but being adept in one craft also makes the difference for when a battle is imminent a king will prefer an adept archer even though he is a śūdra to a brahmin or a khattiya who is not adept in archery.

Why did the Buddha put forward so many arguments to prove that there is no basic difference between people belonging to different castes? Because his intention was to see that such a human society is established where a group of people do not exploit a large section of people by calling themselves superior because of their birth in brahmin caste, because the rights of people to live in a society where there are equality, fraternity and liberty are not violated. Men should not be looked down upon by people and there should be a society where all people are equal. He did not like to see such a society where people are not equal. Even at that point of time he was pained to see "What man has made of man?" Therefore he wanted man to develop such qualities of the head and heart as will nip in the bud all the tendencies to exploit people for his vested interests and deprive them of their rights.

It is true he was not a social revolutionary but what he said about caste system is very scientific and sane. That he did not believe in it is clear from the examples he set. He allowed people of all castes to be ordained. He allowed even the lowest caste people to become Bhikkhus and Bhikkhunis. He accepted the invitation given by courtesans like Ambapāli. In short, he made no distinction between one man and another on the basis of caste which he regarded as a means for the Brahmans to serve their interests. Although he could not demolish the caste system in his life- time he said things against it which if put into practice by rational people now, they can

149. Sn *Vasala Sutta* 142
150. D1.96 (see *Soṇadaṇḍa Sutta*)
151. D1.85 (see *Ambaṭṭha Sutta*)

do away with it. And once this obnoxious caste system is abolished people will not be deprived of their rights, right to drink water from the same well, right to marry a girl or a boy of their own choice, right to exercise their franchise in a way they like and their freedom to speak against some policies of the government or against some imposition made by some persons in society. They will not also be deprived of their right to hold a particular belief and go to a particular religious place.

From the *Kūṭadanta ṣutta*[152] it is clear that the Buddha spoke against taking works from unwilling persons. The bonded labourers had no alternative but to obey the king and do the works they were asked to do most unwillingly. The Buddha said in clear terms to the king that if works are taken from unwilling persons even in performing a sacrifice that sacrifice will not produce great fruits and the king will not earn great merits. All these examples go to prove that the Buddha was aware of people's rights and in no case he wanted them to be deprived of them.

Apart from speaking against the caste system which divides people into high and low and which makes the high deprive the low of their social, political and economic rights, the Buddha came out with what is called the Magna Carta of freedom of thought and gave people freedom to accept only those things which they know from their experience to do good to them and provide their welfare. In the famous *Kesamutti Sutta*[153] he asked the Kālāmas not to accept something even if that has been coming from a long time and about which so many people have spoken well, even if that is there in the scripture, even if that is logical and seems to be true from inference, even if that has been well considered, even if that is approved and even if that is taught by their teacher or somebody with an attractive personality. Unless they know from their own experience that what they are going to accept will be good and beneficial to them they should not accept it. This is a great freedom given to the people by the Buddha. If people are so free how can they accept anything imposed on them?

The Buddha's views about human rights are implied. That he was aware of human rights is clear from all his efforts to do away with the caste system which he thought was a very effective instrument in the hands of the people with vested interests to deprive people of weaker sections and lower castes of their rights so that their vested interest might continue forever. The Buddha went to the root cause of why people are deprived of their rights and who deprive them and showed the way to extirpate the cause by being scientifically aware of the real social situation. Caste system is man made. Therefore man must be aware of ending it by understanding its reality.

152. D1.111

153. A1.216

The Buddha also made people aware of their rights by teaching them dignity. Man is great. Man has immense power. He can make or mar his life. It is in his hands to ameliorate his conditions, cross the ocean of misery and experience *nibbānic* peace. He does not have to depend upon any god or God with a capital G to put an end to his suffering. But he said at the same time that man is also responsible for his suffering. It is his unwholesome actions that cause his suffering and he can end it by walking on the Noble Eightfold Path.

The Buddha showed people that there is no basic difference between man and man. A man or a woman may be poor, he/she may belong to any low caste such as *doma, cāṇḍāla, bhaṅgī* or a woman may be a courtesan like Ambapālī, Abhayamātā, Aḍḍhakāsī, Vimalā or she may be a slave like Khujjuttarā or Pūrṇā or he may be a hungry farmer, or a potter like Dhaniya or a fisherman like Yasoja or he may be a barber like Upāli or he may be a leper like Suppabuddha, all could realize the higher spiritual stage. Their caste and profession as also their physical condition did not come in their way to walk on the Noble Eightfold Path. All these are brilliant examples to prove that caste has got nothing to do in one's spiritual development

According to the Buddha it is the intrinsic quality of a man which is more important than his external label of belonging to a particular caste. As far as intrinsic qualities are concerned, all can develop them by walking on the path shown by the Buddha. The Buddha proved this by giving numerous examples of people belonging to different castes who achieved the same spiritual height by destroying their mental defilements.

Had people listened to the scientific and sane arguments against caste system put forward by the Buddha and acted accordingly, our society would have been free from the violation of human rights. However, we can now wield the weapons he has given and get rid of this curse of our society so that all of us can enjoy equality, fraternity and liberty.

That the Buddha did not only teach and practice equality, fraternity and liberty is clear from the fact that the Buddhist monks did not keep servants. His followers also did the same. If one looks at the history of the spread of his teachings, one finds that wherever his followers taught and propagated they did so peacefully. The sword was never used in propagating his teachings as it was used in propagating some other religion. As a consequence, there was no shedding of blood. Without interfering in their political affairs and without even trying to bring about any change in their belief and practice, Buddhism planted itself in the hearts of the people of the countries it went because it underlined the importance of *sīla, samādhi* and *paññā* and also because it was shorn of rites and rituals. Mahendra did not impose Buddhism forcibly in Sri Lanka. He allowed it to strike its roots naturally. We have the example of Japan where we see how the traditional religion Shintoism and Buddhism have lived and flourished together. The Japanese marry performing Shinto ceremony and bury their dead observing Buddhist rituals.

One most striking thing in Buddhism is that it extended the right to life to all beings. This speaks volume about its concern with not only human rights but with the rights of all living beings. The Buddha underlines the importance of right to life as a principle, not as a rule. Rules either break mankind or it breaks rules but principles become a way of life.

Buddha's Pragmatic Approach to Social Harmony and Material Prosperity

Buddha was not only a spiritual scientist of the first order but he was also a great social scientist. Although his primary aim was to make a quest for peace and inner harmony, he also came out with seminal thoughts for achieving social harmony and material prosperity. His pragmatic approach to life enabled him to put his finger on the real causes of social unrest also. Long before Karl Marx and even other sociologists who saw in poverty the cause of most social evils, the Buddha had expressed the same view. From the *Cakkavattīsīhanāda Sutta* this is clear. The fable narrated here underlines the point that a king fails in his duty if he does not provide people with property so that they can satisfy their basic needs. So even if he makes all arrangements for guarding and protecting people but fails to give property to the needy, he fails to establish law and order in his kingdom and also fails to stem the tide of other social evils that follow poverty.

Poverty is the root cause of many social evils. It is out of poverty that man commits theft. Committing theft endangers his life. He gets capital punishment. Taking a lesson from his example, others who want to commit theft devise ways and means so that they can commit theft without being caught by the king's men. They arm themselves with weapons and forcibly take from others what is not given to them. In the past it happened so. 'Thus, from the not giving of property to the needy, poverty became rife; from the growth of poverty, the taking of what was not given increased; from the increase of theft, the use of weapons increased; from the increased use of weapons, the taking of life increased; and from the increase in the taking of life, people's life- span decreased, their beauty decreased...'[154]

What happened in the past can happen again. This is a universal law. This happens time and again. So the process of degeneration does not stop here. Those who do not commit theft speak against those who do and, as a result, speaking ill of another comes into being. Those who do not take what is not given and those who take are beautiful and ugly respectively and this difference causes envy in some of them, which leads them to commit adultery with others' wives. This compels the sinning people to chatter idly and the persons who are sinned against use harsh speech. Envy makes a person use harsh speech and also makes him full of hatred. And the beautiful makes the ugly covetous. In short, a number of mental defilements and social evils are caused by poverty.

---

154. LDB, pp. 399-400.

The Buddha knew that unless poverty is alleviated social evils cannot be eliminated and unless they are eliminated, they are bound to make society miserable. There can be no peace and harmony in society as there will always be law and order problems. He gives a lot of practical suggestions to alleviate poverty, to achieve material prosperity and create conditions for peace and harmony in society. In the *Kūṭadanta Sutta* of the *Dīghanikāya* the Buddha says how material prosperity and social harmony can be achieved in society. If there is poverty in society many social evils are bound to arise and cause disturbance. How can there be peace in society? And how can a society achieve prosperity? These are important questions. Poverty, as shown above, is the cause of most of social evils. Thieves, dacoits and highwaymen take to committing theft, loot and robbery because they have not enough to live on. So, they commit crimes like theft and murder. No amount of punitive measures taken by a king or a government can eliminate them. Punishment is not a sure cure of social evils and malaise. Corruption and crime cannot be eliminated completely by punishing criminals. It is true that particular criminals will be punished but there will be many in which the seeds of crime will remain. So, whatever punitive measures one takes say, degradation, banishment, fines, bonds and capital punishment, the criminal activities cannot be stopped completely.

The most effective way to get rid of such crimes is to ensure that people have enough to live on. We know that a hungry man is an angry man. Therefore, in order to allay their hunger, it is desirable to see that all sections of society have sufficient to live on. We hear of hunger marches undertaken by the poor and the unemployed people. The Buddha, therefore, suggests that willing farmers and cattle rearers, not the lazy ones, must be given seed and other necessities and must also be provided with capital enough to buy plough, oxen or (tractor in modern times) to carry on agricultural operations and produce crops. The king or the government should also see that there are irrigation facilities. Their crops should not fail even if the monsoon fails. The businessmen must be provided with enough capital to set up and run their business. And, last but not least, all citizens must have employment, particularly the unemployed young men and women whose idle minds are like the devil's workshop. So, if one wants social harmony and material prosperity he must follow the Buddha's advice—'Give seeds and other requisites to farmers, give capital to businessmen to set up and run their business and give employment to the unemployed youth of a society'. In short, if there is economic well-being, there is bound to be social well-being.

Seen from this point of view, it is clear that the Buddha anticipated Marx and other sociologists who see the cause of social evils in poverty. If one gives to each according to his needs then he can demand from each according to his capacity. Therefore providing a congenial atmosphere so that one's capacity flowers up, his basic needs must be taken care of and the basic human need is allaying hunger. That is why the Marxist sociologists give so much importance to equal distribution of wealth, equal opportunity to all and abolition of private property. Such measures will, no doubt, have salubrious effect in curbing, if not completely rooting out, social evils.

The Buddha goes one step further than Marxist sociologists. Greed is a defilement deeply rooted in the human mind. In the *Aggañña Sutta,* through another fable, the Buddha shows how greed gives rise to ugliness, arrogance and lust and how it leads to hoarding (*parigraha*), committing theft, lying, censuring, punishment and many other evil things.[155] And so long as this defilement is not removed, man can still crave for more and more and commit all sorts of crimes even though his basic needs are fulfilled.

How is one to get rid of this defilement?The Buddha prescribes the Noble Eightfold Path consisting of *sīla* (virtue), *samādhi* (concentration) and *paññā* (wisdom). By walking upon this path, man can become virtuous, can concentrate his mind and develop his insight wisdom. With his developed insight wisdom he can see the real nature of things and be aware at the experiential level of the impermanent nature of things he craves for out of ignorance. With the dawning of wisdom upon him that the things they crave for are impermanent (*anicca, anitya*), he realizes the futility of craving for things that do not last. Thus he is able to lessen, if not completely annihilate, his greed.

The division of human beings into different castes in India is another important cause for unrest and many other social problems leading to disharmony and disturbances in society. If people pay attention to the rational observation made by the Buddha and live their life accordingly, they can make their society a veritable paradise. A man is not a Brahmin because he is born of parents belonging to Brahmin caste and not a śūdra because he is born of parents belonging to śūdra caste. A man is high or low, great or small by virtue of his actions, by virtue of his *sīla* i.e. purity of his physical and vocal actions.

Na jacca vasalo hoti, na jacca hoti Brahmano/
Kammuna vasalo hoti, kammuna hoti Brahmano//[156]

The time seems to be ripe now when this magnanimous and glorious message of the Buddha will go straight into the hearts of the right thinking

155. ibid., pp. 410-413. (For details, see the English translation of the *Agganñña Sutta* called 'On Knowledge of Beginnings')

156. Sn 142

people who make no difference between man and man on the basis of caste system introduced by people with their vested interests.

In short, if one follows the path prescribed by the spiritual scientist – the Buddha one can go a long way in achieving not only inner harmony but social harmony too.

Buddha's Spirit of Tolerance

The Buddha is the epitome of religious tolerance. He did not have even a trace of fanaticism in him. He neither extolled his own view nor did he deride others' views. Wrangling arises only when one thinks highly of one's view and looks down upon others' views. The Buddha knew this so well that he never thought of indulging in mean activities. When the Kālāmas asked him whose views should be accepted, because every religious teacher who came to them talked highly of his view and placed others' views in bad light, the Buddha said—"Now, look you Kālāmas, be you not misled by report, or tradition, or hearsay. Be not misled by proficiency in the collections, nor by mere logic or inference, nor after considering reasons, nor after reflection on and approval of some theory, nor because it fits becoming, nor out of respect for a recluse (who holds it). But, Kālāmas, when you know for yourselves - these things are unprofitable, these things are blameworthy, these things are censured by the intelligent, these things when performed and undertaken conduce to loss and sorrow—then indeed do ye reject them Kālāmas."[157]

Isn't this the first ever Magna Carta for freedom of thought? If such freedom of thought is guaranteed to all people, where is the possibility of looking down on others' religious views and igniting the fire of religious intolerance?

In the *Caṅki Sutta*[158] of the *Majjhima Nikāya* the Buddha puts to rout all the Brahmins headed by the brilliant Kāpaṭika who held the view that what was written in the ancient holy scriptures of the Brahmins is Truth. "This alone is Truth, and every thing else is false". The Buddha wanted to know if there was any single Brahmin among them who claimed he personally knew and saw that "this alone is Truth and every thing else is false." Not only did none of them personally know and see the Truth, but even their teacher or teacher's teacher seven generations back could not make such a claim. The Buddha then compares them to a line of blind men where neither the first man, nor the middle one, nor the last one can see.

Belief is one thing and Truth is quite another. Similarly, faith is one thing and Truth quite another. Therefore, those who think that what they believe in and what they have faith in alone is Truth are wrong. Truth is a matter of personally knowing and seeing, not a matter of belief and faith. Faith and belief give rise to attachment, which is nothing but a fetter. In the *Sutta Nipāta* the Buddha says: "To

157. BGS pp. 171-172

158. M2.387

be attached to one thing (to a certain view) and to look down upon other things (views) as inferior—this, the wise ones call a fetter."

The Buddha had no attachment even to the Truth he had known and seen and he clearly warned his disciples that if they were attached to their view, they did not properly understand the importance of Dhamma. Dhamma is for liberation, it is not meant to be clung to. In the *Alagaddūpama Sutta* of the *Majjhima Nikāya* he compares Dhamma to a raft, which is meant for crossing a river and not for taking hold of it and carrying it on one's back after crossing the river. This is sheer foolishness. If this is the view of the Buddha of his own Dhamma, which he had known and seen, how could he have religious intolerance for the views held by others? Religious intolerance arises only when one holds one's view dear and looks down upon others' views.

That the Buddha allowed freedom of thought is clear from what he said to the Kālāmās. From his view of Truth it is clear that it was not a matter of belief and faith. It is clear that Dhamma is not something to be clung to, but something to be put to use very wisely. He is fully aware of the consequences of attachment. Therefore, there is no question of his being intolerant of any religion or point of view.

From the *Upāli Sutta* of the *Majjhima Nikāya*[159] the Buddha's astonishing spirit of tolerance is clear. Upāli--a very rich householder of Nalanda--was a well known disciple of Lord Mahāvira who once sent him to the Buddha to debate with him and defeat him on some points connected with the theory of *kamma.* Upāli was convinced by the arguments put forward by the Buddha and requested him to accept him as a lay disciple. Had there been some other religious teacher he would have been glad to immediately accept him as one of his lay disciples because he was one of the richest men around who could give a lot of *dāna.* But the Buddha, instead of immediately granting his request, asked him to reconsider his proposal and not be in a hurry. But even when the Buddha accepted him as a lay disciple the Buddha requested Upāli not to close the door on his teacher Lord Mahāvira and other friends who once followed Lord Mahāvira. This is the spirit of tolerance *par excellence.*

The Buddha taught the same kind of tolerance when he asked the *Vajjians* not to demolish the *caityas* spread in the length and breadth of the *Vajjian* Republic. In fact, he said that if the *Vajjian* Republic was to have strength and prosperity, if it was to prosper and not meet its decline and fall this was one of the seven *aparihāṇiya dhammā* to be sincerely followed. Why did the Buddha say so? The *caityas* were places of worship. They had been erected in the name of some god or *yakkha.* If they were destroyed,

159. M2.38

the religious sentiments of the people would be hurt, which would cause ill-will and animosity. This would go a long way in weakening the unity of the Republic. The Buddha advised the custodians of the Republic not to stir up a hornet's nest.

This sort of spirit of tolerance is greatly needed in our democracy in modern times. It is easy to play with the fire of intolerance but it will take years and years to make good the loss and damage it causes, the damage which in some cases is irrepairable.

In the third century B.C. the great Buddhist Emperor Asoka, who had been greatly influenced by the noble teachings of the Buddha, followed and practised this spirit of tolerance. He developed understanding for all religions and honoured and supported them. In the Rock Edict XII he declared: "One should not honour only one's own religion and condemn the religions of others, but one should honour others' religions for this or that reason. So doing, one helps one's own religion to grow and renders service to the religions of others too. In acting otherwise, one digs the grave of one's own religion and also does harm to other religions. Whosoever honours his own religion and condemns other religions, does so indeed through devotion to his own religion, thinking "I will glorify my own religion". But on the contrary, in so doing, he injures his own religion more gravely. So concord is good: Let all listen, and be willing to listen to the doctrine professed by others."[160]

One of the most cherished ideals of the Buddha's teachings and Buddhist culture is this spirit of tolerance and understanding. There is no fanaticism and no fundamentalism. Instead, there is understanding and good will. By virtue of this quality, wherever the teachings of the Buddha went, people belonging to different religious traditions and cultures accepted them. The ambassadors of Dhamma were full of the milk of human kindness and they never thought of taking swords in their hands to force their Dhamma on the people of the countries they went to. Two thousand six hundred years have passed but there has been no instance of persecution in the name of this religion. Instead, the fundamental teachings of the Buddha such as *sīla* (virtue), *samādhi* (concentration of mind) and *paññā* (insight wisdom) and *mettā* (loving kindness), *karuṇā* (compassion), *muditā* (sympathetic joy) and *upekkhā* (equanimity) have been accepted by all people and accommodated in all religions. The teachings of the Buddha have lighted many a dark heart and have gone a long way in ennobling mankind. All this has been possible because non-violence is the cardinal principle of the Dhamma of the Buddha. It is its spirit of tolerance which has been instrumental in its smooth spread throughout the world, without shedding even a drop of blood and without ever waging war.

160. 12th Girnara Rock Inscription

Buddha's Altruism

The ubiquitous nature of the Noble Truth of suffering, based on the Buddha's observation, is an undeniable fact of human life. No philosopher worth the name has ever contradicted it. All six systems of Indian philosophy have accepted it as an incontrovertible fact of life. As far as the Buddha is concerned, he propounds his philosophy when he analyses the cause of suffering. This philosophy, unlike most of the philosophies of the world, is not the outcome of intellectual thinking but the direct product of experiential wisdom. By practising Vipassana meditation, which he himself discovered, the Buddha found out the cause of suffering. Suffering does not come from outside, it comes from within. It is not caused by any outside force nor is it caused fortuitously, nor does any god cause it, but rather it is caused by one's own self--by the internal dynamics of one's mind. One is the creator of one's own suffering.

The Buddha then explained at great length that one's suffering is caused by one's cravings and aversions and these arise due to one's ignorance of the real nature of things. By walking on the Noble Eightfold Path he attained wisdom in the light of which he saw that all things of the world are impermanent and so it is not wise to hanker after them, and consequently multiply suffering and keep on moving endlessly in the cycle of birth and death and suffer incalculably. How did the Buddha come to this conclusion? Not by logic and intellect, as said above, but by the experiential wisdom which he attained by practising Vipassana meditation.

The Buddha's practice of Vipassana meditation led him to the conclusion that just as one can cause one's own suffering, so one oneself can also put an end to it. How? By removing the cause of suffering. And how is one to remove the cause of suffering? It is by observing precepts, practising meditation and attaining wisdom. The Buddha came to this conclusion by walking on the Noble Eightfold Path. It would not, therefore, be incorrect to say that the Buddha's philosophy has an in-built action plan. He himself walked on the Noble Eightfold Path and saw that one's suffering is caused by mental defilements (craving and aversion) which arise in ignorance and he also saw that suffering can be annihilated by one's ethical and moral actions which are performed to remove the defilements responsible for one's suffering. In conclusion, he said that it is one's impure mind that causes suffering and to get rid of suffering is to purify the mind. Thus, in the teachings of the Buddha (all of which are utterly pragmatic and realistic) one finds a happy combination of Philosophy, Psychology and Ethics. Here is an in-depth study of the psychology of mind, the dynamics of which make one suffer; an in-depth study of philosophy, which explains the cause of his suffering; and also an in-depth study of ethics, which explains what impurities of the mind are and how they can be removed. One observes ethical precepts and concentrates one's mind and with this purer, more focussed mind he starts to see reality as it is. If he wants to harvest a good crop of peace and happiness, he has to weed out his mind, otherwise there will be a luxuriant growth of weeds as a result of which all prospective plants of peace and happiness will be choked and smothered. What actually is needed for extirpating suffering is to change the dynamics of mind. The dynamo that produces desires is also fuelled by desires. In order to stop this dynamo from going on and on one has to stop fuelling it, which means he has to eliminate desires. This understanding of the rise of desires also includes the understanding of the stopping of desires. An impure and defiled mind is the spring of desires. If one's mind is made pure and free of defilements, the spring of desires will dry up.

The Buddha was not a pessimist as many critics have made him out to be. The charge of pessimism made against him is not tenable. The incomparable physician that he was, he diagnosed the disease man is subject to thoroughly and prescribed the medicine to get rid of it for good. How can such a philosopher be called a pessimist? Understanding man's mind which is the spring of all his actions, it is incumbent, he said, on man to purify the mind and for purifying it he has to walk on the Noble Eightfold Path. To walk wisely on this path, one has to attain knowledge of reality, has to eliminate his desires and has to work hard without ever being unmindful.

So when the Buddha asked monks to go forth for the good and welfare of many, what he meant was going to the people and teaching them the way to put an end to their suffering by walking on the Noble Eightfold Path of *sīla, samādhi* and *paññā*. Why did he ask the monks to go alone and not in a group? There are, to my mind, two reasons for this. One is that a monk is supposed to live a lonely life, which is conducive to his practice of *sādhanā*, and the second reason is that in those days monks were few and suffering people were many. It was necessary for all people to listen to the teachings of the Buddha. How would that be possible? Perhaps the Buddha thought: let one monk go to a particular area and be with the people of that place. One monk would be able to teach the Dhamma to a large number of people. At least one enlightened person would be present where previously there was none. So if monks went individually to different places, many areas would be covered and there would be many green islands 'in this deep wide sea of misery'. As Shelly says—

> "Many a green isle needs there must be,
> In this deep wide sea of misery."

With this end in view, the Buddha exhorted monks to go forth alone "for the gain of many, for the welfare of many, with compassion for people and gods alike."

"Bahujana hitāya, bahujana sukhāya" obviously means that the Buddha's mission was to help people out of their suffering. So, if some people think there is a contradiction between the Buddha's propounding of *Dukkhaṃ ariyasaccaṃ*—the first Noble Truth of suffering–and his mission to take measures to put an end to suffering, I am afraid they have not understood the spirit of the Buddha's teachings. He propounded the first Noble Truth of suffering all right but he never said that suffering cannot end. In fact, he said from personal experience that if the cause of suffering is rooted out then suffering is bound to end. So where is the contradiction? When he exhorted the monks to go forth and work for the gain and welfare of many, it was quite in keeping with his mission as also with his compassionate nature.

The Buddha and his disciples did not only teach people to walk on the Noble Eightfold Path and work out their salvation. Of course, this was the most important thing for them to do. But the Buddha and his disciples did not only put a premium on their spiritual welfare but also took great care of their material happiness and well-being.

I think one would be justified to say that the Buddha's concern was with both, material as well as spiritual matters. One does not see him neglecting people's material well-being. Certainly, the balance seems to tip in favour of the spiritual well-being of people. If the highest spiritual welfare is achieved, the material well-being will take care of itself. That is why one sees the Buddha teaching so many persons and taking them out of their misery. For instance, the Buddha went to Aṅgulimāla to save him from going to hell. He taught him the Dhamma, which changed the course of his life. From a fearsome robber he became an *Arahant.* In other episode, the Buddha explains to Kasibhāradvāja how his agricultural produce pales into insignificance in comparison with his (Buddha's) 'produce', which unlike Kasibhāradvāja's produce, allays hunger for good. For the Enlightened One faith is the seed, austerity the rain and so on. On another occasion he makes it clear to Dhaniya that material comforts cannot compare with the *nibbānic* peace that a samaṇa attains. He explains to so many Brahmaṇas the quintessence of Dhamma. In the *Caṅkī Sutta* it is made clear how one can find out what Dhamma is. He was so compassionate that even when his *mahāparinibbāna* was nearing he taught his Dhamma to a wanderer named Subhadda. Thus, he quenched the spiritual thirst of someone in need, irrespective of his own comfort or convenience. The compassionate nature of the Buddha and his altruistic attitude to help the needy is clear from what he says to Ānanda who does not allow Subhadda to visit the

Buddha anticipating trouble from him. "Ānanda, do not prevent him from coming to me. Whatever Subhadda will ask me (*"yaṃ kiñci maṃ Subhaddo pucchissati"*) it will be with a view to knowing the highest truth (*"sabbamṃ taṃ aññapekkhova pucchissati"*) and not with a desire to give me trouble (*"no vihesāpekkho"*)".[161] Such examples can be mutiplied *ad libitum*. The Buddha's objective was to teach all these people the meaning of the Noble Eightfold Path and to exhort them to walk on it and to break the cycle of birth and death. This is how one can get rid of suffering. To this end he kept on working ceaselessly. Except for when he ate, drank, slept or answered the call of nature, he kept on teaching:

> *"Aññatra asitapītakhāyitasāyitā aññatra uccārapassāvakammā, aññatra niddākilamathapaṭivinodanā apariyādinnāyevassa, sāriputta, tathāgatassa dhammadesanā, apariyādinnaṃye-vassa tathāgatassa dhammapadabyañjanaṃ, apariyādinnaṃyevassa tathāgatassa pañhapaṭibhānaṃ.Annatra aitapitakhayitasayita, aññatra uccārapassāvakamma, aññatra niddākilamathavinodanā apariyādinnayevassa, Sāriputta, Tathāgatassa dhammadesanā, apariyādinnamyevassa ñdhammapadabyañjanaṃ, apariyādinnamyevassa thatāgatassa pañhapaṭibhānaṃ".*[162]

However, it is not possible for all to end their suffering and attain *nibbāna* in one life. Most of us have so many deep layers of *saṅkhārās* that it is not possible to get rid of all of them in one life. It will be several lives before they are all burnt out and every time one is born one suffers from different kinds of physical ailments and mental afflictions. The Buddha was so compassionate that he did not lose sight of such ailments people suffered from. There are examples in the Tipiṭaka of the Buddha himself helping suffering monks. He also asked other monks if they had enough to live by. Like a loving father, he saw to it that monks did not suffer from lack of food or robes or other necessary requisites. Is this not an expression of his altruism? Was he really concerned only with his own salvation, his own spiritual well-being and not with the needs of others? Once when he came to know about a sick monk who was not being attended by anyone, he himself along with Ānanda took great care of him. The monk was so weak that he was not able to get up from his bed. He was soiled with his own urine and excreta. The Buddha asked Ānanda to fetch hot water. He poured water on his body, cleaned him and put him on a clean bed to sleep. He said that monks must help one another when they are ill, otherwise who else will take care of them. The Buddha also said: "One who serves the sick

161. D2 (see *Mahāparinibbāna Sutta*)

162. M1 (see *Mahāsīhanāda Sutta*).

serves me."[163] Is that not a great altruistic thought? Does it not show his infinite compassion for suffering humanity? He equates serving the sick with practising Dhamma.

The altruistic attitude of the Buddha can be seen in what he does for the downtrodden and the depressed–Sopāka, for example. The Dhamma is not meant only for kings and rich people. The Enlightened One taught his Dhamma to the leper Suppabuddha; to the poor Sopāka who was born in a cāṇḍāl family; to the low born Suppiya; to Sunīta who was a sweeper. He showered his compassion on a hunter's daughter, Cāpā. He showered it likewise on Ambapāli, on Abhaya mātā, on Padmāvatī, on Addhakāsī and on Vimalā, who were all sex workers of his times. Once he delayed giving a talk on Dhamma because there was a hungry farmer present. He started teaching Dhamma only after the farmer had been fed. What do all these instances show? They show that the Buddha was not unaware of the need to ameliorate the conditions of the poor and the neglected.

Although his primary concern was to cross the four floods, eradicate cravings and attain *nibbāna*, he did not ignore the material well-being of people. In the *Kuṭadanta Sutta* it is said that it is the duty of a king to provide seed, agricultural implements and other infrastructure to the farmer. It is also the duty of a king to provide a merchant with seed money and other necessaries to enable him to set up business and above all it is the primary duty of a king to see that no young man or woman remains unemployed. He went on further to say that many evils of society would disappear if the minds of the youth were occupied. An idle mind is the devil's workshop. Besides, if all were fruitfully engaged in their work, society would be free from thieves, dacoits and other perpetrators of crime. This seminal thought of the Buddha goes a long way towards taking care of the material well-being of people, making society prosperous, free from crime and other disturbances. The conditions of the poor, the needy, and the unemployed as also the sick and the neglected sections of society must be ameliorated before peace and harmony in society can be achieved. In the *Cakkavatīisīhanāda Sutta* and the *Aggañña Sutta*[164], it is shown how man's mind is defiled by craving, aversion and other polluting factors. This analysis is made so that man can keep himself away from these pollutants. This is altruism *par excellence.*

The four sublime states, viz. *mettā, karuṇā, muditā* and *upekkhā* can assume significance only in a human society, and each one of the states is the direct product of one's altruistic attitude. When one feels love or loving kindness (*mettā*) for people around him, he is taking active interest

163. *Yo, bhikkhave, maṃ upaṭṭhaheyya so gilānaṃ upaṭṭhaheyya.* Mv p. 394

164. See D1

in others. In other words, *mettā* is "*hitesitā*" (thinking of doing good to others), "*anukampā*" (compassion) and "*abyāpādo*" (the absence of hatred). In short, it is "*hita sukha upanayakamatā*"—the desire to bring to one's fellowmen that which is welfare and good. *Karuṇā* is the desire to remove bane and sorrow–"*ahita dukkhāpanaya kamatā*"–or *karuṇā* is when one's heart is moved to see fellow beings suffering. *Muditā* is sympathetic joy, i.e. feeling joy when somebody has made progress and has achieved success, and *upekkhā* is an equanimous attitude--being disinterested in and impartial towards whatever happens to one. The Buddha was continuously practising at least one of these vihāras. This is perhaps one of the reasons why one finds the word '*viharati*' being used in the context of the Buddha. "*Ekaṃ samayaṃ Bhagavā Buddho Sāvatthiyaṃ viharati*". He lived and dwelled in an altruistic mode of consciousness. When, like the Buddha, one takes active interest in others, these sublime states of altruism can develop.

Reading the Jātaka stories it becomes clear how the Bodhisattva always thinks of the welfare and good of others, how he takes pity on those who are in trouble and how he remains equanimous in adverse situations. Is that not altruistic activity? The concept of the Bodhisattva's compassion became so pervasive in Mahāyāna Buddhism that the Bodhisattva became the embodiment of *Mahākaruṇā* (lit. "Being of Great Compassion"). I have analyzed this concept of Bodhisattva in my paper entitled: "Acarya Śāntideva's Humanism".[165]

165. Angraj Chaudhary, Essays on Budhism and Pali Literature, E.B.L. Delhi, 1994, pp. 47-54.

Buddha's Concept of Good Governance

There are a few *Suttas* in the Tipiṭaka, which contain Buddha's seminal thoughts on his concept of good governance.

Good governance consists in maintaining law and order in society. It also consists in creating an economically viable society - a society where people do not die of hunger, where health, education and other items of their well-being are taken care of, where their wives and daughters are safe, where their children are not kidnapped and held to ransom, where they have enough occupation to keep themselves engaged and where they are not required to resort to bad means of earning their livelihood.

Why do people take to bad means of earning their livelihood? We know that food is one of the unavoidable necessities of life. Every body needs food. If one does not get food, he is compelled to adopt any means to get it. He will steal, he will even commit murder to get it. If there are such poor people in society, who find it hard to make their two ends meet then there are bound to be law and order problems. All poor people, of course, do not take recourse to bad means of earning their livelihood but some thieves and robbers are bound to be there in society to do so. They will ravage villages and towns and waylay people on the way to rob them of everything. As a consequence, the peace of society will be disturbed. People will live in fear. Therefore the king or the government will face the problem of eliminating these plagues in order to make people safe and free from fear.

Why there are law and order problems in society has been incidentally told by the priest of Mahāvijita, a king in ancient times, who wanted to perform a sacrifice in order to earn merits for himself so that he could benefit and secure happiness for a long time and also secure a place in heaven after death.[166]

What his priest says is primarily concerned with bloodless sacrifice. No cows, bullocks, goats and sheep were to be killed in sacrifice but it should be performed with ghee, oil, butter, curds, honey and molasses.

He also spoke about the proper time when the sacrifice should be performed.

When the king expressed his wish to perform sacrifice the priest told him that the time was not proper for doing so. How could a sacrifice be performed at a time when there was no peace in society, when it is beset by thieves and robbers and when villages and towns were being destroyed?

---

166. D1 (see *Kūṭadanta Sutta*)

Perhaps he anticipated the king's answer to solve those problems. And, therefore, he said that punishment is no sure cure of such crimes. If a mass fine is imposed on the people of a particular area where theft occurs, injustice will be done to a large number of people. Theft would be committed by a few, but many will be the sufferers. If the fines are imposed on the innocent people, they will grieve, think ill of the king and may even try to do him harm. Even imprisoning and executing them will not solve the problem, because their relatives who will survive will think of harming the kingdom. Punishments like confiscation of property, threats, and banishment are not going to solve the problem.

The priest then goes to the root cause of the problem. Poverty is one of the causes. The second important cause is that people do not have work enough to keep themselves engaged. Unengagement or unemployment is another serious cause for people to take to activities that are harmful for society. It is rightly said that an idle mind is the devil's workshop. Therefore, he suggested to the king to give to them who are engaged in cultivating crops and rearing cattle all that they need so that they are fruitfully engaged in their work. The farmers should be provided with seeds, agricultural implements, bullocks and fodder. If what is given is not sufficient, they should be given again. (*Dinne appahonte puna aññampi bījañca bhattañca kasiupakaraṇabhaṇḍāñca sabbaṃ detūti attho.*) The traders should be provided with capital to set up their business. The king should provide the farmers and traders with money and all they need on easy terms. There must be trust between them and the king. Trust begets trust. Therefore they should be provided with money without asking a signed document containing a written promise to pay back the money taken or without asking somebody to bear witness to it (*Pābhataṃ anuppadetūti sakkhiṃ akatvā paṇṇe anāropetvā mūlacchejavasena bhaṇḍamūlaṃ detūti attho*). The king should give them without expecting them to pay it back. If they do so, well and good; if they do not, they should not be forced to pay and they should never be asked to pay interest. Last but not least, jobs should be provided to young men and women who want to enter into government service and they should be given proper living wages. The priest says that if people are kept engaged in their different occupations, they will never think of harming the kingdom by creating law and order problems.

This, I think, is a very important suggestion given by the priest to the king. The priest has put his finger on the root cause of the problem. In order for a king to govern well this point must be kept in mind. Its neglect by any king or any government will definitely cause troubles.

Besides, the priest asked him to take into confidence all *khattiyas* from town and country, all his counsellors and advisers, the most influential Brahmins and the wealthy householders and ask for their help and assistance. If they are asked by the king to help him, they will not feel neglected. Rather they will feel honoured and do their best to enable the king to achieve success in what he wants to do. This is a great confidence building measure.[167]

In this way, when the common people are helped and trusted and the influential people are consulted and taken into confidence, there will hardly be any grievance by the people and hardly any anger from those who are influential and wealthy. There will be what is called harmony in society. Such an atmosphere will go a long way in eliminating law and order problems and will pave the way for good governance.

Two thousand six hundred years ago the Buddha put his finger on one of the most important causes of disturbance in society and gave the suggestion as to what to do to eliminate this problem and bring peace and prosperity in society.

Buddha's concept of good governance becomes very clear from what he says in the *Mahāparinibbāna Sutta*.[168] He says there that so long as the Vajjians 'hold regular and frequent assemblies', 'meet in harmony, break up in harmony, and carry on their business in harmony, they may be expected to prosper and not decline.' He says further that so long as the Vajjians 'do not authorise what has not been authorised already, and do not abolish what has been authorised by their ancient tradition,' so long as 'they honour, respect, revere and salute the elders among them and consider them worth listening to,' so long as they 'do not forcibly abduct others' wives and daughters and compel them to live with them,' so long as 'they honour, respect, revere and salute the Vajjian shrines at home and abroad, not withdrawing the proper support made and given before,' and so long as they make proper provision for the safety of Arahants, so that such Arahants may come in future to live there, and those already there may dwell in comfort,' they are expected to prosper and not decline.' [169]

Why is it necessary to hold frequent assemblies? There are two obvious reasons for it. One, to inform themselves on the latest happenings in the country, and two, to take immediate action to put down the riot if there is any in any part of the country and to teach a lesson to the perpetrators of crimes such as highway robberies. The sooner they know about the riot and the robbery, the sooner they can lay their heads together and decide what action to take and take immediate action to bring the criminals to book. Carelessness on the part of the people does not pay. Instead it makes the troubleshooters bold and thieves repeat their highway robbery

167. D1 (see *Kūṭadanta Sutta*)

168. D2 (see *Mahāparinibbāna Sutta*)

169. ibid.

without any fear. But if action against them is taken on time, they do not dare repeat their crimes. `Eternal vigilance' is the price of liberty. So, if the people of a country remain careless and are slow to act, problems arising as a spark become conflagrations and catch them unaware. By the time they come to know about them, it becomes too late to put them out. If they know about them in the initial stage, they can nip them in the bud without any difficulty. This is what happened in India when intruders in Kargil caught us unaware and we got a severe jolt. Both our army and government had to pay a heavy price for their negligence and lack of alacrity and vigilance.

The Buddha had also taught the Vajjians to remain united. He had asked them to assemble in unanimity, rise in unanimity and carry out their business in unanimity. Why is the unanimity of the people so important? It is important because any decision taken unanimously becomes all people's decision and any business carried out unanimously becomes their business. So, where is the place for discord and dissent? Where is the cause for raising one's voice against anybody and raising one's finger at anyone? If all unanimously take a decision after laying their heads together, it becomes a collective decision.

What's the acid test of practising unanimity? It is said that if people do not make any pretext to attend the assembly when it is announced, but immediately come out of their homes leaving their works unfinished, come out even in the middle of their having meals and dressing themselves in order to discuss the agenda of the meeting/assembly, then it is clear that they are sincere, dutiful and united. And if they are asked who would go to put down the riot on the border or arrest the thieves and bring them to book all should vie with one another and offer themselves to go first and do the job assigned. This is sincerity, alacrity, awareness and a sense of duty and responsibility. How could they accomplish their responsibility successfully? Because they were never bothered about the security and well-being of the members of their families. When someone went out to put down the riot or arrest the criminals, their works at home and the members of their families were taken care of by others who were left behind. This had a great advantage. Those who went to fight with the enemies never bothered their heads about the security and well-being of their members at home. As a result, they carried out their assigned task with great zeal and enthusiasm with an added sense of responsibility and patriotic feeling. All people stood united in prosperity and adversity alike. This was the cause of their being successful in accomplishing their tasks.

If our army personnel can have such assurance of security for the members of their families and are not anxious about their welfare then they will lay down their lives at the altar of their motherland with a sense of more commitment and patriotic feelings.

The third condition for a republic to prosper and not to decline is not to abrogate old customs and introduce new ones. Realization of octrois and land revenues introduced earlier should be continued, and new octrois and land revenues should not be introduced. Similarly, no new punishment and no new procedure for ascertaining whether one is a thief or not, should be introduced. Introduction of new taxes and new punishment is met with opposition by the people. People begin to suspect the intentions of the powers that be. And if the prevailing taxes and revenues are not realized, the royal treasury becomes empty with the result that the four divisions of army become weak and inefficient inasmuch as they do not get money from the royal treasury to meet their expenses, to maintain themselves and keep themselves in a ready position to fight any impending war with the enemy or punish the perpetrators of various crimes.[170]

Punishing some innocent person without making a thorough enquiry has disastrous consequences. The relatives of the punished suspect the King's intention and his sense of justice and express their anger by siding with the thieves and by creating troubles in the kingdom.[171]

The fourth condition according to the Buddha for a republic to prosper is to respect, honour and revere the elderly and the experienced people. As they are old and wise and have a lot of experience of running a government efficiently, so they are the best persons to advise the king or the powers that be as to how to efficiently manage the affairs of the state. They make the rulers aware of the traditional custom and advise them about the `Do's and 'Dont's. They also instruct them on the strategy of fighting a battle to win it. If the experienced and elderly people are not respected and consulted frequently, those who are at the helm of affairs of the republic remain at a loss and do not know, inexperienced as they are, what to do in a critical situation.[172]

The fifth condition for a republic to prosper is the protection given to women and unmarried girls. If women are molested and insulted and unmarried girls are forcibly kidnapped and raped by the goons, their husbands and fathers become angry, join the band of robbers and thieves and create troubles in the republic. Because their women and daughters are not protected, because the goonda elements are not punished and because they feel insulted, the evil in them comes to the fore and instead of becoming good and law-abiding citizens, they rise in revolt. Protection of women and girls is one of the most important responsibilities of a republic[173]

170. ibid.2.97

171. ibid. 2.97

172. ibid.2.97

173. ibid.2.98

and it goes hand in hand with the observance of precepts. They, who break the *sīlas*, do not care to protect them. As a result, good governance is not possible because observance of *sīla* is the basis of all good works, more so of good governance.

The sixth condition for a republic to prosper is the honouring of *caityas* and paying them the tithe due to them.[174] Why did the Buddha ask people to honour and maintain *caityas*? According to a renowned commentator, he asked them to do so because they are the places where *yakshas* live. So when they are honoured and worshipped, they help people in living a healthy life, free from disease. They also help them in winning a war. But I think that the Buddha underscores here the point of religious tolerance. All *caityas* irrespective of whether they belong to one religion or other, should be protected and worshipped. This will create the atmosphere of religious tolerance and a fellow feeling. Besides, people will develop faith in those, who bring out the best in them.

The seventh condition which is last but not least - for a republic to prosper is to honor the Arahants (the enlightened persons) and provide them with the four requisites of life such as food, robes, place to stay and bed to sleep and medicine. They should always be welcome. They should never be neglected. If they are not welcomed, the message is passed that the people of the country do not respect Arahants. As a result, those staying there leave the country thinking that the people are inhospitable. If they leave and other Arahants do not come, people do not get a chance of learning Dhamma from them. The Arahants are the embodiments of *sīla, samādhi* and *paññā*. They are the symbols of simplicity and sacrifice, and are the living examples of simple living and high thinking. They are also the living examples of all good values. When they are around, people come in contact with them and learn from them better and higher values in life.[175]

The Buddha also asked people to protect Arahantas but not by the police foce. He said that they should be protected in the same spirit as people do not dare catch fish from a sacred pond, nor dare kill sacred animals like cows or horses nor cut sacred trees for fear of transgressing some ethical rules. In the same manner they should never dare neglect the Arahants but take care of them, protect them with the feelings of awe and reverence for them, which will be for the good, and well-being of the people.

Good governance does not mean tackling law and order problems only diplomatically or by efficient policing, but it means that whatever actions are taken by the king or government they should be done with an honest,

174. ibid.2.98

175. ibid.2.99

pure and compassionate heart. Even justice must be tempered with mercy. Such occasions should not be allowed to come when people are compelled to commit crimes. If punishment is to be given to law breakers it must be given after thorough inquiry, not on suspicion, and that also with mercy. No innocent man should ever be punished.

Although the *Cakkavatti-Sīhanāda Sutta* chiefly traces the origin of the tendency to steal, to kill, to tell a lie and to commit adultery etc. to poverty, the duties of a king have also been defined here. In the first place, the king should be Dhammic. Unless he practices Dhamma he cannot establish good governance. The royal sage who is equivalent to the priest in the *Kūṭadanta Sutta* instructs in a way that makes the duties of a king clear. "It is this, my son: Yourself depending upon the Dhamma, honouring it, revering it, cherishing it, doing homage to it and venerating it, having the Dhamma as your badge and banner, acknowledging the Dhamma as your master, you should establish guard, ward and protection according to Dhamma for your own household, your troops, your nobles and vassals, for Brahmins and householders, town and country folk, ascetics and Brahmins, for beasts and birds. Let no crime prevail in your kingdom, and to those who are in need, give property." [176]

The sage also says that the king should listen to what the ascetics and Brahmins who have renounced the life of sensual pleasures ask him. If they want to know what is wholesome, unblameworthy and harmless and what is just the opposite, they should be told. For good governance what is practically needed is that there shouldn't be a nexus between the king and the criminals. If there is, the criminals will commit crimes without the fear of any punishment. This has been said in the *Mahācora Sutta* [177]of the *Aṅguttara Nikāya.* If the king or his ministers are in league with the criminals, what good can one expect from them? How can good governance be achieved?

---

176. LDB, pp. 396-7
177. A1.178 and A2.120

Was the Buddha a Misogynist?

As the doctrine of the Buddha is basically monastic in character so his attitude towards women is determined by it. It is typical of monastic sentiments not to have any sympathy with women because she is a great snare. She is the most attractive but at the same time most insidious and dangerous. When Ānanda asks, "Master, how shall we behave before women" the Buddha says, "you should shun their gaze and if you happen to see her, you should not speak to her, and if you should speak to her, you must watch over yourself"[178]

As far as the monastic view is concerned, there 'can be no falling in love, because it is a kind of *moha*, infatuation'. As Ananda K. Coomaraswamy says, "To compare *nibbāna*—as the Bṛhadāraṇayaka Upaniṣad compares the bliss of *Ātman* intuition—to the self-forgetting happiness of earthly lovers locked in each others' arms would be for Buddhist thought a bitter mockery."[179] He further says, "No less remote from Buddhist sentiments is the view of Western chivalry which sees in woman a guiding star or that of Vaiṣṇavas or Platonic idealism which finds in the adoration of the individual an education to the love of all."[180]

In answer to a question put by Ānanda, the Buddha once said, "Women are soon angered, Ānanda; women are full of passion, Ānanda; women are envious, Ānanda; women are stupid, Ānanda, etc."[181] But he never disdained to accept the hospitality and the gifts of devout lay women like Khemā, Uppalavaṇṇā, Paṭācārā, and Visākhā etc. He not only accepted offerings from the respected women, but also from the sinners. He accepted Ambapāli's invitation and refused the alternative invitation from the Licchavī princes.

In this paper, I shall try to bring out the Buddha's overall view of women.

There are at least a few passages in the Tipiṭaka where the Buddha has directly or indirectly expressed his opinion about women.[182] There are some passages among them on whose basis one can prove his misogynic

---

178. D2.106

179. BGB, p. 160

180. ibid. pp. 160-61

181. See below f.n.7

182. To get through to the Buddha's view of women it is appropriate to concentrate on the earlier layers of the Tipiṭaka and not on its later layers and Aṭṭhakathās such as the Jātaka Aṭṭhakathās which do not faithfully represent the Buddha's view of women.

outlook. One such passage occurs in the Cūlavagga where the Buddha says to Ānanda, "if, Ānanda, women had not received permission to go out from the household life and enter the homeless state under the doctrine and discipline proclaimed by the Tathāgata, then would the pure religion would Ānanda, have lasted long. The good law could have stood fast for a thousand years. But since, Ānanda, women now have received that permission, the pure religion, Ānanda, would not last so long; the good law will now stand fast for only five hundred years."[183]

The tone here is confessedly apprehensive of the dangers that the Order would be exposed to and the repetition of the name of Ānanda as pointed out by I B Horner for as many as four times more than confirms the Buddha's acknowledgement of his colossal mistake in permitting women into the Order. What he seems to imply by 'one thousand years' and 'five hundred years' is that the religion he took so much pain to spread would not last long and he seems here like a tired man who has staked something very dear to him by giving them permission to enter the Order. He seems to rue the fact that women had been given permission to enter the Order. On the face of it, it is quite clear, that the Buddha in the heart of his hearts, perhaps, did not approve of the idea of women entering the order. But he acceded to the request made by Ānanda on behalf of women, because he loved Ānanda so much that he could not think of disappointing him. It was Ānanda who had pleaded the case of women headed by Mahāpajāpati Gotamī. To Mahāpajāpati Gotami who brought him up after the death of his mother, he could say 'a flat no', "Enough oh Gotamī, let it not please thee that women should be allowed to do so",[184], but to Ānanda's request he acceded although he was full of misgiving and apprehension that were to follow as a necessary consequence. On the basis of this passage one can glibly say that the Buddha did not hold women in high esteem, thought them incapable of leading a religious life and so looked down on them.

There are other passages in the Saṃyutta Nikāya and Aṅgutttra Nikāya where the evils of women as a race are brought out at length. "Women folk are uncontrolled, Ānanda; women folk are envious, Ānanda; women folk are greedy, Ānanda; women folk are weak in wisdom, Ānanda, that is the reason, that is the cause why women folk do not sit in a court of justice, do

---

183. *Sace ānanda nālabhissa mātugāmo tathāgatappavedite dhammavinaye agārasmā anagāriyaṃ pabbajjaṃ, ciraṭṭhitikaṃ, ānanda, brahmacariyaṃ abhavissa vassasahassaṃ saddhammo tiṭṭheyya. Yato ca kho, ānanda, mātugāmo ...pabbajito na dāni brahmacariyaṃ ciraṭṭhitikaṃ, ānanda, bhavissati. Pañcevadāni ānanda, vassasatani saddhammo ṭhassati.* Cv. Nalanda edition p. 377

184. *Alaṃ gotamī, mā te rucci mātugāmassa tathāgatappavedite dhammavinaye agārasmā anagāriyaṃ pabbajā'ti.* Cv Nalanda Edition, p. 373

not embark on business, do not reach the essence of the deed."[185] "Monks, women folk end their life unsated and unreplete with two things. What two? Sexual intercourse and child birth"[186] "It is woman that doth stain the higher life."[187]

The very fact that a woman is said to possess the above mentioned evils proves beyond doubt her inferiority to man.

There is another passage in the Majjhima Nikāya where very authoritatively and forcefully the Buddha proves the inferiority of women. "It is impossible, it cannot come to pass that a woman who is a perfected one could be a Fully Self Awakened One... but the situation occurs when a man who is a perfected one could be a Fully Self Awakened One... this situation occurs... it is impossible, it cannot come to pass that a woman should be a wheel- turning king... could be a Sakka... a Māra... a Brahmā... but this situation occurs when a man might be a Sakka, a Māra, a Brahmā... this situation occurs."[188]

It is clear from this passage that a woman can attain Arahantship, and may become perfect but she cannot rise to the status of a Sakka, a Māra, a Brahmā let alone to the status of a Buddha. On the strength of this passage one would naturally arrive at the conclusion that the Buddha saw some inherent weaknesses in women on account of which they cannot achieve the perfections of a Fully Self Awakened One. This passage, therefore, most seriously stresses the inferiority of women and it is this passage once again which more than anyone else reveals the Buddha's misogynic outlook. Perhaps, passages like this were later responsible for the development of the view that *purisa indriya* is superior to *itthi indriya* and also that the former is acquired by observing higher morality (*mahantena kusalakammena*),[189] and the latter by observing lesser morality (*mandena kusalakammena*).[190] It has been said in the Buddhavaṃsa[191] that

---

185. *Kodhano Ānanda, mātugāmo, issukī Ānanda, mātugāmo, maccharī, Ānanda, mātugāmo, dupañño Ānanda, mātugāmo-ayaṃ kho Ānanda, hetu, ayaṃ paccayo yena mātugāmo neva sabhāyaṃ nisīdati na kammantaṃ payojeti na kambojaṃ gacchatī ti* A 2.87, (Nalanda Edition)

186. *Dvinnaṃ dhammānaṃ, bhikkhave, atitto appaṭivāno mātugāmo kālaṃ karoti. Katamesaṃ dvinnaṃ? Methunasamāpattiya ca vijāyanassa ca.* A 1.72, (Nalanda Edition)

187. *Itthi malaṃ brahmacariyassa, etthāyaṃ sajjate pajā* S 1.36 (Nalanda Edition)

188. MLS III p. 109, *Aṭṭhānametaṃ anavakāso yaṃ itthi arahaṃ assa sammāsambuddho, netaṃ ṭhānaṃ vijjatī ti pajānāti. Thānaṃ ca kho etaṃ vijjati yaṃ puriso arahaṃ assa sammāsambuddho, ṭhanametaṃ vijjati pajānāti.* M 3 p. 128,129, (Nalanda Edition)

189. (Ed) P.V. Bapat, *Aṭṭhasālinī*. p. 259

190. ibid. p. 259

191. *Manussataṃ liṅgasampatti, hetu satthāradassanaṃ/*

one has to have eight attainments (*sampatti*) before one can become a Buddha. One of the attainments obviously is to be born a man.

Buddhaghosa explains it in the *Sutttanipāta Aṭṭhakathā* that *paṇidhi* (aspiration, resolve) can be fulfilled only by men, not by women. *"liṅgasampattī ti purisabhāvo, mātugāmanapuṃsakaubhatovyañjakānam hi manussajātiyaṃ ṭhitanam pi paṇidhi na samijjhati."*[192]

In the *Atthasālini* also it has been explained at length that faculty of male sex is caused by strong *kusala kammas.*

> *"Tasmā purisaliṅgaṃ balavakusalena kammena antaradhāyati, itthi liṅgaṃ dubbalakusalena patiṭṭhā ti. Itthi liṅgaṃ pana antaradhāyantaṃ dubbala akusalena antaradhāyati, purisaliṅgaṃ balavakusalena patiṭṭhā ti. Evaṃ ubhayaṃ pi akusalena antaradhāyati, kusalena patiṭṭhāti ti veditabbaṃ."*[193]

On an analysis of these three passages one finds that all of them, in a way, point to the inferiority of women as a race. The second passage concerns itself primarily with making a psychological analysis of her character but the first and the third which are chiefly concerned with her capacity or otherwise to adopt a religious or ascetic life and achieve Buddhahood prove that women are inferior to men as a race.

Before we make a thorough critical analysis of these passages and bring out their real import, it will be better to refer to some more passages from the Tipiṭaka which prove that the Buddha was not a misogynist. On the contrary, he was full of compassion for women. He poignantly felt their five woes,[194] deeply cared for their hopes and aspirations and even looked beyond his age as has been pointed by I.B. Horner 'to secure for them a status' social as well as spiritual which most of the social philosophers and ascetics of his time could not even conceive of. It was the Buddha and Mahāvira who had the courage of conviction to rise above the prejudiced public opinion. They actually took good care to see that women got their just and right place.

For quite a long time women were looked down upon, were regarded as no better than chattels and were subjugated by men. A time came when daughters were regarded as unwelcome. Dowry may have been one of its

---

Pabbajjā guṇasampatti, adhikaro ca chandatā/
Aṭṭhadhammasamodhānā abhinīhāro samijjhatī ti. Bu. (Nalanda Edition) p. 309

192. (Ed) Angraj Chaudhary, SnA p. 60

193. (Ed) P.V.Bapat, *Aṭṭhasālinī* p. 259

194. S.4 212 -213 (Nalanda Edition) See *Āvenikadukkhasuttaṃ*

BKS, Vol. IV, pp. 162-163 ... a woman at a tender age goes to her husband's family; is subject to menses, is subject to pregnancy, is subject to bring forth... has to wait upon a man.

reasons. The second and perhaps the most important reason was the belief that a son by performing rites could secure for father (parents) a place in heaven but a daughter could not do so. As a result, daughters gradually lost their prestige which they had during the Vedic period and even during the early Upaniṣadic period. We hear of women such as Maitreyī and Gārgī who were great seers, perhaps as great, if not greater, as ṛṣis like Yajñavalkya. But, by the time of the Buddha women came to have a very low place. One instance among many will make this amply clear. When a messenger told king Pasendi that Queen Mallikā had given birth to a daughter, he became very sad.[195] The Buddha's outlook which is evident from what he said to Pasendi on the occasion is quite different from the general public opinion which prevailed at that time. His appreciations of the qualities of women are couched in excellent language.

> *A woman child, O lord of man, may prove*
> *Even a better offspring than a male.*[196]

He doesn't have any doubt in his mind that women do have virtues and qualities and at times they can be better than men.

If we take into account the time when the Buddha pronounced this view of women his revolutionary idea about them will be obvious. I am not using the term 'revolutionary' in the modern sense which implies some kind of demolition, but I am using it in the sense in which one can be revolutionary without resorting to violence and demolition and by just holding a view which is unheard of in one's time. The Buddha was very much advanced for his age and he saw clearly that women did deserve a higher status than they had been given and also they deserve more sympathy and compassion than they were given. He took a liberal view in an age the atmosphere of which was not congenial for it. From this point of view the Buddha can be said to be the holder of new view of women, the view which centuries later came to be known as the 'Emancipation of Women'--a movement which epitomized their hopes and aspirations. It may legitimately be said that the Buddha fully espoused the cause of women and in his own way fought hard to secure for them a status which they had lost for quite some time.

Now let us see what he thought of them from the religious or spiritual point of view. Did he consider them inferior to men as far as religious aspiration and ascetic practices are concerned? It will be clear from what

---

195. S1. p. 85. (Nalanda Edition)
196. ibid. p. 85 *Itthi pi ekacciyā, seyyā posa janādhipa/*
Medhāvinī sīlavatī, sassudevā patibbatā//
Tassā yo jāyati poso, sūro hoti disampati/
Tādisā subhagiyā putto, rajjaṃ pi anusāsatī ti //

he said to Ānanda that women were not incapable of ascetic practices and were not inferior to men as far as living a spiritual or religious life is concerned. When Ānanda asked him, if he thought women incapable of practicing religion and making a spiritual progress he gave a categorical reply in the affirmative.

Bhabbo nu kho, Bhante, mātugāmo Tathāgatappavedite dhammavinaye agārasmā anagāriyaṃ pabbajitvā sotāpattiphalaṃ vā sakadāgāmīphalaṃ vā, anāgāmīphalaṃ vā Arahattaphalaṃ vā sacchikātunti"
Bhabbo, Ānanda, mātugāmo....... sacchikātunti.[197]

He has absolutely no prejudice against women and unlike others[198] very frankly admits that the door of salvation is not closed for women nor are they unfit by their nature to attain *nibbāna.*

"And be it woman, be it man for whom such chariot doth wait by that same car into *nibbāna*'s presence, shall they come."[199]

His view that both mother and son can overcome the three terrors by walking on the Noble Eightfold Path is explicit from what he says in the *Aṅguttara Nikāya.*[200]

From what has been quoted above it is clear that the Buddha did not say anywhere that women cannot lead a religious life nor are they incapable of attaining *nibbāna.* He never presumed that the nature of women stands in the way of their realizing *nibbāna.*

Somā replies boldly to Māra that being a woman does not mean that *nibbāna* is impossible for her.

Itthibhāvo no kiṃ kayirā, cittamhi susamāhite/
Ñānamhi vattamānamhi, sammādhammaṃ vipassato//[201]

What shall one say about the Buddha who emerges out of these passages? Can one justifiably call him a misogynist? The Buddha who is so full of sympathy for women, who almost took up arms against those who wanted to keep them subjugated and did not allow them to have

197. Cv. p. 374. (Nalanda Edition)

198. The Digambar sect of the Jains holds that women are incapable of salvation.

199. *Yassa etādisaṃ yānaṃ, itthiyā purisassa vā/ Sa ve etena yānena, nibbānsseva santike //*

S. 1.31 (Nalanda Edition)

200. *Ayaṃ kho bhikkhave, maggo, ayaṃ paṭipadā imesañca tiṇṇaṃ samātāputtikānaṃ bhayānaṃ imesañca tiṇṇaṃ amātāputtikanaṃ bhayānaṃ pahāṇāya samatikkamāya saṃvattatī ti* A 1.167 (Nalanda Edition)

201. How should the woman's nature hinder us. Whose hearts are firmly set? Psalms of the Sisters (Tr) Mrs C, A. F. Rhys Davids, p. 45

their social status, who thought women as capable as men of tasting the *Dhammarasa*, who unequivocally declared that women are capable of attaining *Arahantship* cannot be labeled as a women hater. In fact, he is a real revolutionary who is trying to get for women the status, social as well as spiritual, that they once enjoyed and lost during the centuries that intervened between the glorious Vedic period and the rise of Buddhism.

It is unthinkable that the Buddha who declared in emphatic terms that people attained superiority and greatness not by birth but by their actions[202] and did not attach any importance to caste, should have thought women inferior to men and relegated them to a lower position. Had it been so, he would not have so readily accepted the invitation extended to him by Ambapālī, the courtesan. The verses of the *therīs* simply bear it out that he espoused their cause and when occasion demanded, he gave them sermons to lead a religious life so that they could work out their own salvation and release themselves from the shackles of suffering as also from the rounds of births and deaths.

Now, while interpreting the passages mentioned in the beginning one must remember this aspect of the Buddha. One should not interpret them in isolation. If he does so he will miss their real import. It is only when one reads them in isolation and out of context that one is inclined to call him a misogynist.

Let one take the third passage first where the Buddha says that it is impossible for a woman to become a Cakkavattī, a Sakka, a Māra, a Brahmā or a Buddha. As a matter of fact, he is not giving vent to his prejudice against women nor is he looking down on them when he says so for any inherent weakness in them but he is making a statement of fact here just as he does when he says there is suffering in the world. It is possible for a woman to attain Arahantship, it is also possible for her to put an end to her suffering and better her lot, but it is impossible for her to become a Sakka, a Māra, a Brahmā or a Buddha.

We know that for becoming a Perfectly Enlightened One, one has to work very hard. One has to fulfill all the *pāramitās*[203] (perfections), *upapāramitās* and *paramattha pāramitās* in order to attain Buddhahood. Besides, one has also to have what is called *paṇidhāna* (resolve) and *abhinīhāra* (aspiration). To fulfill all these one is required to be born several times and make immense efforts. Women in general are tender by nature

---

202. *Na jaccā vasalo hoti, na jaccā hoti Brāhmaṇo/ Kammunā vasalo hoti, kammunā hoti Brāhmaṇo//*

203. Ten pārmitās are: *Dāna pāramitā, Sīla pāramitā, Nekkhamma pāramitā, Paññā pāramitā, Vīiriya pāramitā, Khanti pāramitā, Sacca pāramitā, Adhiṭṭhāna pāramitā, Mettā pāramitā, Upekkhā pāramitā.*

and not capable of hard labor. Their physical build is such as does not enable them to make sustained efforts and keep hard vows. If we also take into account what the Buddha said in the second passage where he has made an objective psychological analysis of women's nature it will be clear that physically, physiologically and psychologically they are not strong enough to fulfill conditions for becoming a Buddha.

Had the Buddha said that they are incapable of attaining Arahantship and salvation, his observation would have smacked of prejudice against them. But what he said about them is based on psychology which could have been ignored only at the cost of being unrealistic. A realist as he was he knew that women in comparison to men are physically and physiologically weak and psychologically weak-minded. But the second passage should not be interpreted to mean that he regarded women inferior to men from social and spiritual points of view.

The first passage too should not be taken to mean as pointed out by Horner, any kind of discourtesy to women. The Buddha hesitated to admit them into the Order because he thought the time was still unripe for this revolutionary step. Almost all contemporary philosophers and ascetics were against women pursuing religious and spiritual life and none of them except Mahāvira had established an Order for them (*Bhikkhuṇi Saṅgha*). 'The dead weight of public opinion' according to I.B. Horner was too heavy to shake off. He was not a narrow-minded and conservative Hindu, but a broad-minded and liberal one. I do not agree with I.B. Horner who says that 'a man is bound by the chains of the past and these go clanging in his ears too insistently to be ignored.' This may be true of an ordinary man but this cannot be true of the Buddha. He was not prejudiced as others were against women. But he hesitated to admit women into the Order because of 'a whole host of reasons in their complicated relationship in the India of that time'. Public opinion was one of them. He did not want to stir up a hornet's nest.

So when Mahāpajāpati Gotamī accompanied by a large number of women strongly desirous of renouncing the world and tasting the elixir of *Dhamma* approached him and requested for being allowed to do so three times, he gave the same reply, "Enough, oh Gotamī, let it not please thee that women should be allowed to do so". Mahāpajāpati Gotamī and other women accompanying her were indeed very sad by this refusal, but they did not lose heart. After some time they again went to him. This time they first met Ānanda who made out a case for them. Finally, the Buddha did agree to admit them into the Order, but he did so hesitatingly because he thought that some unnecessary complications would arise if women were admitted into the Order and there would be obstacle in spreading the *Dhamma* as a consequence.

It is quite likely that the Buddha would not have invited women of his own accord to join the Order. But knowing their keenness, sincerity and a strong desire he could not have ultimately denied their entry into it.

We have made a detailed study of the Buddha's views of women and in the light of what has been said it does not appear reasonable to call him a misogynist. He was full of the milk of human kindness and in no case he would have allowed public prejudices against women to get the better of him. 'That he hesitated to admit them into the order and he prescribed rules such as a nun even one hundred years old must stand in reverence before a newly ordained monk, can be surely ascribed to monk-editors of the texts' as has been rightly observed by I.B. Horner, 'who possibly could not rise above their prejudices against women.'

Buddhism and Modern Issues

What has the Buddha or Buddhism (in the sense of Buddha's teachings) to say about modern issues that confront us? Do his teachings have any bearing on our problems today? Do they help us in tackling the various issues that stare us in our face? Can humanity save itself by following the teachings of the Buddha? One may well ask a question here. Isn't it foolish to think of solving modern issues in the light of his teachings given two thousand six hundred years ago? Isn't it ridiculous to look for the solutions of modern problems in the teachings given two thousand six hundred years ago? A poet or a philosopher or for that matter a religious teacher is very much a product of his times. What he writes, propounds or teaches is of course relevant and meaningful in his times but to expect him to foresee future difficulties and problems and prescribe ways and means to obviate and solve them will be nothing short of absurdity. It will be too much for us to look for the answers of our problems in Buddha's writings and teachings but a great poet or a philosopher or a religious teacher does not only see through his times but goes beyond them and transcends them. In his writings or philosophy or in his teachings he gives vent to certain feelings and comes out with certain observations which are universal in nature and remain relevant to all time to come. His writings, observations and teachings become timeless. They are not confined to a particular period of time but they become a perennial source of light in the most disturbing situations and hold good forever.

The Buddha is such an unfailing source of light for us even in the most troubled times. What he said and taught was a balm not only to suffering human beings of his time but also to suffering humanity for all time. He was not a philosopher like Leibnitz whose speculations do not enable us to solve our existential problems nor was he a philosopher like Heraclites who propounded the philosophy of flux when he said that one cannot dive into the same river twice. This was also at best a speculation, an observation of an intellectually scintillating mind but not a universal truth realized at the experiential level with *bhāvanāmayī prajñā*. Because Heraclites could not do so, so he could not develop *nirveda* (non-attachment) and consequently could not earn as much reverence as the Buddha did. The Buddha was also greater than the greatest of poets. Although the writings of poets like Kālidāsa and Shakespeare are timeless, yet they are not the product of *yathābhūtañāṇadassana* which we find in the Buddha through and through. About the poet it is said,

> The poet's eye, in a fine frenzy rolling
> Doth glance from heaven to earth, from earth to heaven,

And as imagination bodies forth,
The forms of things unknown, the poet's pen
Turns them to shapes and gives to airy nothing,
A local habitation and a name.

Like a poet the Buddha did not imagine but said things from his experiential knowledge.

How can the Buddha be of great help in tackling the issues that we have to confront today. Before I say how the Buddha shows us the way out of the darkness created by the issues, let me name a few of the issues that create problems for us and make our life hell. The first burning issue is different kinds of wars and conflicts among individuals, communities and nations. Why do we fight? Why do we go to war? Why do we have communal riots? We fight because we have aversion or greed in us or we fight because we want to prove ourselves superior to others or because we consider ourselves belonging to a superior race. We hate others because we do not like what they eat and how they worship their gods. We go to war because we have greedy eyes on some nation's mineral wealth or we want to extend our territory or we want to show others down. There may be several reasons why we fight and go to war. But its two basic causes are greed and aversion. Greed or desire is a hydra- headed monster. You satisfy one and the other crops up, you satisfy the other and yet others crop up, the more you try to satisfy your desire the more anguished you feel because it is like a bottomless pit, which cannot be filled. Aversion, which also is one form of desire, is never quenched.

Na hi verena verāni, sammantīdha kudācanaṃ/
Averena ca sammanti, esa dhammo sanantano.//

(Hatreds never cease through hatred in this world: they cease through love alone. This is an eternal law)

This is the eternal truth, eternal law that the Buddha teaches.

In the *Aggañña Sutta* of the Dīgha Nikāya which anticipates the Book of Genesis and graphically shows how man lost his innocence because of his greed, the Buddha shows through a fable how greed gives rise to ugliness, arrogance and lust and how it leads to hoarding (*parigraha*), committing theft, lying, censuring, punishment and many other evil things. So long as this defilement is there in man, he can still crave for more and more and commit all sorts of crimes even though his basic needs are fulfilled. Marxist sociologists talk of alleviating poverty and they believe that most of the social evils will disappear if wealth is equitably distributed, if equal opportunity is given to all and if private property is abolished. In the *Cakkavattīsīhanaāda Sutta* it has been underlined that a king fails in his duty if he does not provide people with property so that they can satisfy their basic needs. Even if the king makes all arrangements of guarding and protecting people but fails to give property to the needy, he fails to establish law and order in his kingdom and also fails to stem the tide of other social evils that follow poverty. In the *Kūṭadanta Sutta* the Buddha says how material prosperity and social harmony can be achieved in society. Poverty is the cause of most of the social evils. Thieves, dacoits and highwaymen take to committing theft, loot and robbery because they do not have enough to live on. No amount of punitive measures taken by a king or a government can eliminate them. Punishment is not a sure cure of social evils and malaise as has been said above. Corruption and crime cannot be completely eliminated by punishing criminals. It is true particular criminals will be punished and liquidated but there will be many in which the seeds of crime will remain. The most effective way to get rid of such crimes is to ensure that people have enough to live on. The Buddha, therefore, suggests that all sections of society should be taken care of. Farmers and cattle rearers must be provided with seeds and other agricultural equipments to carry on agricultural operations and produce crops. The businessmen must be provided with enough capital to set up and run their business and, last but not least, all willing citizens must have employment, particularly the unemployed youth whose idle minds are likely to become devil's workshop. In short, economic well-being will ensure social well-being.

The measures suggested by the Buddha are very relevant today. If we go by his suggestions many modern problems like unemployment and other social evils like kidnapping, looting of banks etc. will be solved. If the Heads of states follow his prescriptions much of the law and order problem will be solved and much of the unrest in society will disappear.

It is true that these measures will have a salubrious effect in curbing social evils, but so long as greed is there in one's mind there are bound to be social and political evils. The Buddha is not satisfied with prescribing temporary measures to achieve material prosperity and social harmony. But he prescribes a path by walking on which man can become virtuous, he can develop insight by concentrating his mind and understanding the utter futility of greed for things which are in a constant state of flux; he can purify his mind of defilements like greed and aversion. One must remember that both philosophy and religion have a happy union in his teachings as has been said in one of the essays collected here. It is said that the philosophy lived in life becomes religion. The Buddha does not only propound philosophy but lucidly chalks out an action-plan so that it can be practiced and lived in life. The technique of Vipassana clearly shows the path and also points out how to confidently walk on this path to reduce, if not completely root out, various defilements that pollute our mind.

The third burning issue, particularly in India is the caste system, which is the bane of a civilized nation. The Buddha came out with this clarion call not to divide human beings on the basis of where one is born but he said that a man is great or small, high or low by virtue of his actions.

Na jaccā vasalo hoti, na jaccā hoti Brāhmano/
Kammunā vasalo hoti, kammunā hoti Brāhmano//[204]

(Man is great or small, not because of his birth in a particular caste, but because of his actions)

Now-a-days bioethics has come up as a new science. It means the ethics of medical and biological research. Researchers in this field are making various researches to discover medicines for different kinds of diseases. But in course of discovering such medicines they make experiments on innocent and mute animals which suffer severe pains and some of them die during the experiment. What does the Buddha have to say about it? Had the Buddha been alive today, could he have shut his eyes to these cruel crimes perpetrated on mute animals? Before answering this question, one would like to put two counter questions. If one of the disciples of the Buddha were to suffer from a disease and the doctor prescribed such medicines as are discovered in the way described above, could he have forbidden his disciple to take such medicines? And could he have allowed scientists to experiment the discovered medicines directly on human beings and risk their lives? I think the answer is an emphatic NO. Man's life is rare. It is man who can become the Buddha, not an animal. *Manussattaṃ liṅga sampatti, hetu satthāradassanaṃ* etc. Therefore man's life must be saved. It is clear from the Vinaya Piṭaka that he allowed the use of tallows as medicines for example tallow from animals such as bears, swine, donkeys and fish. Didn't the Buddha know that tallows are got from killing these animals?

Nowadays one talks of transplanting human organs and saving human lives. The Buddha would have definitely liked the idea of donating one kidney to save a precious human life. Of course, he would have strongly objected to the racket of supplying kidneys to the needy ones for fabulous money. He would also have objected to taking out the kidney of a patient without his knowledge. This is highly unethical. But if transplanting the heart of a pig could save a heart patient he would have allowed it knowing full well that this heart was got by killing a pig.

Different kinds of pollution such as air pollution, noise pollution, water pollution etc. pose a big problem today. The Buddha anticipated these problems. There are many places in the Tipiṭaka where he spoke against noise. He felt extremely annoyed when a group of five hundred novices

---

204. Sn 142

came to the monastery where he was living and started making noise. He, therefore, prescribed noble silence. Either the Bhikkhus should discuss Dhamma or observe noble silence. There are rules in the Vinaya Piṭaka where he asked monks and nuns not to pollute water.

The Buddha did not like to disturb ecology and wanted to maintain a balance. That he liked nature and wanted to live in natural surroundings is proved by the fact that he was born in a forest, he practised austerity far away from the madding crowd, he attained Bodhi under a tree, he set the wheel of Dhamma in motion in the Deer Park at Sarnath and attained Mahāparinibbāna in the Sālavana of the Mallas. Very often he would sit under a tree and meditate.

He wondered how one could think of cutting a tree, which gives us shade to rest and fruits to eat. Monks and nuns were even prohibited from injuring plants and seeds. He asked them time and again not to pollute water by throwing undesirable things in it. So, he had very seminal thoughts to control pollution and save ecology. If we want to save ecology we must eliminate the defilement of greed from our mind. It is our greed which impels us to take more resources than the earth can give us. It is out of greed that we devastate nature, rape it and take far more resources than we actually need. Resources are limited but human greed is limitless.

The Buddha has drawn up a clear action-plan as has been said above, to reduce greed, if not completely root it out.

The Buddha is very relevant even today. He can still show us the path.

Bioethics and the Buddha

Bioethics means the ethics of medical and biological research. Researchers in these fields have made a quantum leap in the present century. Medical researchers are making various researches to discover medicines for different kinds of diseases. Some of the medicines discovered indeed have miraculous effects. But these medicines are discovered by making experiments on mice, guinea pigs, cows and horses. Researchers test different kinds of medicine on them and ascertain the suitability or otherwise of medicines for mankind. During these experiments, the innocent and mute animals suffer severe pains and even die during the process. The question is: is it ethically justified to make experiments on the mute and innocent animals, cause them severe pain and even cause their death. The answer to this question can partly be found in another question: can the discovered medicines be directly experimented on human beings. This is what some of the scientists of Hopkins Institute in collaboration with some Indian scientists did recently and with what ghastly results! They are still feeling a lot of guilt conscience.

There are some thinkers and social workers, who are dead against making experiments on animals because in the process a lot of injury and pain is inflicted on them. This, according to them, is cruelty towards animals and highly unethical. But will they allow scientists to experiment discovered medicines directly on man? And what would the Buddha have said about it?

On the one hand, the Buddha could not have shut his eyes to the cruel acts perpetrated by researchers on mute animals. On the other hand, he could not have forbidden his disciples also to take those medicines and get cured because their life was very precious.[205]

To my mind, as the Buddha considered man's life very valuable, perhaps more valuable than the lives of other creatures in the world, and as his philosophy is exclusively humanitarian, geared to the spiritual development of man besides solving other problems of life, he would have definitely cared more for their physical and mental health.

We know that the Buddha regarded man as the greatest of all beings. To be born as man is of the highest advantage especially from the spiritual point of view because it is man who can become a Buddha, it is he who can practise Dhamma and attain *nirvāṇa*. This view of the Buddha is corroborated by what he says in the *Buddhavaṃsa—Manussattaṃ liṅga sampatti, hetu satthāra dassanaṃ* etc. Out of the eight chief conditions, which are necessary for

205. See my essay entitled 'Buddhism and Modern Issues'.

attaining Buddhahood, to be born as man is the first important condition. The other conditions follow from this. It is man who can attain *vijjā* (*paññā*) and *caraṇa* (*sīla*)—*Vijjācaraṇasampanno, so seṭṭho devamānuseti*, other beings cannot. So in the scale of values man occupies the highest place.

The second point the Buddha makes is that in order to walk on the Noble Eightfold Path one must have fairly good health. It is only healthy people free from diseases who can perform the uphill task of walking on the Noble Eightfold Path. *Sarīramādhyam khalu dharmasādhanam*. To begin with, a healthy body is the primary requisite for practising religion.

So man's life being valuable, must, on all accounts, be saved. Medical researchers who make experiments on animals in order to discover suitable and efficacious medicines for mankind cannot be ethically blamed because, in the first place, their intention is not to take their life. Killing or murder is said to be committed when five conditions are fulfilled viz. there must be a being to be killed, there must be a killer, it must be his intention to kill, he must have a weapon to kill (he can use his hands and legs as weapons) and when the act of killing is actually committed. We also know that many bacteria are killed when we breathe in and breathe out but we commit no murder as our intention is not to kill them.

And, in the second place, the medicines they discover save precious human lives. In short, the *akusala kamma* they do (if at all they do it) is more than compensated by the wholesome actions they do. Just as a ball of iron immediately sinks into the sea but a ship made of tonnes of iron does not, so the *kusala kamma* done in discovering medicines to save precious human lives acts as a ship which can carry several balls of iron symbolising *akusala kamma* without sinking. Researchers make experiments without having the intention to kill the animals they experiment on. So, their intention is pure. They are not ethically blameworthy. Besides, *kamma visaya* is the subject of the Buddha, it is *acintanīya* for one. One never knows in what proportion and in what way one gets the results of the *kammas* he does

Buddha's great concern was to root out the cause of suffering and annihilate it. In order to do so, he prescribed a way for purifying mind from pollutants like craving and aversion--the cause of suffering. But although he prescribed a way all right he did not make it binding for all to walk upon it. He was not a theoretical philosopher like many others who only think about a problem intellectually. He was a realist. He knew very well the different capacities of individuals and, therefore, he did not expect all to follow what he prescribed. Of course, as he established an Order of monks who had left home for leading a homeless life in order to attain *nibbāna*, (*amata*, deathlessness), he prescribed the great mass of rules for its members with a view to guiding them in such a way that they could live a monastic life smoothly without violating the ethical codes of conduct which are the backbone of leading a spiritual life. So he made the great mass of Vinayic rules binding for them. He prescribed in detail the do's and dont's for monks and nuns. What kinds of shoes and sandals the monks might wear and whether they should make use of animals' skin or hides have been discussed in detail. It is clear from the *Vinaya Piṭaka* that whatever the Buddha prescribed and what he objected to is based on sound reason. Nothing that he said, prescribed or not allowed is arbitrary. He was not rigid, but he was always open to conviction and adapted himself to the changed circumstances. He did not make it compulsory for a Soṇa Kolivisa who was delicately nurtured to go without a sandal nor did he ask a monk with corns in his feet to negotiate the road without shoes, nor did he ask the monks to make use of animals' skins when he did not consider them necessary. Of course, his intention was not to take life, however infinitesimal. So he did not allow monks to use animals' hides, but when he saw it was necessary for monks living in the border country where, perhaps, the winter was not kind he prescribed, animals' hides for them to keep themselves from inclement weather. Wooden shoes were objected to because monks wearing them might slip on insects and kill them besides disturbing the monks who were meditating.

It is true one of the most important five ethical precepts is to abstain from killing, but it must be remembered that the Buddha did not prescribe it for all. When soldiers fight in the war in order to defend their country from enemies, they are bound to kill them and the Buddha considered it their bounden duty. That is why when he came to know that the king's soldiers stealthily entered the Order and some monks ordained them as monks, he admonished them and did not allow such soldiers to be ordained. He knew that there are different duties to be performed by different persons and performing different duties is essential for making a society stable and smooth going. He did not confuse worldly obligations with spiritual ones, So he did not interfere in others' affairs. But personally, he liked to walk on the Noble Eightfold Path, observe *sīla*, practice *samādhi* and attain *paññ.* to know the true nature of reality, to realize at the experiential level the transitory and fleeting nature of worldly objects in order to develop non-attachment (*nirveda*) to them and break the strong bonds that bound him to the wheel of life and death. He kept on giving this message to all and sundry, but never made it binding for all. Of course, he hoped his message was driven home to many so that they could realize the sweeter and higher values of life and being inspired by their conviction they could walk on the path of virtue. It is true he was greatly concerned with spiritual life, but he did not lose sight of the material life and material well-being here and now.

If one reads the section on medicines in the *Mahāvagga*, it will soon be amply clear that the Buddha was not rigid and whatever he prescribed as medicines he did not do it arbitrarily. In the beginning when he prescribed five medicines such as ghee, fresh butter, oil, honey and molasses to monks and nuns he prescribed them knowing full well that they 'are medicines and are also agreed upon as medicines'. This phrase is very important because the Buddha accepted those as medicines, which people regarded as medicines. People must have accepted them as medicines after seeing their efficacy in curing diseases and for determining their efficacious nature some sort of experiments must have gone on even in those days and, may be, they were experimented on animals and birds. He did not bother his head to know how they were procured, by killing animals or by any other means. If ill monks had need of tallows as medicines he allowed them. "I allow you monks, to make use of tallows as medicines by using them with oil: tallow from bears, tallow from fish, tallow from alligators, tallow from swine, tallow from donkeys..."[206] Didn't the Buddha know that the tallows are got from killing these animals? On another occasion when he came to know that a monk who had a non-human affliction got cured when he ate raw flesh and drank raw blood of a swine in a swine's slaughter- place, he allowed other monks suffering from it to take it. "I allow, monks, when one has a non-human affliction, raw flesh and raw blood"[207] Didn't he know that raw flesh and raw blood of a swine can be obtained only by killing it?

The Buddha was able to make a distinction between what is necessary and life saving and what is not. Therefore, he did not allow monks to wear shoes of palmyra palm leaves, because when they are cut, they wither and die. But he did allow them to use roots of turmeric, ginger, orris root, white orris root, garlic, black hellebore, khus-khus, nut grass or whatever other roots there are that are medicines, knowing full well that when their roots are dug up, they will die.

In the light of what has been said above the Buddha would have allowed such medicines as were available in the market, although they were procured from animals which suffered severe pain and even died. But this is another question whether the Buddha, if asked for permission, would have allowed scientists to inflict so much pain on innocent animals to discover medicines?

We know he did not allow a monk to treat patients but he did not make it ethically binding for all, who can, not to make researches in medicine and discover life-saving medicines. After all, the Buddha did not hesitate in taking the services of Jīvaka Komārabhacca, whose fame as a great surgeon had spread far and wide and who 'having cut open the skin of his (a merchant of Rajgir) head, having opened a suture in the skull' drew out two

206. BD Vol. 4, pp. 270-271.

207. ibid. p. 274.

living creatures and cured the disease of his head'. The Buddha knew it but he did not regard him as a violator of the first ethical principle although the two creatures he had drawn out from the merchant's head must have perished soon. but there is no reference to his transplanting human organ. This is a contribution of modern science and modern bio-medical research.

Ecological Reflections in Pāli Canonical Literature

Ecology is a branch of biology dealing with relations of organisms to one another and to their surroundings. But here in this paper we are not so much concerned with this ecology as we are with Ecological Ethics which makes relations between man and man on the one hand and between man and the flora and fauna on the other smooth, easy and happy so that not only people, birds and beasts live happily without any fear, but also their surroundings and sanctuaries also grow without any fear of destruction and pollution from people.

Men and ecology are interdependent. They can protect and destroy each other. If the relationship between them is smooth and happy, both grow and flourish but if the relationship is strained both are affected. That the two are deeply interrelated has been shown by the Buddha. As man thinks, so does he become. This is true of man, but as man thinks and acts, so does ecology become. This is also as true. Ecology is affected by what man thinks and does. For relations to be good and happy between man and man and also between man and ecology, Lord Buddha enunciated some basic ethical principles. Broadly speaking these are five. They are abstaining from killing, stealing, committing adultery, telling lies, and drinking liquor. The Buddha says that if people's physical and vocal actions are pure, they will live a happy and peaceful life and if they indulge in immoral physical and vocal actions, not only will there be disturbance, tension and unrest in human society but also ecology will be badly affected.

But why did the Buddha have to enunciate these ethical principles? It's because he saw that man's roots of immoral actions are craving (*lobho*), aversion (*doso*) and ignorance (*moho*). It's also true that man is capable of moral actions--their roots being *alobho, adoso* and *amoho*. But his general tendency is to work under the influence of the first three immoral roots of actions. Besides, man far surpasses animals in matters of greed and lust and even in matters of jealousy. It is only man's greed and lust, which are insatiable. Animals are not that greedy and lustful. So, the Buddha had to enunciate five social ethical principles for man to follow and observe so that peace and harmony can be established in human society.

Killing, stealing, committing adultery, telling lies and drinking liquor are the grossest broad immoral actions and all other actions that a man does are but the permutations and combinations of these. And all of these actions stem from man's craving and aversion, which are like the two sides of a coin. It is true that craving and aversion arise out of ignorance and if man can dispel the darkness of ignorance, knowledge will dawn on him and he will be rid of them i.e. craving and aversion. But that state is not to be easily achieved. That's why Lord Buddha has prescribed the five precepts of social ethics so that man can reduce the quantum of greed and hatred and thereby live in human society peacefully and harmoniously i.e. if these ethical rules are observed by man, his mind will not be polluted. And if his mind is unpolluted, he will live peacefully with his fellow beings and there will be peace, harmony and prosperity in human society.

Greed or craving is one of the greatest pollutants of mind. A greedy mind is not only a threat to one's own peace and happiness, but it is a great threat to others' peace and a great hazard to ecology. How man's greed can affect ecology has been very graphically shown by the Buddha in the *Aggañña Sutta* of the *Dīghanikāya.* As this Sutta traces the genesis both of man and human society it is rightly called a Book of Genesis. But incidentally it also shows how people were happy when their minds were not polluted and how they began to feel unhappy and experienced different kinds of troubles and sufferings when their minds were polluted by craving, aversion and other negativities. Human beings are pure when they are born into this world from the World of Radiance. "And they become made of mind, feeding on rapture, self-luminous, traversing the air, continuing in glory and remain thus for a long long period of time"[208] To them who were without any greed, the earth with its savour was spread out in the waters 'even as a scum forms on the surface of boiled milky rice that is cooking'[209] and eventually became 'endowed with colour, with odour and with taste'.[210]

Then greed appeared in some of them. They tasted the savoury earth, liked it and developed craving for it so much so that they started taking lumps of it with their hands. Their action done out of greed robbed them of their luminance. They were reduced to the same kind of state as Adam had been when he was expelled from Eden for disobeying God and eating the forbidden fruit. So instead of lighting their way themselves they now had to depend upon the light of the sun and the moon which manifested themselves.

These beings continued to feast on the savoury earth. As a result, their bodies became solid and their beauty was lost in direct proportion to the amount of the earth they ate. Some ate the savoury earth more than others. Those who ate less were more beautiful than others. So they became proud of their beauty. They began to despise those who were less beautiful.

---

208. DB, III, p. 82
209. ibid. p. 82
210. ibid. p. 82

Because of their greed, conceit and hatred the savoury earth disappeared. This was the first change in ecology caused by their three defilements. Then for those beings 'outgrowths appeared in the soil'[211]. They were like mushrooms which had colour, odour and taste. They continued to feed on them for a long time. As a result, their bodies became more solid. Some became more beautiful than others causing in them pride for their beauty and hatred for others' ugliness.

What one sees here is the gradual pollution of their minds. As the pollution became more and more, the mushroom like growths also vanished and in their place grew creeping plants, which had colour, odour and taste. This was the second big change in ecology brought about by their greed, pride and hatred.

Then they began to feast on these creepers and the more they fed on them the more solid their bodies became causing some to be more beautiful and others to be less so. This again increased the pride and hatred of the more beautiful beings.

As their minds became more polluted with these negativities, even the creepers disappeared. Ecology once again was greatly affected.

Then appeared the rice, which had no powder and husk. The grains were clean and fragrant. So long as these beings held back their cravings and took only that much as was sufficient for them in the morning and evening, rice kept on growing and ripening. Rice gathered in the morning for breakfast, grew and ripened again in the evening to be gathered for dinner. They kept on feeding on such rice. As a result, their bodies became more solid and some became distinctly more beautiful than others. The beings were then differentiated into men and women. They felt attracted towards each other. Man began to contemplate woman and woman man. Passion for each other grew and they began to burn for each other's company. Then they satisfied their lusts.

Too much of indulgence in passion made them lazy. So instead of going in the morning and in the evening to gather rice necessary for breakfast and dinner, they gathered enough for the two meals together. Others following them gathered enough for two days, for four days and even for eight days. The tendency to hoard rice grew in them as they were both greedy and lazy. The lust, greed and laziness drastically affected ecology and the rice which had no powder and husk was clean and fragrant developed powder and husk and 'the reaped or cut stems did not grow again; a break became manifest (where the reaper had cut), the rice stubble stood in clumps'[212].

211. ibid. p. 83
212. ibid. p. 86

With the passage of time when rice stubbles did not grow and stood in clumps, then they thought of dividing the rice-fields and set boundaries.

Excessive greed led some to steal from others' plots. When they were caught red-handed they were punished. With this punishment came fear, hatred and revenge. In this way men's growing greed greatly affected not only ecology but also their minds.

The story narrated in the *Aggañña Sutta* may be taken as a fable which realistically describes what happens to man when he has too much of craving. He meets the same fate (tragedy) as did the man in the fable who killed the goose that laid a golden egg everyday or he meets the same fate as did Midas of the Greek mythology who had enough of gold but no food to eat. Out of insatiable greed he may wish to play these roles in order to make money, say by harming ecology by cutting trees from the jungles and killing animals for their skins and amass gold like Midas but he cannot escape the tragedy that will fall on him. He will die of hunger.

Let us see what greed has made of man. It has made him ever insatiable, ever dissatisfied. It has made him establish big industries to manufacture different kinds of goods to make money. But with what horrible results! The entire atmosphere is polluted by industrial areas. The water of the nearest river is also polluted. Thus, along with stress he is condemned to breathe in carbon dioxide and carbon monoxide gases dangerous for lungs and hazardous for health. Industrialization also causes depletion of the ozone layer with the result that the temperature of the earth is increasing. Its horrible consequences will be the melting of snow and coming of floods submerging a greater part of the earth under water. Partial destruction of jungles leads to erosion of the soil which fills the beds of rivers causing heavy floods leading to famine. Scarcity of food materials causes many negativities in man to arise and what does a hungry man not do, how low does he not stoop to satisfy his hunger? All such negative feelings affect the peace and harmony of society.

In the name of green revolution, he has greatly interfered with nature. He makes the land produce more than its natural capacity with the help of fertilizers. The result is that we are getting prone to all kinds of diseases.

Man's excessive craving causes burning and restlessness not only in him, but also in his immediate society. The relationship between him and other people gets strained. The peace and harmony of the society get affected.

So long as the king and the people of a nation observe *śīla* i.e. the five ethical precepts and follow the Aryan Path, the nation and the people are prosperous. But if they turn away from the Aryan Path, do not follow the Law of truth and righteousness, do not honour and revere it, and if the king forgets his duty to give full protection to people, birds and beasts and does not give enough to the poor to live by, the nation and the people fall into adversity.

How following the *Aryan* Path leads to prosperity and how the contrary causes adversity has been clearly shown in the *Cakkavattisīhanāda Sutta*. Purity of mind causes the well-being of people; polluted mind causes unhappiness and misery. So long as the king gave property to the poor, he achieved social harmony. How social harmony can be achieved has also been described in the *Kūṭadanta Sutta*.[213] But when he did not give wealth to the poor 'poverty became widespread'[214]. It led people to commit theft. A time came when people became so greedy that even if the king gave them enough to live by, they would still steal to get more and more. To stop this, the king introduced punishment, but instead of punishment being a deterrent, it made them violent. They began to behead those whose wealth they stole. Murder became frequent. Next stage was that people for fear of punishment began to tell lies and speak evil of others. There still came a time when the ugly coveted the comely and committed adultery. With each negativity and pollutant growing in the mind people began to lose their life-span and beauty. Thus, one sees that the effect of evil dispositions is tremendous on human beings.

What havoc can be created by mental impurity has been graphically described here. But if the mental purity is retained or cultivated by man, such evil dispositions will not arise in him and he will enjoy peace and harmony with enough prosperity.

These evil dispositions or pollutants of mind do not only affect immediate relationship between man and man but go a long way in affecting ecology as well. As five social ethical precepts prescribed by the Buddha are to be followed for peace and harmony in society, so also they should be observed to save ecology. To make it more explicit let us take the first of the five precepts--refraining from killing. Man indulges in killing out of hatred, anger, fear and greed. One hates somebody, so to get rid of him one kills him. He abuses him or threatens him, makes him angry and frightens him, so he kills him out of anger and fear or because he wants to grab his property out of greed to which he protests, so he kills him. It is clear from this that so long as man is motivated by these negative feelings, there can be no peace in society. There will be only tension, fear, anger and burning. If these negativities are removed, peace and harmony, love and friendliness will reign supreme and human society will become a veritable heaven.

If one observes the first precept of *sīla* i.e., if he refrains from killing living beings, he will not kill birds and beasts and thus save ecology. One

---

213. See the *Kūṭadanta Sutta* in the D1 and the article entitled "Buddha's View of Harmony" collected in my book entitled *Essays on Buddhism and Pali Literature*.

214. D3 (see *Cakkavattisīhanāda Sutta*)

has seen that one commits the act of killing out of greed and fear. One kills tigers for their skins and also to prove that he is stronger than they. He also kills other animals, even snakes for their skins so that he may make huge money by selling them. He also indulges in killing other animals for their exotic and tasty meat. He kills birds for their tasty meat, downs and plumages. Poachers stealthily kill tigers even at the tiger sanctuary and export their different parts to countries where expensive medicines are made from them. These indiscriminate killings create a sort of imbalance in ecology. If there are no tigers in the jungles, people are not afraid to go to those jungles and cut trees. They cut trees for making money. As a result deforestation takes place which leads to shortage of rainfall or no rainfall, which causes famine. Famine causes poverty which gives rise to many negativities mentioned earlier. In order that there is a balance between man and ecology, man should not indulge in indiscriminate killing. Observance of Buddha's ecological ethics can enable us to achieve this end.

The balance between man and ecology goes a long way in making our life happy and enjoyable. Lord Buddha says again and again that ecology should be preserved and man should follow the principle of 'live and let live' as the fauna and flora also have as much right to live.

Most important events of Lord Buddha's life took place in the lap of nature. He was born in Lumbini forest, he practiced meditation in Uruvela near Gaya--a very beautiful spot on the bank of river Nerañjarā, attained bodhi under the Bodhi tree, set the Wheel of the Dhamma in motion in the Deer Park at Sarnath and attained *mahāparinibbāna* in Pāvā lying down between two *sāla* trees.

Going through the *Sutta Piṭaka* one finds Lord Buddha immensely praising natural surroundings such as jungles, parks, rivers, hills and mountains etc. which he found to be conducive to meditation. He taught many of his *Suttas* either in forests or on the banks of rivers or in mango-groves. He becomes ecstatic while describing the delightful beauty of the *cetiyas* as is clear from the *Mahāparinibbāna Sutta*. Lord Buddha's preference for living in a jungle at the foot of a tree has been described in no uncertain terms. His liking for silence is well-known. Once he expelled even Sāriputta and Moggallāna who were responsible for noise in the Vihāra.[215]

From the *Theragāthā* it is clear that the *theras* are never tired of praising the salubrious effects jungles, rivers and mountain caves have on them in practising meditation and perfecting their *brahmacariya* life. Birds like peacock also inspire them to practise meditation. The green forests and the rains falling gently or in torrents provide very congenial atmosphere to sit in meditation. Had there been no jungles, no mountain caves, where would have they gone to get silence and peace necessary for attaining *nibbāna*?

---

215. D2 (*Mahāparinibbāna Sutta*) p. 66

Tālapuṭa's longing for dwelling in the jungles is expressed in the following words-

Kadā aniccaṃ vadharoganīḷaṃ, kāyaṃ imaṃ maccujarāupaddutaṃ/
Vipassamāno vītabhayo vihassaṃ, eko vane taṃ nu kadā bhavissati//

O when shall I, who see and know that this my person, nest of dying and disease, oppressed by age and death, is all impermanent.

"Dwell free from fear lonely within the woods,
Yea, when shall these things be?"

Human society where there is so much noise must be abandoned to experience peace. Lord Buddha compares noise found in human society with thorns (*sadda kaṇṭakā*). It never allows man to experience peace and realize at the experiential level the various kinds of sensations that arise in us by equanimously watching which he can attain insight into the real nature of all things and phenomena. And what else can give physical and mental repose except environment constituted by forests, parks and gardens and hills and mountains and flowing rivers? How nature has inspired *theras* to attain *nibbāna* and arhathood has been described in my article entitled '*Nature in the Theragāthā*'.[216]

As has been said earlier all one's immoral actions spring from his craving and aversion. If he follows the social ethics taught by the Buddha and even if he observes only the first precept of abstaining from killing in both its negative and positive aspects (not killing beings is the negative aspect *vāritta sīla* and developing kindness and compassion for them is the positive aspect *cāritta sīla*), he will reduce his craving and aversion which wIll enable him to save ecology. Buddha's ecological ethics are the same as his social ethics, but they give more importance to the ecology in general and so to the saving of the flora and fauna in particular.

216. See my book entitled *Essays on Buddhism and Pali Literature*.

Causes of the Enduring Greatness of the Nalanda Mahāvihāra

The very name of Nalanda conjures up before our mind's eye all that is best and most excellent in education. In other words, it has become the symbol of the best kind of education that humanity can be proud of.

There are very good universities in different parts of the world today. Some of them like Sorbonne or Paris University in France, Oxford and Cambridge in England have been in existence for a very long time. There are others like Harvard, Wisconsin and Philadelphia in America and yet others in other parts of the world but none commands as much respect as Nalanda did, none has got that prestigious and privileged position as it still enjoys today, although the Nalanda Mahāvihāra (the name of the ancient university) was demolished as far back as in the beginning of the thirteenth century. A small Institute started in 1951 by lovers and patrons of culture in order to resuscitate the ancient glory of Nalanda is regarded as the Nalanda University by all Buddhist countries and even by those western scholars who are greatly interested in Buddhist Studies. This is why when the Government of India wanted to honour the prince of Laos by conferring on him a degree *honoris causa* in the early 1960s, they did not think of Delhi, B.H.U., Pune or even Santiniketan. The only university they could think of was Nalanda

The excellence and distinction of Nalanda lay in several factors. Nalanda was so great that to get a degree from here or to be somehow or other associated with it was the hall-mark of distinction and recognition and still it is so. To have taken a course here was a matter of prestige and many usurped the name of Nalanda students.[217]

In the ancient university of Nalanda the admission was so difficult that only two or three out of ten were selected and the rest were rejected by the learned dwarpandits. Some of them who were rejected stayed around Nalanda and equipped themselves so that they could not be rejected next time. The present Nava Nalanda Mahāvihāra enjoyed the same prestige and distinction at least in its early years of establishment.

In the early sixties Nava Nalanda Mahāvihāra or Pāli Institute as it is popularly called had not come out of its swaddling clothes but special provisions were made in the Constitution of Nava Nalanda Mahāvihāra to hold convocation and confer the degree of Vidyā Vāridhi *honoris causa* on great scholars and patrons of Buddhism.

217. BuddhistMM

It is true that Sorbonne, Oxford and Cambridge were started in the medieval age and since the beginning they have been real great universities but even they are not so revered as Nalanda.

What are the causes of such a prestigious position of Nalanda University? Why is it that Nalanda is regarded as the 'university of all universities'[218] that have been in the past and that are now in the world? Why is it that it is regarded as non-pareil? Why is it that it is regarded as something more than a university as we understand it today?

One of the reasons is that other universities of the world were set up long after the establishment of Nalanda--almost at the time when Nalanda fell into ruins. At that distant time when there was no university worth the name in the world there was a university here where blazed a torch the light of which spread far and wide into several parts of the world. As Santosh Kumar Das rightly says, 'Thus Nalanda was an international centre in the 7th century when Europe was in the darkest watch of the long night of the Middle Ages, when even the Saracenic schools and Arabic seats of learning had not yet been founded'[219]. Not only did the light of logic and philosophy, religion and literature emanate from here but also the message of peace, amity, non-violence, sympathy, compassion, joy and equanimity spread from here which went a long way in ennobling the mankind of a great part of the world. The message that spread from here lighted many a dark heart and filled it with the milk of loving kindness.

Before Nalanda University came into existence, there was only one university in the whole world. It was Taxila University in India (now in Pakistan). In Pāli literature we find its name mentioned with great reverence. Jīvaka Komārabhacca who was the personal physician of Lord Buddha received his education both theoretical and practical at Taxila which at that time was a great centre of medical learning besides other secular subjects. But even Taxila which was by all reckonings perhaps the first ever university much before the time of Lord Buddha is not so much revered as Nalanda. Taxila which was at its acme of name and fame at the time of Lord Buddha must have been in existence for at least two hundred years before it could acquire such a prestigious position.

Why is it that Nalanda Mahāvihāra which came into being at least one thousand years after the Buddha became so famous? What are the reasons for it? What was its special contribution which has sunk into our psyche to regard it as the symbol of the best kind of education?

Education as conceived and understood by the custodians and professors of Nalanda university did not mean only passing information to

218. Nal Uni, p. 170

219. Edu, Sys Hin. p. 369.

students but it meant their all-round development i.e. intellectual, moral, spiritual and aesthetic development. It also meant physical development, but not the kind of development as is exampled by wrestlers, but physical fitness enough to put in strenuous efforts and hard work.[220] The education imparted here enabled the students of the university to develop self-confidence and thinking capacity in depth. For developing these qualities in students the great professors (the majority of them were renowned) adopted tutorial and discussion methods besides lecture method. The tutorial system enabled them to take individual care of students as the ratio between the teachers and the taught was one to seven.[221] It also enabled them to develop a sense of morality and a sense of greater and sweeter values of life which people live by. It was borne in on them that a student who clutters his mind with a lot of information and does not live a moral and religious life and care for his spiritual well-being is just like a cowboy who counts the cows of his master but does not and cannot drink their milk.[222] This type of education is meaningless. The professors of Nalanda did not only teach philosophy but inspired the students to live it. The difference between philosophy and religion is that the former is belief but the latter is behaviour. When we live our life according to the philosophy we believe in, then only we live a religious life. Nalanda university symbolised the ideal and happy blending of philosophy and religion, *pariyatti* (teaching) and *paṭipatti* (practice) which makes it surpass all other universities set up in the past and all that are existent in the present.

It is said that at Nalanda University secular subjects were also taught. By secular I mean medicine, image casting and even snake charming as has been suggested by some. It is not impossible to include snake charming in the syllabus as the curriculum in the time of Pāṇini included this subject.[223] Besides these, philosophy, logic, literature and religion were taught here. But one thing is quite apparent that the teachers of Nalanda knew their priorities and geared all their efforts to achieve them. Their priority was the cultivation of a spiritual and moral life. But this was impossible without a healthy physical life. So consideration of physical fitness was there as has been said above because they thought it was almost impossible to undertake the arduous spiritual journey to *nibbāna* without being physically fit. Annihilation of cravings leads to freedom from suffering and it is really a Himalayan task to put an end to them. Only a physically fit person can fulfil

220. One should be *appābādho* (free from illness) to take up the hard work required for walking on the Noble Eightfold Path.

221. Nal Uni pp. 171-173.

222. Dh 19.

223. Nal Uni pp. 5-7.

such an enormous and uphill task. Science of medicine was perhaps taught with this end in view. In an area which was and still is infested with snakes, snake charming was as necessary to be taught.

Philosophy and logic which are definitely abstruse subjects were taught for making one's mind sharp, alert and agile. In this field the contribution of the professors of Nalanda is great.[224] But the chief stress was on inculcating moral values in the students here.

Another singular and distinct feature of Nalanda Mahāvihāra was that it was monastic in character throughout its existence. The only university in the continent which had this character at least in the beginning was Paris University which attracted the most celebrated professors in Europe all of whom were ecclesiasts, as were the students. 'Like the schools that preceded it in the twelfth century, the university continued to attract the most celebrated professors as were the students themselves.'[225] This character of the University did not last long and Oxford and Cambridge which were set up in the early twelfth century and were modelled on the pattern of Paris University were not like it in that not all professors and students even in the beginning were ecclesiasts.

But even in Paris University which had monastic character in the beginning, the alumni did not lay as much stress on inculcating a moral and spiritual life and taking upon themselves the uphill task of striving for and achieving the *summum bonum* of life as did the alumni of Nalanda University. This is clear from the subjects taught there. The Faculty of Arts included 'the arts of trivium (grammar, rhetoric and logic) and the arts of quadrivium (arithmetic, geometry, astronomy and music)'. In addition to the Faculty of Arts there were three other Faculties–the Faculty of Theology, the Faculty of Law and the Faculty of Medicine.[226] But no where do we find stress laid on living a life up to the theological ideals. On the other hand, all monk alumni and monk professors of Nalanda Mahāvihāra strenuously followed the Noble Eightfold Path as taught by Lord Buddha for their spiritual well-being.

It is true that at Nalanda Mahāvihāra also not only monks but also others were admitted in later centuries. There was a natural transition and as S. Dutt says "these seats of learning" developed, though never foregoing their original monastic character, into educational seminaries where admission was thrown open not only to monks but also to other

224. See my article 'Nalanda and Logic' collected in Nalanda, Past and Present published on the occasion of Silver jubilee celebrations of Nava Nalanda Mahāvihāra.

225. Encyclopaedia Britannica Reprinted 1995.

226. See Encyclopaedia Britannica under `Cambridge University'. Reprinted 1955.

seekers after knowledge, irrespective of sect, religious denomination and nationality. They partook of the character of the *studium generale* of medieval Europe, and from the fifth or sixth century onwards several of them were organized as universities and functioned as such.[227]

From what has been said above it can be safely presumed that the monk students at Nalanda Mahāvihāra far outnumbered the 'strangers'. And all monk alumni of this Mahāvihāra who had left home thinking that the worldly life is full of dust and defilements and ordination is liberation supreme did not only learn the teachings of Lord Buddha but also practised them. They sincerely tried to live up to the ideals shown by the Master. In none of the universities of the world the ideal of a student was so high and glorifying. Even in Sorbonne, Oxford and Cambridge where religion was a subject in the curriculum the students did not take upon themselves the task of living an ideal religious life. On the other hand, the monk students of Nalanda Mahāvihāra were sincerely wedded to the cause of their spiritual well-being and hardly cared for worldly gains. Even the 'strangers' also lived like *brahmacārins* and cultivated the higher values of life. It is in view of this professed aim of life that other subjects that had no direct bearing on spiritual well-being were excluded from the curriculum. The observations of Santosh Kumar Das are most relevant.

"It will be noticed that the curriculum in these monastries excluded all technical sciences. It was, therefore, a deterioration from Taxila where the curriculum was more varied. But there is nothing strange in this when we bear in mind that the monks in them had no care about food, lodging and clothing which were supplied to them *gratis*. In fact, the monks had hardly any secular care and their whole endeavour was given to intellectual and spiritual improvement. Moreover, there is no evidence that Law, Mathematics and Astronomy were cultivated in these monastries. Probably Law was already regarded too much as an exclusive possession of the Brahmins to make intrusion by others impossible, while Buddhism would not have more need of astronomy than Brahminism had for ascertaining auspicious times for sacrifices and other ceremonials."[228]

Hyuen-Tsang described the curriculum in these words: "The priests belonging to the convent or strangers (residing therein i.e. who came from outside and joined it) all study the great vehicle and also the works belonging to the eighteen (Hīnayāna) sects and not only so but even ordinary (i.e. secular) works such as the Vedas and other books, the Hetu Vidyā (logic), Śabdavidyā (Grammar), Philosophy and Cikitsā vidyā (medicine), the works on magic (Atharva-veda) and Sāṇkhya (system of philosophy). Besides

227. 2500 years, p. 170.

228. Edu Sys Hin pp. 169-170.

these they thoroughly investigate the miscellaneous works by which is probably meant works of literature and General Knowledge."[229]

Sorbonne, Oxford, Cambridge Wisconsin and Harvard are great universities in their own way. Oxford's contribution to literature, Cambridge's contribution to science, Sorbonne's contribution to French language and literature and Harvard's contribution to science, literature, philosophy and theology are well known but none can be compared with Nalanda whose contribution to humanity is singular and unique in so far as almost all the alumni that it trained were living examples of not only high learning but also of high morals and spiritual development that go a long way in enriching human life and ennobling it. However, in making such a comparison my intention is not to detract from the merits of other great universities of the world, but to underline the exclusive and absolute importance given by the university to turn out alumni who were not only highly educated but whose morals were high and whose conduct showed what ennobling and sweetening effect education imparted there had on them. The monk scholars from foreign countries who came to study at Nalanda Mahāvihāra were real cultural ambassadors of India. Their contribution in the field of Buddhist learning and philosophy, in preserving the texts of Buddhist philosophy and canonical literature through extensive translation and exposition as also in disseminating Lord Buddha's message of love and non-violence in the different countries of the world is staggeringly and incredibly great. One example will amply illustrate it. Hyuen-Tsang translated a number of texts into Chinese and wrote commentaries on difficult philosophical texts which are still an intellectual treat to the scholars. He was a great scholar and a very great debator. His power as a debator 'suggests the capacity of the university which could convert a traveller into such a learned debator, one who could talk on all the then known philosophies with so much accuracy'[230]. The greatness of this university lies in training many other scholars, Chinese, Tibetan and Indian whose contribution in the field of translation work is very great. Had they not burnt their mid-night oil and translated Buddhist texts into their mother tongues, we would forever have been deprived of the rare texts embodying the quintessence of high thoughts and noble values of life. The invaders set fire to the three libraries of Nalanda Mahāvihāra and nothing remained. But as these texts fortunately exist in Chinese and Tibetan translations, there is hope for their restoration into Sanskrit. There is also hope of knowing the high thoughts and noble values enshrined there through translation from those languages into Hindi and English.

229. L Hie p. 112

230. Nal Uni p. 226.

Thus, the lasting contribution in the academic world of the professors and alumni of Nalanda Mahāvihāra is very clear at this distant time.

Although Taxila was the oldest university of the world and indeed a very famous one, yet it could not command that respect from the people at large and it could not sink into the psyche of the people because it did not ever think of drilling into the minds of its students the ideals of life. They were perhaps not underlined here as much as they were at Nalanda. Education was related to life in Taxila also but at Nalanda it was chiefly related to that aspect of life which gives one permanent peace and enables one to pursue and follow a path which would ultimately lead to *nirvāṇa*. This was the speciality of Nalanda which no university of the world could ever emulate in the past nor any one is doing it in the present on a scale as Nalanda did.

It is true there were some old philosophical schools in Greece whose character resembled that of Nalanda University. The Academy of Plato and the Lyceum of Aristotle were such schools where emphasis was laid on inculcating both intellect and virtue. Socrates was a great philosopher who put premium not only on intellect and reasoning but also on virtue. He wanted people to develop zealously that quality in them which distinguishes humans from all other beings. This quality is wisdom which is the outcome of a sound reasoning and living a virtuous life. Logic and philosophy studied in isolation are barren. They become productive only when they are related to life. Unless they have a wholesome bearing on life their pursuit is futile. Socrates' ideal was a happy blending of knowledge and character, intellect and virtue which the Academy of Plato and the Lyceum of Aristotle imparted. Socrates, Plato and Aristotle were not only philosophers puzzling out solutions to hypothetical questions but they laid emphasis on cultivating wisdom. They applied their sharp intellect and thinking capacity which is the faculty that humans are gifted with and concluded that virtue and wisdom were the highest values of life and they should be cultivated. It is wisdom that enables one to make a distinction between good and bad and right and wrong. They laid so much emphasis on wisdom and virtue that they ethicised and moralised even beauty. Physical beauty was no longer a great consideration in life according to them, but they believed in handsome is that handsome does. Beauty thus became a matter of virtuous action and no longer remained a thing only of exterior look.

Buddha's definition of beauty is exactly the same. Beauty consists in virtuous action, in uprooting and eliminating the roots of *akusala cittas* and in cultivating *kusala cittas*. It is the presence of *lobho* (craving), *doso* (aversion) and *moho* (ignorance) that makes one ugly. Their removal gives rise to real beauty in one.

The professors and alumni of Nalanda (the majority of them were monks) knew more than the teachers and students of these Greek schools that craving, aversion and ignorance could be removed only by walking on the noble but difficult Eightfold Path or by practising Vipassana. So they lived together (it was a first ever residential university in the real sense of the term) and the alumni emulated the ideal life of the professors there who were inspired by the teachings of the Buddha to live a pure, virtuous and simple life.

Dialogues of Plato and the *suttas* taught by the Buddha have the same tone and tenor. They use sophisticated arguments to bring to the fore the higher values of life which one should cultivate and imbibe. But the professors and students of Nalanda University tried more than their counterparts of the above-mentioned Greek schools to cultivate and imbibe the higher values of life besides contributing enormously to the field of philosophy and logic. Intellectual pursuit was not at a discount here but what was most important is the spiritual attainment. This gave Nalanda Mahāvihāra a rare character of its own. In the words of I-Tsing Nalanda could claim to be 'the most magnificent Temple of learning in Jambudvīpa' or to use a modern phrase 'the premier and pioneer National University in India'.[231] This is why it is still regarded as the 'university of all universities'.[232]

231. Nal Uni. p. 274.
232. ibid. p. 170.

Four Noble Truths

Four Noble Truths form the most important teaching of the Buddha. In fact, this is the cornerstone of his philosophy. Both the schools of Buddhism viz. Hīnayāna and Mahāyāna, in spite of their differences in some respects, regard the Four Noble Truths as his basic teaching. The Buddha understood these truths at the experiential level. He did not propound them by exercising his intellect or by making use of his logical acumen either as other philosophers do their philosophy. But he propounded them because he experienced them. Of the three kinds of *paññā* (knowledge) *sutamayā* (knowledge based on hearing from others), *cintāmayā* (knowledge based on one's own reading books and reflection) and *bhāvanāmayā* (knowledge born out of one's own experience) these truths are born out of his *bhāvanāmayā paññā*. Therefore, they are truths that cannot be controverted. Theories propounded by virtue of intellect and logic are not always infallible, but the theories propounded at the experiential level are always infallible. The Buddha who became an *ārya* (noble) after attaining *nibbāna* by extirpating all desires saw these truths. Therefore, they are called *ārya satyas* or noble truths i.e. the truths seen by an *ārya*.

'Ariya saccāni' has been defined as the truths penetrated and taught by the Tathāgata who became an *ārya*.

> *Tathāgato ariyo tasmā 'ariya saccānī'ti yasmā ariyena tathāgatena paṭividdhattā desitattā ca tāni ariyasantakāni honti, tasmā ariyassa saccattā, ariya saccānīti attho*[233].

It is said that they are called *'ariya saccāni'* because their realization makes one a noble (*ārya*) or they have been penetrated by the noble.

> *'Ariya saccānīti ariyabhāvakarāni, ariyapaṭividdhāni vā saccāni*[234].

These truths are, therefore, incontrovertible facts of life.

In the *Tatha Sutta* of the *Saṃyutta Nikāya*[235] it is said that these truths are real truths, facts of life, not imaginary, nor supertitious tenets of any philosophical school.

These ubiquitous truths are four in number. They are suffering (*dukkha*), its cause (*dukkha samudaya*), its cessation (*dukkha nirodha*) and the path leading to its cessation (*dukkhanirodhagamini paṭipadā*)

---

233. SA 3.329,

234. AA 2.158.

235. *Imāni, kho bhikkhave, cattāri ariyasaccāni, tathāni, avitathāni, anaññathāni, tasmā 'ariya saccānīti vuccanti.* S 3.408

The Buddha propounded them when he set the wheel of the Dhamma in motion at Isipattana Migadāya.

He explained to the five bhikkhus each of them from the view point of *sacca ñāṇa* (the knowledge of truth), *kicca ñāṇa* (the knowledge gained by trying to understand the truth thoroughly) and *kata ñāṇa* (the complete knowledge).[236] All that is suffering has to be completely comprehended (*pariññeyyaṃ*) and when one comprehends it, it is said it has been comprehended (*pariññātaṃ*). The second truth is that suffering has a cause. This cause has to be abandoned (*pahātabbaṃ*) and when one abandons it, it is abandoned (*pahīṇaṃ*). The third truth—the cessation of suffering is to be realized (*sacchikātabbaṃ*) and when one has realized it, it is said that it has been realized (*sacchikataṃ*). The fourth noble truth must be developed, must be made to become (*bhāvetabbaṃ*) and when it is developed and made to become i.e. when one has walked on it, it is called developed (*bhāvitaṃ*). Thus each truth has three aspects (*tiparivaṭṭaṃ*) and only when all four truths are understood in twelve ways (*dvādasākāraṃ*) the vision of knowledge (*ñāṇadassana*) is purified[237]. Only after Samaṇa Gotama had purified his vision of knowledge like this, he became the Buddha, 'thoroughly awakened with the supreme full awakening'.[238] When he thoroughly comprehended each truth, 'vision arose, knowledge arose, wisdom arose, higher knowledge arose, light arose about something not heard before.[239]' This was his vision of knowledge–*ñāṇa dassana,* not only knowledge but its vision at the experiential level. He came to know at the experiential level that 'Freedom of mind is for me unshakeable, this is the last birth, there is not now again-becoming.'[240] While the Buddha was giving this discourse 'Dhamma vision, dustless, stainless, arose to the Venerable Koṇḍañña that "whatever is of the nature to uprise, all that is of the nature to stop".'[241] In other words, Venerable Koṇḍañña was convinced that suffering could be ended. Suffering has a cause. If its cause is removed suffering ends. This was the first ever success achieved by the Buddha when he set the Dhamma-wheel in motion. In the *Dhammacakkappavattana Sutta* the Buddha explains each of the four Noble Truths thoroughly.

The first aspect of the first Noble Truth is that there is *dukkha. Dukkha* is not only physical suffering but it is also mental. And these two kinds

236. (for definitions of different *ñāṇas* see SA,3.327)

237. CDB (See the English translation of *Dhammacakkappavattana Sutta*)

238. BD, p. 15.

239. ibid.

240. ibid.

241. *Yaṃ kiñci samudayadhammaṃ sabbaṃ taṃ nirodhadhammaṃ.* (*Dhammacakkappavattana Sutta*)

of suffering are there because one is born again and again with five aggregates (*khandhas*) such as *rūpa, vedanā, saññā saṅkhāra* and *viññāna*. It is not only suffering, pain, misery and sorrow but in the words of Walpole Rāhula it 'has a deeper philosophical meaning and connotes enormously wider senses'.[242] In addition to suffering it includes deeper ideas such as imperfection, impermanence, emptiness and insubstantiality etc.[243]

In order to understand *dukkha* thoroughly one should understand it from three view points. The first view point is that it is ordinary suffering (*dukkha dukkha*) realized by common people. The second view point is to understand it as change (*vipariṇāma dukkha*) and the third view point is to understand it as conditioned states (*saṅkhāra dukkha*).

Birth, old age, disease and death are physical suffering. Association with persons one does not like, separation from near and dear ones and not getting what one desires etc. are mental suffering. They are *dukkha-dukkha*, universally accepted suffering.

Many a time in life one has pleasant sensations and he feels happy. But these pleasant sensations do not last forever. They change. The happy condition of life also changes and produces pain. All these can be grouped under *vipariṇama dukkha*.

But the third type of *dukkha* is a little difficult to understand. And this is where the philosophy of the Buddha comes in. One suffers from the above mentioned *dukkhas* because one is born. One is born with five *khandhas* (aggregates) viz, *rūpa, vedanā, saññā, saṅkhāra* and *viññāṇa*. These aggregates constitute what is called a 'being'. An individual consists of these aggregates. Out of the five aggregates one is matter (*rūpa*) and the rest four are mind (*nāma*). So long as one has strong attachment to these aggregares he will be born again and again and is likely to suffer incalculably.

The Buddha says that the five aggregates and *dukkha* are not two different things. 'O, bhikkhus, what is *dukkha?* It should be said that it is the five aggregates of attachment.'[244] It will be good if one goes a little deeper to understand why these five *khandhas* (aggregates) are *dukkha*.

To understand that there is inescapable *dukkha* in life is *sacca ñāṇa*. To have understood the different kinds of *dukkha* is *kicca ñāṇa*. This is called the *pariññeya* (to be understood accurately) aspect of the first Noble Truth. When one has thoroughly understood all kinds of *dukkha* at the experiential level one has comprehended (*pariññātaṃ*) it. This is the third aspect of the first Noble Truth and is known as *kata ñāṇa*. *Sacca ñāṇa* and

242. WBT p. 17

243. ibid.

244. *Katamañca, bhikkhave, dukkhaṃ ariyasaccaṃ? 'Pañcupādānakkhandhā dukkhā' tissa vacanīyaṃ*. S. Khandha Sutta p. 489

kicca ñāṇā can be attained by *sutamayā* and *cintāmayā paññā* but *kata ñāṇa* is exclusively attained by *bhāvanāmayā paññā.* (*sutamayā paññā* is 'wisdom gained from listening to others', *cintāmaya paññā* is wisdom gained by intellectual analysis, and *bhāvanāmayā paññā* is wisdom gained from direct personal experience)

Why are the five aggregares called *dukkha*? Because they are in a constant state of flux. *Rūpa* changes, *vedanā* changes, *saññā* changes, *saṅkhāra* changes and *viññaṇa* changes. They are not the same for two consecutive moments. So the Buddha says, "whatever is impermanent is *dukkha* (*yad aniccaṃ taṃ dukkhaṃ*)."[245] This is what he means when he says that 'in short, five aggregates of attachment are *dukkha.*'[246]

Because one is born with five aggregates which are impermanent, so one is bound to suffer.

In the same way the second Noble Truth should be understood. That *taṇhā* (craving) is the cause of *dukkha* is *sacca ñāṇa.* Broadly speaking there are three types of *taṇhā, kāma taṇhā* (sensual craving), *bhava taṇhā* (craving for existence) and *vibhava taṇhā* (craving for non-existence). If one thoroughly understands why they arise and where then he will thoroughly understand the second aspect of the second Noble Truth. This is *pahātabbaṃ* i.e. the cause of craving should be eliminated. And when one has eliminated the cause of craving that aspect of the second Noble Truth is called *pahīnaṃ* (eliminated).[247]

The first aspect of the third Noble Truth is that *dukkha* can cease to be. The Buddha saw it clearly. He explained through the law of *paṭiccasamuppāda* that a cause gives rise to an effect and he also explained it as clearly that if the cause is removed no effect can come into being. *Dukkha nirodha* is *sacca ñāṇa.* The cause of *dukkha* has got to be eliminated is *sacchikātabbaṃ.* This is the second aspect of this truth. And when one has realized that the cause is removed is the third aspect of this truth. This is *sacchikataṃ.*[248]

The fourth Noble Truth also, like others, has three aspects. That there is a path leading to the cessation of *dukkha* is what is called the *sacca ñāṇa* of the fourth Noble Truth. In order to end suffering one has to walk on this path. This aspect of the truth is called *bhāvetabbaṃ.* It means one has to walk on this path again and again, time and time again (*bhāvetabbaṃ*) because without walking on the path one cannot end *dukkha*. The Buddha

---

245. (*Yadanicca Suttaṃ*, S 2.21)
246. *saṅkhittena pañcupādānakkhandhā dukkhā* See *Dhammacakkappavattana Sutta*
247. See *Dhammacakkappavattana Sutta*
248. ibid.

said '*Tumhehi kiccamātappam akkhātāro thatāgatā.*'[249] One who has walked on the path of *sīla, samādhi* and *paññā* and extirpated *dukkha* is said to have developed the path (*bhāvitaṃ*).[250]

The way the four Noble Truths have been arranged is very scientific and reminds us of the method adopted by Āyurveda. This branch of science talks of disease, its cause, its cure and its medicine. Unless a physician puts his finger on the cause of the disease, how can he cure it?

The Buddha had a very comprehensive understanding of suffering. He does not only talk of physical and mental suffering which are obvious to many but he also talks of the root cause of these two types of suffering. These two types of suffering occur to one who is born. So one who is subject to birth is subject to suffering. Birth and suffering go hand in hand. One who is born is not free from suffering. And one is born with five *khandhas* (aggregates). So long as one has these constituents one is bound to suffer. In other words, so long as one moves in the cycle of birth and death one suffers.[251]

The second Noble Truth is *dukkhasamudaya i.e. dukkha* has a cause.

Why is one born again and again and why does he suffer? The Buddha saw its cause at the experiential level. One is born because of his desire. A desireless person ceases to be born but one with desire is bound to be born. Desire in Pāli is called *taṇhā. Taṇhā* has been variously defined. It is *duppūrā* (difficult to satisfy), *uparivisāla* (extended on top), and *visaṭagamini* (covering a great area)[252].

Taṇhā is craving for the various objects of the world. All one's six sense organs have their respective objects in the outside world, which he crave for. He sees beautiful objects of the world with his eyes, hears melodious sound with his ears, smells good perfumes with his nose, tastes dainty dishes with his tongue, touches soft things with his body and thinks of good thoughts with his mind. He likes them because he has pleasant sensations and he wants to have more and more of them without knowing that they do not last forever. Because he is ignorant of the real nature of things he has inordinate attachment to and passionate clinging for them. When different objects of the world come in contact with their respective sense organs and they do not produce pleasant sensations he develops aversion for them and desires to get rid of them. In both the cases he either craves for or develops aversion to things. This, in short, is *taṇhā* (desire).

249. Dh 276

250. *Dhammacakkappavattana Sutta*

251. Psycho.AEB

252. (*Uparivisālā duppūrā, icchā visaṭagāmini*, see *Mittavinda Jātaka* no 369)

Where *taṇhā* arises has been very clearly explained in the *Mahāsatipaṭṭhāna Sutta*. Wherever in the world of mind and matter there is something enticing and pleasurable, there this craving arises and gets established.[253]

But what in the world of mind and matter is enticing and pleasurable? All sense organs, their respective objects, their consciousess, their contact with their respective objects, the sensations arising from the contact, their perception, the mental reactions, the cravings, thought conceptions of different objects, rolling in thoughts of them are enticing and pleasurable. It is there that *taṇhā* arises and gets established. (See *Mahāsatipaṭṭhāna Sutta*)

This realization at the experiential level must have been a sort of 'eureka' for the Buddha. He saw where *taṇhā* arises. It must not have taken him long to conclude how *taṇhā* could be eliminated. It is *vedanā* which causes *taṇhā*. When one likes it or when he doesn't like it in both the cases *vedanā* produces *taṇhā*. If at this point one does not react to sensations but remains equanimous, one will be able not to allow *taṇhā* to arise and multiply. One creates desires by reacting. If, on the other hand, one does not react then desires are not produced. How this process works can be understood with the help of a simile. When a black-smith hones a knife against a moving whetstone so many sparks arise. If somebody keeps oil and wick in a lamp ready there to catch a spark each spark can become a conflagration. But in their absence sparks die out. If one does not react, desires do not multiply but they are exhausted. This is what is expressed in the statement made by the Buddha.

> *Khīṇaṃ purāṇaṇ navaṃ natthi sambhavaṃ, virattacittā āyatike bhavasmiṃ.*[254]

Taṇhā accompanied by pleasure and lust finding its delight here and there leads to re-birth.[255]

Craving is threefold, craving for sensual pleasure (*kāma taṇhā*), craving for existence (*bhava taṇhā*) and craving for non-existence or for life to end (*vibhava taṇhā*) as said above. In short, it is craving of one kind or another which causes suffering. *Taṇhā* is a fetter that binds one to the wheel of birth and death. The Buddha aptly compares it to a seamstress who brings two ends together i.e. who joins two existences.[256] *Taṇhā* supplies oil which keeps the lamp of life burning.

---

253. *Yaṃ loke piyarūpaṃ sātarupaṃ etthesā taṇhā uppajjamānā uppajjati, ettha nivisamānā nivisati* (*Mahāsatipaṭṭhāna Sutta*)

254. (See *Ratana Sutta* in the Sn)

255. *Yāyāṃ taṇhā ponobbhavikā nandirāgasahagatā tatratatrābhinandini.*

256. *Phasso Kho, āvuso, eko anto, phassasamudayo dutiyo anto, phassa nirodho majjhe,*

By realizing the Law of Dependent Origination the Buddha knew the cause of suffering. By realizing the same law he also knew that if *taṇhā* is removed suffering will end.[257]

This realization made him pronounce confidently that suffering can be ended. The third Noble Truth (*dukkha nirodha*) is related to this.

One must go a little deeper to understand whether *taṇhā* is the first cause of *dukkha* and how it is responsible for one's being born again and again and suffer. If one just looks at the Law of Dependent Origination it becomes clear that *taṇhā* is not the first cause of *dukkha. Taṇhā* is caused by *vedanā* (sensation) and *vedanā* is caused by *phassa* (contact). In this way the cycle goes on. But it is clear, however, that although *taṇhā* is not the first cause, it is the most palpable and immediate cause. Why palpable and immediate? Because as it is said in the *Abhidharma samuccaya*[258] it is the principal cause (*pradhānyārtha*) and it is ubiquitous (*sarvatragārtha*). In the Pāli Vibhaṅga[259] therefore *taṇhā* comes first in the list of other defilements such as *kilesā, sāsava dhammā* that cause *dukkha.*

Taṇhā is a very comprehensive term. It is 'not only desire for. and attachment to sense pleasures, wealth and power' as lucidly explained by Walpola Rahula, ' but also desire for and attachment to, ideas and ideals, views, opinions, theories, conceptions and beliefs."[260] In the *Sammādiṭṭhi Sutta* of the *Majjhima Nikāya*[261] this is called *dhamma taṇhā.* All quarrels and battles between individuals or the nations have their roots in this selfish kind of desire. It will not take one long to see that selfish attitude causes tremendous suffering, be it a quarrel between two brothers, two families or two nations.

So far, I think, it is easy to understand. But what is not easily grasped is how this *taṇhā* causes one's rebirth.

In order to understand this one has to understand the deeper philosophical aspect of the second Noble Truth and to clearly understand this one has to understand the theory of *kamma* and rebirth which may be called the most important teaching propounded by the Buddha.

One should first try to understand how do beings sustain their lives. For their existence they require nourishments. According to

---

taṇhā sibbini, taṇhā hi naṇ sibbati tassa tasseva bhavassa abhinibbattiyā. A. Chakka Nipāta,2.105.

257. (*imasmiṃ sati idaṃ hoti, imasmiṃ asati idaṃ na hoti*) (See *Mahānidāna Sutta* in the Dīgha Nikāya).

258. Quoted from W B T f.n.4 p. 29

259. Vbh

260. op. cit. p. 30

261. M. 1.65

Abhidhamma Philosophy there are four kinds of nourishments, material food (*kabaliṅkāra*), contact of our six sense organs with their respective objects (*phassa*), consciousness (*viññāṇa*) and volition or mental volition (*manosañcetanā*).

What is mental volition? It is the will to exist, to exist again and to continue to exist again and again. This will manifests itself in one's actions, wholesome or unwholesome. The Buddha has said that volition is *kamma.*[262] All actions that one does are not 'volitional actions'. The volitional actions that produce results are the actions that matter as far as the theory of *kamma* is concerned. Involuntary actions do not matter. This has been well explained in the first two *gāthās* of the Dhammapada.[263] This nutriment of mental volition is closely related to the three kinds of *taṇhā* mentioned above. Whatever actions produce their results are products of mental volition. These actions are responsible for one's well-being or otherwise. If the volition is good, the action that one does is wholesome and this ensures his well-being. If the volition is unwholesome the action is unwholesome. So how can it ensure one's well-being?

Wholesome or unwholesome actions have the force to respectively drive one in a good direction or in a bad one and so make him move in the cycle of birth and death. In short, one moves in *saṃsāra* because of his *kamma.* As one does one's actions with attachment, with desire, so he produces their results, good or bad, as seeds germinate. In the case of an arahant, his actions do not produce any result, because he does his actions without attachment and clinging. His actions are like fried seeds which are incapable of germinating and producing fruits.

The theory of *kamma,* therefore, is the theory of cause and effect, of action and reaction. It is a natural universal law. If one does good, one reaps good, if one doesn't do so, he doesn't. This law has got nothing to do with the law of retribution i.e. with the law of reward and punishment. It is unfortunately this interpretation of the law that people think and they are made to think by those who have vested interests that their condition

---

262. A2 118 *cetanāhaṃ, bhikkhave, kammaṃ vadāmi.*

263. Dh 1&2 *Mano pubbaṅgamā dhammā, manoseṭṭhā manomayā/*
Manasā ce paduṭṭhena bhāsati vā karoti vā/
Tato naṃ dukkhamanveti, cakkaṃ va vahato padam//

Manasā ce pasannena bhāsati vā karoti vā/
Tato naṃ sukhamanveti chāyāva anapāyini//

Mind is the forerunner of all evil or good states. Mind is chief. They spring from mind. If one speaks or acts with impure or pure mind suffering follows one even as the wheel follows the hoof of the draught or happiness follows one even as one's shadow that never leaves respectively.

pitiable or otherwise is due to their past *kammas*. They tend to become fatalists and do not try to ameliorate their conditions. The theory of *kamma* according to the Buddha is the law of cause and effect. As is the cause so is the effect. Just as seeds produce sweet fruits or bitter fruits according to their nature, so also the nature of one's volitional actions is responsible for his moving in a good or bad direction. The Buddha says that one is free to work. One's hands are not tied by his past actions. The results of one's past unwholesome actions can be eliminated by his present wholesome actions. So, there is no fatalism here, but there is great freedom to choose to do wholesome actions.

So far it is clear that wholesome and unwholesome actions produce respectively good or bad results in this life. One may be happy or unhappy depending upon his past *kammas* but they have nothing to do with one's birth in a brahman or a śūdra caste. The caste system is not universal. The theory of *kamma* applies to all people of the world and not only to the people of India where unfortunately there is caste system.

This aspect of the theory of *kamma* is easy to understand but what is difficult to understand is how these *kammas*, of course, the volitional ones, continue to manifest themselves in a life after death. The theory of *kamma* explains this.

One knows that a human being consists of five aggregates (*khandhas*), only one of which is physical. The rest four are mental. They are actually energies and they can be extirpated when their source dries up. The Buddha says that death is that state when physical body totally stops to work. But do all these energies die out? What Buddhism says about them has been nicely described by Walpola Rahula. "Will, volition, desire, thirst to exist, to continue, to become more and more, is a tremendous force that moves whole lives, whole existences, that even moves the whole world.'[264] This comes very close to 'libido' as the psychologists say and 'will' as Schopenhaeur has shown in his famous book entitled 'The World as Will and Idea.' Will Durant in his book 'The Story of Philosophy' says, "Will indicates want and its grasp is very strong. Desire is infinite and fulfilment only limited."[265]

This force which does not cease with the death of the body keeps on continuing itself in different forms causing rebirth. But who is born is still a difficult question to grasp. Nagasena says in his authoritative book *Milindapañho* that it is neither the same nor another.[266] How it is so can be understood only when one understands the process philosophy of

264. (op. cit. p. 33)
265. (op. cit. p. 33)
266. *Na ca so, na ca añño*

the Buddha.[267] One gets curd or yoghurt from milk and gets butter from yoghurt, but neither yoghurt can be called milk nor butter can be called so. But one cannot get any of them without milk. In the same way the force that survives the death of the body keeps on changing under the influence of other *kammas* and manifests itself in another form. The force continues to be because of one's desire or *taṇhā*. When *taṇhā* is rooted out the force also like the body dies out. And one's movement in the cycle of birth and death stops forever. This is called *nirvāṇa*.

The third Noble Truth is *dukkha nirodha* i.e. *dukkha* can cease. If one does not hanker after any thing and if he has no desire left in him, he does not suffer and *dukkha* ends.

Dukkhanirodha is nothing but *nibbāna* or *nirvāṇa* as it is called in Sanskrit. This is the *summum bonum* of human life according to the Buddha. When the root of *dukkha* is eliminated suffering in life and continuity of life i.e. being born again and again in the cycle of birth and death stop forever. This state is called the state of desirelessness (*taṇhākkhaya*) which is characterized by complete extinction of desire.

What this state of *nirvāṇa* is cannot be answered adequately and perfectly in human language which is not capable of describing experiences beyond one's sense organs. It is here that the limitation of language becomes obvious. However, there are terms, though negative, which attempt to describe it. *Taṇhākkhaya* (extinction of desire), *asaṅkhata* (unconditioned), *nirodha* (cessation), *virāga* (non -attachment) and *nibbāna* (extinction) are such terms. From these terms at least one gets an idea that *nibbāna* is the absence of desire, extinction of desire and non -attachment to the various objects and viewpoints and dhammas of the world. In the *Saṃyutta Nikāya*[268] it has been defined by the Buddha himself as 'the complete cessation of that very *taṇhā*, giving it up, renouncing it, emancipation from it, detachment from it.' In the same *Nikāya* it has been defined as 'calming of all conditioned things, giving up of all defilements, extinction of all 'thirst', detachment, cessation, *nibbāna*.[269] In the same *Nikāya* Sariputta defines it as *rāgakkhayo* (extirpation of desire), *dosakkhayo* (extinction of aversion) and *mohakkhayo* (extinction of ignorance).[270] In the *Mahāhatthipadopama Sutta*[271] Sāriputta pithily defines *nibbāna* as the destruction of desire and craving for the five

267. D1 *Poṭṭhapāda Sutta*

268. S3.484 *Yo tassāyeva taṇhāya asesavirāganirodho cāgo, paṭinissaggo, mutti, anālayo.*

269. ibid S1.162. *Sabbasaṅkhārasamatho sabbūpadhipaṭinissaggo taṇhākhayo virāgo, nirodho, nibbānaṃ.*

270. S 2.24

271. M 1 252 (*Yo imesu pañcasu upādānakkhandhesu chandarāgavinayo, chandarāgappahānaṃ so dukkhanirodho'ti*).

aggregates of attachment. Musila, one of the disciples of the Buddha, says that *bhavanirodha* (cessation of continuity and becoming) is *nibbāna.*[272] In short, it is a state where one ceases to burn from the three fires of craving, aversion and ignorance.

The Buddha identifies *nibbāna* with truth.[273]

An important point should be considered here. When one says that *taṇhakkhaya* is *dukkha nirodha* does it mean that the extinction of *taṇhā* is the cause of *nibbāna*? No. *Nibbāna* is not produced or caused. It is not *saṅkhata* (produced). It is *asaṅkhata* (unproduced). Walpola Rahula gives an apt simile to bring this point home to one. 'There is a path leading to the realization of *nirvāṇa.* But *nirvāṇa* is not the result of this path. You may get to the mountain along a path, but the mountain is not the result, not an effect of the path. You may see a light, but the light is not the result of your eyesight.'[274]

The fourth Noble Truth is *dukkhanirodhagāminī paṭipadā.* It is a path walking on which one extirpates one's desire and ends one's suffering. The path leading to the cessation of suffering is popularly known as *Majjhimā paṭipadā* (*sk. Madhyama mārga*). Why? Because it avoids the two extreme paths of *kāmesukāmasukhallikānuyoga* (happiness through the pleasures of the senses) and *attakilamathānuyoga* (happiness through self mortification) The Buddha had the experience of both. He did not find them of any help. One was 'low, common, unprofitable and the way of the ordinary people' and the other was 'painful, unworthy and unprofitable.'[275]

The word 'path' has been used here as a metaphor. It does not mean the path, say, from Sāvatthi to Rajgir by walking on which one makes outside journey. But it is a path which enables one to make inward journey from a state full of *raga, dosa* and *moha* to a state where in addition to their absence there are non-attachment, compassion and wisdom. One begins from a point at the path where he is full of defilements, from a point where he does not observe *sīla*, practice *samādhi* and does not have *paññā*, to reach that point of the path where he is free from all defilements and where he has attained wisdom by observing *sīla* and practicing *samādhi.* By walking on this path he is qualitatively transformed. He walks on the path and in the course of this inner journey he goes from darkness to light, from ignorance to wisdom. Unlike the geographical mile he does not just come a long way but he comes a long way completely transformed. The path, say, a national highway on which he makes outside journey is made by others. He

272. S1 102 *Bhavanirodho nibbānan'ti* (*Kosambi Sutta*).

273. M 3.294 *Taṃ saccaṃ yaṃ amosadhammaṃ nibbānaṃ*

274. (op. cit. p. 40,)

275. op. cit. See English Translation of the *Dhammacakkappavattana Sutta.*

simply walks on this to reach his destination. But this Noble Eightfold Path is made by one as he goes along. He has been simply told that there are three milestones on this path such as *sīla, samādhi* and *pannā*. As he begins to walk on this path he begins to transform himself. His mind is defiled when he begins the journey. As he goes along the path his mind is purified. He begins to abandon the root cause of his suffering and when he comes to the end of journey suffering comes to an end.

Who can walk on this uphill path? One who observes five moral precepts and thus enables his mind to concentrate and see things as they are with his developed wisdom can walk on this path. This path has eight constituents. Three of them such as right speech, right action and right livelihood come under *sīla,* three others such as right mindfulness, right effort and right concentration come under *samādhi* and the rest two such as right view and right resolve come under *paññā. Sīla, samādhi* and *pañña* go hand in hand. One supports the other two and they in turn strengthen the one. Walking on this path means developing *sīla, samādhi* and *paññā* simultaneously. When they are developed, made much of, *dukkha* comes to an end. The four Noble Truths are to be comprehended (*pariññeyaṃ*), to be abandoned (*pahātabbaṃ*), to be realized (*sacchikātabbaṃ*) and to be developed (*bhāvetabbaṃ*) respectively.

Complete realization of any one of the Four Noble Truths enables one to realize the other three. The third aspect of the first Noble Truth is *pariññātaṃ* (comprehended). It is not possible to have full comprehension of it unless one knows its cause, unless one walks on the Noble Eightfold Path to remove the cause and unless one has realized that with the eradication of the root cause of *dukkha* it has ended.

There are many who call the Buddha a pessimist. Why? Because they say that he talks only of *dukkha.* But a little careful thinking will clear him of this charge. A physician talks of disease, but doesn't he talk of the cure of disease at the same time? It is true the Buddha talks of *dukkha* but he also talks of its cessation. He also clearly points out how it can be eliminated. He propounds the fourth Noble Truth of the cessation of suffering showing the path to end it (*Dukkhanirodhagāmini paṭipadā*). How can he be called a pessimist?

The beauty of the Buddha is that he does not only propound his realistic philosophy but he also gives an action-plan to live this philosophy in life. The second Noble Truth (*dukkha samudaya*) is his philosophy and the fourth Noble Truth (*dukkhanirodhagaminī paṭipadā*) is his action -plan. This is also called the Noble Eightfold Path. Walking on this path enables one to root out the ever growing creeper of desire (*taṇhā*)- the cause of suffering for good and experience peace and happiness. In short, the Noble Eightfold Path is the path of progressive self culture in the sense that by observing *sīla* (precepts) one gets rid of defilements like craving, aversion anger, hatred etc., trains oneself to concentrate one's fleeting mind to see reality as it is, attains wisdom, develops non-attachment and realizes *nibbāna*—the highest good of human life.

Four Noble Truths respectively denote disease, its cause, its cure and the medicine to cure it.

Brahmavihāra

Mettā (loving kindness), *karuṇā* (compassion), *muditā* (sympathetic joy) and *upekkhā* (equanimity) are called the four *brahmavihāras*. They are one's sublime states of mind. They are virtues which when cultivated make one good, great, noble and serviceable. One is endowed with immense and inconceivable potentialities. One can become a criminal. One can also become a saint. What is required is the exertion of one's will power to cultivate good qualities and make oneself noble, kind, sympathetic and equanimous.

One should develop loving kindness towards all beings and compassion for all those who are in trouble. One's heart should melt when one sees beings in trouble and one should have the will to remove it. One should never feel jealous of others. Even if one makes more progress and achieves greater prosperity, one should not have an iota of jealousy in oneself. On the other hand, one should feel appreciative joy in oneself. Whenever anything happens to oneself that tries to destroy the mental equipoise, one should remain undisturbed, unperturbed and indifferent. One should not mind what happens to oneself. One must cultivate these exalting qualities in order to bring about a qualitative change in oneself for the better. Persons endowed with these virtues never think only of themselves but they think of other human beings, nay, all living beings and work for their good.

What can be greater and more sublime than these virtues? Cultivating these virtues and practicing them sublimates one. It ennobles them. One knows that anger is a great vice. It is so destructive that it destroys one's peace. When one is angry, one burns and causes others to burn. Anger makes one so blind that one cannot distinguish between right and wrong and he commits such crimes, which he would not have committed had he not flown into a rage. Anger is a great evil.

It is said in the *Itivuttaka*;

Anatthajanano kodho, kodho cittappakopano/
Bhayamantarato jātaṃ, taṃ jano nāvabujjhatīti// (*Iti, 239*)

Anger causes harm, misery and misfortune; it upsets the mind and causes fear in one. One does not realize that anger is a great evil. This evil force can be subdued by practicing loving- kindness. Loving-kindness is an antidote to anger. It sweetens our life and does not poison it as anger does. In the *Suttanipāta* (*Uraga Sutta*) anger has been compared with the poison of snake, which spreads all over one's body (*Yo uppatitaṃ vineti kodhaṃ, visaṭaṃ sappavisaṃ va osadhehi*). Therefore, it must be kept at arm's length. It must be subdued and put away. This is possible only by practicing loving- kindness.

Cruelty is another vice. When one's heart is not soft, when it does not melt to see others in grief and pain, one becomes hard- hearted. It is this hard heartedness, this cruelty that impels one to commit so many crimes and atrocities. Thus, cruelty is also a great evil. It is because of cruelty that one fights war, kills innocent men and women, deprives them of the necessities of life, takes away their freedom and liberty, subjugates them, drops atom bombs on them, causes the holocaust and perpetrates many other such crimes. The antidote to cruelty is compassion (*karuṇā*).

Jealousy is also a great vice. It leads to unhealthy rivalries and competitions. Why has she stood first in the class? Why not I? Why has he succeeded in his business? Why is it that I cannot compete with her? I must compete with her and leave her far behind. This sort of thinking is because of jealousy. A jealous person always burns. One cannot tolerate the progress and achievements made by others. The most effective remedy for this poison is to cultivate a state of joy and happiness at the success of others. One should be happy at the success of others; should be glad when others, even if they are his rivals, prosper and make achievements.

When one feels pleasant sensations, one is attached to them and when one feels unpleasant sensations one feels aversion for them. In both the cases one is normally upset. One loses the balance of one's mind. In the first case, one feels exalted and in the other case one feels depressed. In the first case, one feels attraction and in the other case one feels revulsion. It is by practicing equanimity (*upekkhā*) that these opposite states of mind can be eliminated and one can maintain a balance on both occasions of attraction and revulsion.

Mettā, karuṇā, muditā and *upekkhā* are sterling qualities. In the words of Narada Thera, "These virtues tend to elevate one. They make one divine in this life itself. They can transform one into a superhuman. If all try to cultivate them, irrespective of creed, colour, race, or sex, the earth can be transformed into a paradise where all can live in perfect peace and harmony as ideal citizens of one world."[276]

Mettā (*Sansk. maitrī*) is a sublime state of mind. When one is in this state, one is filled with altruistic feelings. One sincerely wishes the welfare and happiness of others and is ever ready to do good to them. In this state, one never thinks of harming others and causing injury to others. How does one feel when one is endowed with this divine and sublime state? One feels like the mother, 'who protects her only child even at the risk of her life.'[277] Similarly without caring for one's own life, nay, at the risk even of one's

---

276. B&H p. 614,

277. (*Mātā yathā niyaṃ puttaṃ, āyusā ekaputtamanurakkhe/Evampi sabbabhūtesu, mānasaṃ bhāvaye aparimāṇaṃ// Karaṇīyametta Sutta*)

own life one tries to save the life of others. In fact, one cultivates boundless loving kindness towards all living beings. One always sincerely thinks of the welfare of others. One's love for others is not tinged with passion. It is pure, unselfish love without expecting anything in return. *Mettā* is qualitatively different from ordinary affection.

Mettā transcends all boundaries of caste, race, nation, religion, political affinity, professional brotherhood and any other consideration, which divides people into different groups. *Mettā* is shown to all without any discrimination, without any distinction of friend and foe and without any distinction of love and hate. In the words of Narada Thera, "Just as the sun sheds its ray on all without any discrimination, even so sublime *mettā* bestows its sweet blessings equally on the pleasant and the unpleasant, on the rich and the poor, on the high and the low, on the vicious and the virtuous, on man and woman, and on human and animal."[278]

Mettā is opposed to anger, ill will and aversion.[279] *Mettā* cannot co-exist with them. In *mettā* is such quality that it conquers anger. Hatred can be ended by loving kindness, not by hatred.[280]

In the *Mettānisaṃsa Sutta* (*Aṅguttara Nikāya*) blessings of *mettā* are enumerated. One practicing it has a good and sound sleep without any trouble. One also wakes up in the morning feeling fresh and light. In one's sleep, one is not disturbed by bad dreams. One endears oneself to all. As one loves others so others also love him. One also endears oneself to non-humans. When one permeates one's mind with loving kindness, even ferocious animals, snakes and scorpions are also attracted towards oneself. Practicing *mettā*, the colour of his face is brightened. *Mettā*, therefore, has great power to make one beautiful and lovable. As the face reflects the state of the mind so when one is angry or jealous he cannot have that placidity and serenity on his face, which can make him beautiful. But if one is full of loving -kindness the calmness will be reflected on one's face and the chemistry of one's face will be different. Such a person quickly attains the concentration of mind and when death comes, one dies remaining mindful and alert.

For understanding the power of *mettā* we have to understand the chemistry of our thought. There is a great difference between the chemistry of hateful thoughts and that of loving thoughts. Whereas loving thoughts produce healthy physical effects, hateful thoughts produce just the opposite. The former make one happy and calm but the latter make

278. ibid. p. 617

279. DT3.212 *Akopo ti adoso, mettāti attho.*

280. Dh 5 *Na hi verena verāni, sammantīdha kudācanaṃ/ Averena sammantī esa dhammo sanantano//*

one disturbed and unhappy. In the words of Narada Thera, " When one gets angry, the heart pumps blood twice or three times faster than the normal rate. Heated blood rushes up to the face, which then turns red or black. At times the face becomes repulsive to sight. Loving thoughts on the contrary, gladden the heart and clarify the blood. The face then presents a lovable appearance." (See B&H,p. 622)

Who is fit to practice *mettā* and how to practice it? In the *Karaṇīyamettasuttaṃ* the qualities of one who is fit for practicing *mettā* are described. One should be physically fit and mentally free from pollutants like pride, anger and jealousy. One should be extremely simple and straightforward. There should be no crookedness in oneself. One should be wise, one's sense must be calm. One should not have attachment in oneself. One must fill his mind with loving kindness for all living beings and one should always think of protecting others just as a mother protects her only child at the cost even of her own life. One must be free from all kinds of negative thoughts and fill oneself with positive ones, one should be happy and free from anger and other defilements before one can practice *mettā.*

If people of this world, particularly the heads of states practice loving-kindness and think the welfare of all people then the world can be a veritable paradise. Narada Thera says. "This chaotic, war-weary, restless world of today, where the nations are arming themselves to the teeth, frightened of one another, where human life is endangered by nuclear weapons which may be released at any moment, is sorely in need of this universal loving kindness so that all may live in one world in perfect peace and harmony like brothers and sisters." (See B&H,p. 626)

More than anything else what is badly needed in this world, which is in the process of being globalized is loving- kindness.

Compassion (*karuṇā*) is the second virtue which when cultivated makes one sublime, makes one soft, makes one rid of hard- heartedness and cruelty. It is defined as that which affects one to see others in trouble and suffering. (*Paradukkhe sati sādhūnaṃ mana kampetīti karuṇā ti. Majjhima nikāya Ṭīkā* 1.1). When one is endowed with this feeling one does not want to inflict pain on others. One's heart melts to see others suffering and wants to remove all their suffering. One makes all efforts to do so. One wants to help others even at one's own cost, without caring for one's own comfort and convenience, without caring for even one's own life. *Karuṇā* is synonymous with *avihiṃsā* (non-injury, mercy, friendliness, love). One endowed with this exalted feeling combats the sufferings of others and destroys them (*Kināti vināseti vā paradukkhanti karuṇā. Abhidhammāvatāra ṇāmarūpaparicchedādi*, p. 22). The characteristic of *karuṇa* (compassion) is to remove the sufferings of others, its function is not to tolerate others' sufferings, it is manifested in *avihiṃsā* and its immediate cause is the helplessness of the sufferers. (*Sā paradukkhāpanayanākārappavatti lakkhaṇā, paradukkhāsahanarasā, avihiṃsāpaccupaṭṭhāna, dukkhābhibhūtānaṃ anāthabhāvadassana padaṭṭhānā.* ibid., p. 22)

Compassion is opposed to cruelty, to hard-heartedness. There are many in this world, who badly need compassion. The physically ill and the mentally sick, the poor and the downtrodden who live their life in abject poverty, the illiterate who do not understand what their rights are and how can they ameliorate their conditions, the servants who are ill treated and justice is not meted out to them, the women who are treated as second rate citizens of the world, the old who are not looked after by their children, the beggars who are compelled to go begging--all need one's compassion. Unless one has compassion for them how can he open charitable hospitals to treat the sick, to start schools to educate the poor children, to start orphanages to take care of the children who do not have any body to look after. Compassion makes one do altruistic works. It is because of this sublime virtue that many compassionate persons are engaged in doing many social activities for the poor and the needy. This is called 'Socially Engaged Buddhism' in the present time.

Inspired by this sublime virtue the rich can make the best use of their wealth and the experts in their fields can do works to ameliorate the poor conditions of a large section of humanity. The Buddha with his great compassion always looked for the poor, the ignorant and the depraved and helped them better their life. He himself served the sick. He exhorted his disciples to attend upon the sick. (*Yo, bhikkhave maṃ upaṭṭhaheyya, so gilānaṃ upaṭṭhaheyya. Mahāvagga*, p. 394)

Muditā (sympathetic joy) is the third sublime virtue. It is not merely sympathy, which in most cases is passive. But it is active in so far as it completely destroys jealousy. *Muditā*, therefore, is antidote to jealousy. Narada Thera says the following about jealousy: "One devastating force that endangers our whole constitution is jealousy. Very often some cannot bear to see or hear the successful achievements of others. They rejoice over their failures but cannot tolerate their successes. Instead of praising and congratulating the successful, they try to ruin, condemn and vilify them. In one way *muditā* is concerned more with oneself than with others as it tends to eradicate jealousy, which ruins oneself. On the other hand it aids others as well since one who practices *muditā* will not try to hinder the progress and welfare of others."(ibid. p. 635).

One can easily rejoice over the success of one's near and dear ones but it is very difficult to be happy at the success of one's enemies. *Muditā*, therefore, is very difficult to practice, more difficult than *mettā* and *karuṇā*.

But if *muditā* is practiced sincerely, if the poor rejoice over the rich, if the developing nations rejoice over the developed ones, if the people belonging to one religion are not jealous of the people following another religion, if one institution is not jealous of another, if the unsuccessful are not jealous of the successful, a lot of trouble, tension and suffering caused by jealousy will not arise. Shakespeare calls jealousy 'a green eyed monster' that can cause havoc.

So, if the individuals and groups practice *muditā* (appreciative joy) the world will become a paradise.

I remember one incident of jealousy in my life. Some of my classmates who were from town were very jealous of me because I, coming from a village used to stand first in the class. One of them became so jealous of me that one day he persuaded me to go to a garden nearby where he would give me guavas. I went there but lo and behold instead of giving me guavas he took out a blade and wanted to cut one of my right-hand fingers. I felt helpless because he was physically a bully. But fortunately, an elderly man appeared on the scene and the bully ran away. On being asked why I looked sad and afraid I told him all about it and he himself being a town dweller must have taken the boy to task. Even now sometimes I think what would have happened to me if he would have cut the index finger of my right hand.

Muditā, in fact, is a great sublime mental state. It must be cultivated to drive out jealousy.

The fourth sublime virtue which makes one remain undisturbed, unshaken is *upekkhā* (equanimity).

Upekkhā means 'discerning rightly' and 'viewing justly'. If one sees rightly, one will not be attached. Right seeing also will lead one to develop no *rāga* (attachment, clinging) and no *dosa* (aversion). There are eight *loka dhammas* (worldly conditions) that affect all humanity. They are loss (*hāni*), gain (*lābha*); fame (*yasa*) infamy (*apayasa*); blame (*nindā*) praise (*pasaṃsā*); and *duhkha* (pain) *sukha* (happiness). They are such *dhammas*, which affect all humanity. People become happy and feel elated when they gain, when they earn name and fame, when they are praised and when they feel happy. But they are depressed and sad when their opposites happen to them. If one can remain undisturbed, unperturbed, unmoved and stable in such conditions of life one will really be practicing equanimity (*upekkhā*). Equanimity is a great virtue, which makes one *sthitaprajñā* (established in wisdom). If in any circumstance one does not lose one's mental balance, does not lose one's cool and equipoise one is practicing *upekkhā*. Because one has developed wisdom and known that nothing is permanent so whatever situations arise in life one is neither elated nor depressed. One does not allow elation and depression to overpower him but one overpowers them instead. If one is elated to hear praise, one is bound to be depressed to hear blame. If one feels happy on gaining something, one is bound to feel unhappy when one suffers loss. Therefore the Buddha has exhorted one to remain calm and equanimous particularly in that circumstance of life when one feels like retaliating. In the *Dhammapada* he says:

Sace neresi attānaṃ, kaṃso upahato yathā/
Esa pattosi nibbānaṃ, sārambho tena vijjati//

'Retaliate not. Be silent as a cracked gong when you are abused by others. If you do so, I deem that you have already attained nibbāna although you have not realized *nibbāna*.'

The Buddha regards *upekkhā* as the greatest good, as the highest welfare.

Phuṭṭhassa lokadhammehi, cittaṃ yassa na kampati/
Asokaṃ virajaṃ khemaṃ, etaṃ maṅgalamuttamaṃ//

When faced with the vicissitudes of life, one's mind is unshaken.
Sorrowless, stainless, secure–this is the highest welfare.

One finds several occasions when the Buddha practiced equanimity and won his foes and revilers. When Akkosaka Bhāradvāja incensed at the conversion of his eldest brother by the Buddha goes to him and insults him he does not feel offended at all. Instead he asks him what does he do when he gives some present to some body who does not accept it and getting the answer that he keeps it with himself the Buddha said calmly that he does not accept his abuses, so let him keep them with him. This remark of the Buddha brought about a complete transformation of character in Bhāradvāja. In all adverse circumstances a wise one should remain unshaken, undisturbed steadfast like a solid rock which is not shaken by fierce winds.

Selo yathā ekaghano, vātena na samīrati/
Evaṃ nindāpasaṃsāsu, na samiñjanti paṇḍitā//

Upekkhā is a great quality, which abandons *rāga* and *dosa*. The chief characteristic of *upekkhā* is impartial attitude. One makes no distinction between the good and the bad, between the saint and the sinner. If this sublime and ennobling virtue is practiced, one will really become great and noble.

Thus, the four Brahmavihāras are qualities of mind which make people noble, kind, sympathetic and equanimous. In the words of Narada Thera. "*Mettā* embraces all beings, *karuṇā* embraces sufferers, *muditā* embraces the prosperous, and *upekkhā* embraces the good and the bad, the loved and the unloved, the pleasant and the unpleasant." (ibid. p. 640)

Upekkhā (equanimity) is like the quality of the earth, which remains indifferent in all circumstances. Whatever sweet or foul is thrown on it, it does not react. It remains undisturbed, indifferent and equanimous. One practicing *upekkhā* should be like the earth.

"Just as the earth whate'er is thrown
Upon her, whether sweet or foul,
Indifferent is to all alike,
No hatred shows, nor amity.
So likewise one in good or ill,
Must even-balanced ever be."

Buddha's Anattavāda: Why?

It is difficult for one to grasp the Buddha's concept of *anattā* because of his mind set. One has inherited this mind set from his fathers and forefathers and also from a large number of poets, philosophers, thinkers and religious teachers who talk of the impermanent nature of his body and say that the soul (soul and self are synonymous) that lives within the body is eternal. It does not die with the body. It enters into another body after death (*Vāsānsi Jīrṇāni yathā vihāya, navāni gṛhaṇāti naroparāni —Gītā*). The bird and the cage simile is greatly responsible for one's having this mind set. The bird is the soul and the cage is the body. When one dies the soul flies away like a bird and the cage i.e. the body is left behind. Apparently, this seems to be a very apt simile to explain the relationship between body and soul. But, if one goes a little deeper and tries to know the nature, shape and size of the invisible or disembodied soul he is confronted with many questions. What is the nature of soul? Is it eternal or not? Where did it come from? What becomes of it on the dissolution of the body? Where does it go after the dissolution of the body? In what form does it exist 'hereafter'? How long does it remain there? Is it small or large? Is it sentient or not sentient? Is it happy or miserable after it leaves the body? Does it remain unaffected by one's actions or does it get affected? What are its functions?

The answers given to these questions are not the same. Some answer them in one way and others do so in quite the opposite way. If one looks at the different views found regarding soul in the *Brahmajāla Sutta* he will see the contradictions there.

Those who call themselves eternalists regard soul as eternal and they come to this conclusion by remembering their past lives for an unimaginably long stretch of time. This they do by attaining mental concentration and one of the six *abhiññās* called *pubbenivāsānussati ñāṇa* They recall their past lives and remember that wherever they were born they had this name or that and so they think their souls are eternal. Among eternalists there are some who prove their eternality by taking recourse to logic.

What happens to soul or self after death? The following answers are given: the self after death is healthy and conscious and (1) material, (2) immaterial, (3) both material and immaterial (4) neither material nor immaterial, (5) finite, (6) infinite, (7) both (8) neither (9) of uniform perception, (10) of varied perception, (11) of limited perception, (12) of unlimited perception, (13) wholly happy (14) wholly miserable, (15) both and (16) neither.

There are others according to whom the self is not conscious after death. They declare that 'the self after death is healthy and unconscious and (1) material, (2) immaterial, (3) both, (4) neither, (5) finite, (6) infinite, (7) both and (8) neither.

There are still others who regard self as neither conscious nor unconscious after death and declare that the self after death is healthy and neither conscious nor unconscious and (1) material, (2) immaterial, (3) both (4) neither, (5) finite (6) infinite, (7) both and (8) neither.

There are others who believe that the self is annihilated and destroyed after death. According to them the self is of seven kinds. The first kind is material, composed of the four great elements, the product of mother and father. The second kind of self is divine, material belonging to the sense sphere fed on real food. The third kind is divine, material, mind-made, complete with all its parts, not defective in any sense organ. The fourth, fifth. sixth and seventh kinds relate to the four kinds of *arūpāvacara jhāna.*

Those who propound such views do so by speculating. They have no direct experience of the self. They do so just as the brahmins are shown to do when they show one the path to one's union with Brahmā. They claim to know the path leading to Brahmā but they have never walked on it nor have they met Brahmā face to face. They are themselves blind. How can they show the path to others? Similarly, these views are based on speculation. How can they really talk about the nature, shape and size of self?

One question that agitated Poṭṭhapāda most was 'Is the soul the same as the body or is the soul one thing and the body another?'[281] The Buddha answered many of his questions, one being - 'Is perception a person's self, or is perception one thing, and self another?'[282]

Poṭṭhapāda's mind was moving in an accustomed rut and what the Buddha said was incomprehensible to him. So, the Buddha said to him that he thought it useless to try to answer these questions inasmuch as they had no bearing on leading a *Dhammic* life. Leading a *brahmacariya* life is one thing and trying to know the answers to these questions is quite a different thing. There is no relation between them. Just as the Buddha said to Mālukyaputta that he left ten metaphysical questions unanswered and called them indeterminate (Ten metaphysical questions are: Is the world eternal or not eternal? Is the world finite or not finite? Is the soul the same as the body or are they different? After death, the Tathāgata exists or does not exist, both exists and does not exist and neither exists nor does not exist) because such questions 'are unbeneficial, they do not belong to the fundamentals of

281. D 1, *Poṭṭhapāda Sutta,*

282. LDB, p. 163

holy life, they do not lead to disenchantment, to dispassion, to cessation, to peace, to direct knowledge, to enlightenment, to *nibbāna*.[283]

He further said that to insist on getting answers to these questions is as foolish and unprofitable as one afflicted with an arrow refusing to be treated by a doctor unless he knew all about the arrow and the person who shot it.

He further said that he declared the four noble truths such as 'This is suffering, This is the origin of suffering, This is the cessation of suffering and This is the way leading to the cessation of suffering', because this declaration 'is beneficial, it belongs to the fundamentals of holy life, it leads to disenchantment, to dispassion, to cessation, to peace, to direct knowledge, to enlightenment, to *Nibbāna*.'[284]

This satisfied Mālukyaputta because he understood that the most important problem before mankind is to get rid of suffering. Other questions do not have any immediate bearing on the existential problem that mankind faces.

Poṭṭhapāda also understood what the Buddha said about the existential problem of mankind and although the wanderers who were with him sneered and jeered at Poṭṭhapāda from all sides saying that whatever the ascetic Gotama says Poṭṭhapāda agrees with him - "So it is Lord, so it is Well-Farer." He does not mind their satirical remark and replies to them, "I do not understand either about whether the world is eternal or not...or whether the Tathāgata exists after death or not, or both, or neither. But the ascetic Gotama teaches a true and real way of practice which is consistent with Dhamma and grounded in Dhamma."[285]

The most important point to be noted here is both Mālukyaputta and Poṭṭhapāda understood the importance of practice underlined by the Buddha rather than knowing the theory.

Dialogues such as these (and there are many such dialogues in the *Sutta Piṭaka*) bring out a very important aspect of the Buddha's philosophy. His philosophy is not based on intellectual analysis but it is based on the practice of Vipassana and direct experience. The most important words that Poṭṭhapāda uses here are *bhūtaṃ tacchaṃ tathaṃ paṭipadaṃ dhammaṭṭhitataṃ dhammaniyāmataṃ*.

There is a great difference between the Buddha as a philosopher and other philosophers. The Buddha was a pragmatic and practical philosopher.

---

283. MLD, p. 536

Na hetaṃ, mālukyaputta, atthasaṃhitaṃ na ādibrahmacariyakaṃ na nibbidāya na virāgāya na nirodhāya na upasamāya na abhiññāya na sambodhāya na nibbānāya saṃvattati.

284. MLD, p. 536

285. LDB, p. 165

Like Leibnitz, he never talked of things that have no direct bearing on human life. How is Leibnitz's monad going to help one in eliminating suffering? He saw that suffering is a fact of life. Therefore, his primary concern was to get rid of it. Like a wise doctor he knew that unless he knew the cause of suffering, he would not be able to eliminate it. While practicing *sādhanā* he had realized that nothing arises without a cause. Thus, he discovered the Law of *Paṭiccasamuppāda* which may be regarded as a great discovery on the spiritual path. When he looked for the cause of suffering he found that desire is at its root. He also very clearly saw how desire is caused and how it can be extirpated.

In one of my essays entitled *Mechanism of Vipassana*[286] I have shown how sensation gives rise to desire, how desire becomes strong and how it leads one to be born again. Buddha's deep knowledge of human psychology and his understanding of the role of ethics in controlling this monkey mind stood him in good stead. And so, he discovered the Noble Eightfold Path by walking on which one can end desire. That the cause of suffering is desire is his philosophy and walking on the eightfold path can eliminate desire is the action-plan of his philosophy. The action-plan of his philosophy is leading an ethical life. His philosophy unlike others' is not barren, not a product of intellectual thinking but it is a product of his own realization, product of his knowing and seeing. Unlike other philosophers, he relied more on *bhāvanāmayā paññā* and not on *sutamayā* and *cintāmayā paññā.* The philosophy that stems from intellectual thinking has its limitation but the philosophy based on direct experience is true philosophy as it is based on seeing reality as it is i.e. *yathābhūta ñāṇadassana.* The two most important attributes of the Buddha are *jānato* and *passato* i.e. one who knows and sees. Therefore, it is a real philosophy inasmuch as he saw the universal problem of mankind and also saw how it can be solved. He said time and again that his philosophy is to be lived in order to reap its benefit. One who only recites the sacred texts but does not act accordingly is like a cowherd who only counts the cows of others but cannot drink their milk. In order to enjoy the fruits of Holy Life one has to act according to what is said in the scriptures.

Bahumpi ce saṃhitaṃ bhāsamāno, na takkaro hoti naro pamatto/
Gopova gāvo gaṇayaṃ paresaṃ, na bhāgavā sāmaññassa hotī'ti//[287]

Had Siddhartha Gotama followed the rut, he would not have been the Buddha. He would have ended as one of the heretical thinkers. One

286. Angraj Chaudhary, Aspects of Buddha-Dhamma, Eastern Book Linkers, Delhi, 2009.

287. Dh 19

knows that some of them did believe in an eternal soul, but what they preached ran counter to what could give peace to mankind and bring harmony in society. Pūraṇa Kassapa propounded the theory of inaction, Makkhali Gosāla propounded the philosophy of fatalism, Ajita Kesakambali propounded the doctrine of annihilation and Pakudha Kaccāna regarded seven things as stable and permanent but their teachings did not inspire people to lead an ethical life. Puraṇa Kassapa denied any merit in doing wholesome actions and according to him unwholesome actions produced no demerit. According to Makkhali Gosala people are so helpless that they cannot do any wholesome action on their own. Even if they want to, they cannot lead a religious life. Ajita's annihilationism goads people to live this life as best as they can even by fair means or foul for there is no future life to reap what they sow in the present life. Pakudha Kaccāna's philosophy exempts murderers because the life principle - one of the seven stable things - cannot be murdered.

This was the ethical milieu in which the Buddha found himself. There was great confusion. In such a situation, how could people feel inspired to lead an ethical life? How could there be peace and harmony in society when murder was not condemned? People were free to let their greed and aversion run riot and not even think of living a religious life.

As all such views were based on speculation, assumption and imagination they had no bearing on ending human beings' universal problem of suffering. What the Buddha propounded stemmed from his direct experience. He said nothing which he did not directly experience. So what he said was the product of his *bhāvanāmayā paññā* i.e. insight wisdom. While practicing Vipassana he saw how things are impermanent, how they arise to pass away. He saw nothing that can be called eternal, permanent and stable. If there is nothing permanent, how can there be happiness?

Sabbe saṅkhārā aniccāti yadā paññāya passati.[288] He saw every phenomenon arising and passing away. He also saw that whatever is impermanent is suffering. *Sabbe saṅkhārā dukkhāti yadā paññāya passati.*[289] While practicing Vipassana he saw this phenomenon so clearly that he was convinced of the impermanence of things and the suffering caused by them.

Immediately after he set the *Dhammacakka* in motion, he taught the *Anattalakkhaṇa Sutta* to five bhikkhus so that they might not fall a prey to the false belief of *attā* and to many ills that go with it.

Practicing Vipassana, the Buddha had clearly seen with *bhāvanāmayā paññā* characterized by *sati* (mindfulness) and *sampajañña* (knowing *anicca,*

---

288. Dh 277

289. ibid. 278

dukkha and *anatta* characteristics of all phenomena) that which constituted his personality. He had seen no self there - the self that is permanent. *Sabbe dhammā anattāti, yadā paññāya passati.* Of course what people called self in common parlance was there but it was a conventional truth, a convenient symbol to refer to a person. It was *nāma-rūpa* (mind and matter).

Vajirā Bhikkhuṇi rightly says about this self:

"Yathā hi aṅgasambhārā, hoti saddo ratho iti;
Evaṃ khandhesu santesu, hoti satto ti sammuti,"[290]

Just as, with an assemblage of parts
The word 'chariot' is used,
So, when the aggregates exist.
There is the convention 'a being".

Nāgasena takes up this example and proves that 'Nagasena' is just a conventional truth; in the ultimate sense there is no 'Nāgasena'. The self should be understood in the same way. It is the combination of five *khandhas* i.e. *rūpa* (material qualities), *vedanā* (feeling), *saññā* (perception), *saṅkhāra* (formations) and *viññāṇa* (consciousness).

One may ask questions like where does this consciousness come from? How does it come from *rūpa* (matter)? The answer is just as the magnetic field is induced by the electric field, consciousness is induced by the combination of four elements such as, earth, water, fire and air. Just as the combination of lime, *katthā* (catechu), betel nut and betel leaf gives rise to red colour, different parts of a flower give rise to the smell so the combination of the elements induces consciousness. And this consciousness knows, feels and has the volition to act. So it does all three cognitive, emotive and volitional functions. If it does all the three functions, what is left for the soul to do? Therefore there is no *attā.*[291]

What the Buddha found in his being was mind (*nāma*) and matter (*rūpa*). And both of them are in a constant state of flux. The two are divided into five *khandhas* - *rūpa, vedanā, saññā, saṅkhāra* and *viññāṇa.* They are impermanent (*anicca*) and consequently there is suffering (*dukkha*) without any *attā* (*anattā*).

"Bhikkhus, form is non-self. For if, bhikkhus, form were self, this form would not lead to affliction, and it would be possible to have it of form: 'Let my form be thus, let my form not be thus,' but because form is non-self, form leads to affliction, and it is not possible to have it of form: 'Let my form be thus, let my form not be thus'."

290. S I.160
291. B&HD pp. 263-264

Why *anattā*? Because it is not under one's control, it is not its owner, it is void and it is contrary to *attā* (self). *Anattāti avasavattanaṭṭhena* (not being under one's control), *asāmikaṭṭhena* (not being owner), *suññataṭṭhena* (being void), *attapaṭikkhepanaṭṭhenāti* (being contrary to *attā*), *evaṃ catūhi kāraṇehi anattā.*[292]

The same will apply to other four *khandhas* viz, *vedanā* (feeling), *saññā* (perception), *saṅkhāra* (formations) and *viññāna* (consciousness).

As *khandhas* are impermanent, subject to change so they are suffering because what is not permanent is suffering. It cannot be happiness.

"What do you think, bhikkhus, is form permanent or impermanent?"

"Impermanent, Venerable sir."

"Is what is impermanent suffering or happiness?"

"Suffering, Venerable sir."

"Is what is impermanent, suffering, and subject to change fit to be regarded thus: This is mine, this I am, this is my self?"

"No Venerable, sir."

The Buddha says that being induced by craving one says 'this is mine' (*Etaṃ mama*), being induced by conceit we say 'this I am' (*Eso hamasmi*) and being induced by wrong views we say 'this is my self' (*Eso me attāti*).

The Abhidhamma Philosophy he propounded gives a detailed description of the different kinds of *citta* (consciousness), *cetasika* (concomitant factors) and *rūpa* (matter). Its study clearly shows that there is no permanent soul. All *dhammas* that go to make up one's personality are constantly changing. There are as many as eighty nine or one hundred twenty-one kinds of *cittas*, fifty two *cetasikas* and twenty eight *rūpas*. They have been minutely analyzed to show that both mind and matter are impermanent. So if all are changing why crave for them, why regard something as 'my self'?

The importance of Abhidhamma studies in bringing about a change in one's outlook 'from the view point of self to that of non-self' has been underlined by Venerable Nyānapoṇika Thera in these words: " Once one has grasped intellectually the doctrine of non-self, one can certainly succeed in applying it to the theoretical and practical issues if only one remembers it in time and deliberately directs one's thoughts and volitions accordingly. But except for such deliberate directing of thought which in most cases will be relatively rare, the mind will continue to move in the old accustomed ruts of 'I' and 'mine', 'self' and 'substance' which are deeply ingrained in our daily language and our modes of thinking and actions too will still continue to be frequently governed by our ancient egocentric

---

292. *Sāratthadīpanī Ṭīkā* 3.168

impulses."[293] In order to come out of this habit pattern, he says "The only remedy is for bad or wrong habits of action, speech and thought to be gradually replaced by good and correct habits until the latter becomes as spontaneous as the former are now. It is, therefore, necessary that right thinking, that is, thinking in terms of *anattā* be made the subject of regular and systematic mental training until the power of wrong habits of thought is reduced and finally broken."[294]

But mere study of Abhidhamma will not be of great help as practice of Vipassana will be because one will be having the direct experience of impermanence while practicing Vipassana.

The Buddha denied *attā* because there was no proof of it. Those who talked of it had no experience of it and they were saying things about it which they had heard from others. They just speculated about it. The Buddha put no premium on speculation. He gave importance to what he realized, what he saw and experienced within himself. His philosophy proceeded from his direct experience, not from intellectual thinking. Intellect according to him is not an unfailing guide.

He also denied eternal *attā* because this belief led people to become hedonists and enjoy sensuous and sensual pleasures. The other corollary of this belief was to do austere penances to liberate this eternal soul from impurities caused by one's unwholesome actions. The Buddha did not favour either. He had seen what harm indulgence in sensual pleasures could do and what harm austere penances could do.

"Tassa evaṃ ayoniso manasikaroto channaṃ diṭṭhīnaṃ aññatarā diṭṭhi uppajjati. 'Atthi me attā'ti vā assa, saccato thetato diṭṭhi uppajjati; 'natthi me attā'ti vā assa saccato thetato diṭṭhi uppajjati; 'attanāva attānaṃ sañjānāmī'ti vā assa saccato thetato diṭṭhi uppajjati; 'attanāva anattānaṃ sañjānāmī'ti vā assa saccato thetato diṭṭhi uppajjati; 'anattanāva attānaṃ sañjānāmī'ti vā assa saccatothetato diṭṭhi uppajjati; atha vā panassa evaṃ diṭṭhi hoti-'yo me ayaṃ attā vado vedeyyo tatra tatra kalyāṇapāpakānaṃ kammānaṃ vipākaṃ paṭisaṃvedeti so kho pana me ayaṃ attā nicco dhuvo sassato avipariṇāmadhammo sassati samaṃ tatheva ṭhassatī'ti. Idaṃ vuccati, bhikkhave, diṭṭhigataṃ diṭṭhigahanaṃ diṭṭhikantāraṃ ṭṭhivisūkaṃ diṭṭhivipphanditaṃ diṭṭhisaṃyojanaṃ. Diṭṭhisaṃyojanasaṃyutto, bhikkhave, assutavā puthujjano na parimuccati jātiyā jarāya maraṇena sokehi paridevehi dukkhehi domanassehi upāyāsehi; na parimuccati dukkhasmā'ti vadāmi.[295]

'This speculative view, bhikkhus, is called the thicket of views, the wilderness of views, the contortion of views, the fetter of views. Fettered

293. Abh Sts pp. 9-10.

294. ibid.

295. M1.12

by the fetter of views, the untaught ordinary person is not freed from birth, ageing and death; from sorrow, lamentation, pain, grief, and despair; one is not freed from suffering, I say.[296]

There was another great reason why the Buddha did not believe in a permanent self. That was his self realization, his experience, his direct knowledge which made it clear to him that all phenomena are impermanent—*sabbe saṅkhārā aniccāti.*[297]

Buddha's *anattavāda* is a veritable panacea for all the ills that people are subject to. And this is based on truth. The truth is that all things are impermanent, hence without any soul.

This realization at the experiential level enables one to develop non-attachment. With the development of non-attachment craving goes away and so goes away one's suffering.

What he denies when he propounds the philosophy of *anattā* is a permanent soul as it had been conceived by other philosophers of his time. But he had in mind a kind of 'self' which is ever changing, creating a new identity every moment but not completely losing the previous one. Thus, his philosophy can be called a process philosophy. When King Menander asks Nagasena - "who is born," Nagasena replies - "neither he nor someone else (*Na ca so na ca añño*)." Continuous change without losing a previous identity and creating a new identity every moment can be understood by the simile of milk becoming curd - curd becoming butter - and butter becoming ghee. Ghee is not the milk from where it has come but one cannot have ghee without the milk.

"Seyyathāpi, citta, gavā khīraṃ, khīramhā dadhi, dadhimhā navanītaṃ, navanītamhā sappi, sappimhā sappimaṇḍo. Yasmiṃ samaye khīraṃ hoti, neva tasmiṃ samaye dadhīti saṅkhaṃ gacchati, na navanītanti saṅkhaṃ gacchati, na sappīti saṅkhaṃ gacchati, na sappimaṇḍoti saṅkhaṃ gacchati; khīraṃ tveva tasmiṃ samaye saṅkhaṃ gacchati. Yasmiṃ samaye dadhi hoti ...pe... navanītaṃ hoti... sappi hoti... sappimaṇḍo hoti, neva tasmiṃ samaye khīranti saṅkhaṃ gacchati, na dadhīti saṅkhaṃ gacchati, na navanītanti saṅkhaṃ gacchati, na sappīti saṅkhaṃ gacchati; sappimaṇḍo tveva tasmiṃ samaye saṅkhaṃ gacchati. Evameva kho, citta, yasmiṃ samaye oḷāriko attapaṭilābho hoti ...pe... yasmiṃ, citta, samaye manomayo attapaṭilābho hoti ...pe... yasmiṃ, citta, samaye arūpo attapaṭilābho hoti, neva tasmiṃ samaye oḷāriko attapaṭilābhoti saṅkhaṃ gacchati, na manomayo attapaṭilābhoti saṅkhaṃ gacchati; arūpo attapaṭilābho tveva tasmiṃ samaye saṅkhaṃ gacchati.[298]

296. MLD, p. 93
297. Dh 277
298. D 1 *Poṭṭhapāda Sutta*, p. 178

Self changes, does not remain the same even for two consecutive moments. Why does it change? Because of actions that one does in life. According to the law of *kamma,* whatever wholesome or unwholesome actions one does in life create a potential called 'infraconsciousness' as said by Ven. Saddhatissa,[299] which are responsible for the next life. Ven. Saddhatissa goes on to say that 'the stream of consciousness, flowing through many lives, is as changing as a stream of water.' This is the *anattā* doctrine of Buddhism as it concerns the individual being.[300] If one understands the *anattā* doctrine propounded by the Buddha he will realize the other two characteristics (*anicca* and *dukkha*) of all phenomena of the world at the experiential level, develop detachment, he will not allow his desires to grow and multiply his miseries and become wiser to do wholesome actions in life equanimously in order to finally extirpate all desires. True understanding of the *anattā* doctrine will enable one to get rid of craving, conceit and wrong view, develop detachment and attain *nibbāna.*

299. BE, p. 22
300. ibid., p. 23

Paṭiccasamuppāda (The Theory of Dependent Origination)

Paṭiccasamuppāda is the Law of Dependent Origination or conditioned arising. It is applied to explain *dukkha* and *saṃsāra*, the cycle of birth and death i.e. repeated existence. It is a causal chain with twelve links.

The twelve links are *avijjā* (ignorance), *saṅkhārā* (karma-formations), *viññāṇaṃ* (consciousness), *nāma-rūpaṃ* (mind and matter i.e. mental and physical phenomena), *saḷāyatanaṃ* (six faculties), *phasso* (contact), *vedanā* (sensation), *taṇhā* (desire), *upādānaṃ* (clinging), *bhavo* (process of becoming), *jāti* (birth) and *jarā-maraṇa, dukkha domanassa,* etc. (decay, death, lamentation, pain, etc.).[301]

These twelve links extend over three lives and span them. The first two belong to the past life, the last two represent the future i.e. rebirth and the rest of the links i.e. eight links from *viññāṇaṃ* to *bhava* represent the present life. Each of the links is an effect of the preceding link, which acts as a cause.

Every link of this chain originates depending upon the preceding link and gives rise to the succeeding link. Here nothing arises independently. Everything has a cause to arise. *Imasmiṃ sati idaṃ hoti* (this being, that becomes). *Imass'uppādā idaṃ uppajjati* (from the arising of this, that arises). This law also speaks about the opposite. Nothing happens without a cause. Nothing happens fortuitously. *Imasmiṃ asati idaṃ na hoti* (this not becoming, that does not become), *imassa nirodhā idaṃ nirujjhati* (from the ceasing of this, that ceases) i.e. when the cause ceases, the effect also ceases. In the complete absence of cause there is no possibility of the arising of effect.[302]

This law is very deep and profound. How profound it is is clear from what the Buddha says to Ānanda when he says that although it is profound 'yet it appears to me as clear as clear.'[303] The Buddha says that 'through not understanding, not penetrating this doctrine, this generation has become like a tangled ball of string, covered as with a blight, tangled like coarse grass, unable to pass beyond states of woe, the ill destiny, ruin and the round of birth and death.'[304] The twelve links of this causal chain are: *avijjā, saṅkhāra, viññāṇa, nāmarūpa, saḷāyatana, phassa, vedanā, taṇhā, upādāna, bhava, jati, jarā maraṇa, soka parideva* etc. In the *Mahāpadāna Sutta* of the *Dīghanikāya* only ten links of the chain are given in backward order from

301. D2 *Mahānidāna Sutta*
302. For these laws see ibid.
303. See *Mahānidāna Sutta*: The Great Discourse on Origination, p. 223 in LDB
304. ibid., p. 223.

dukkha manifested as old age and death to *viññāṇa*. This order has been put into the mouth of Vipassi Buddha. But in the *Nidāna vagga* of the *Saṃyutta Nikāya* twelve links of the chain of causation are given—the other two being *avijjā* and *saṅkhāra.*

This law is not based on axioms as the laws are in Euclid's Geometry, nor is it based on intellectual inference observing phenomena happening in the outside world as Newton's laws of gravitation. It is a product of direct experience, which one has by looking within oneself with a mind free from defilements. The laws applicable in Geometry and Physics are different from those of *paṭiccasamuppāda* as the latter, unlike those of the former two, apply to the animate world where one's 'will' is important as it is the driving force. For realizing the truth of these laws one is required to experiment within one's own fathom long body and not in outisde laboratories. Besides, one has to develop one's body and mind i.e. insight and concentration to realize these laws that operate within. One has to drive out the defilements from one's mind in order to be fit to experience the truth of these laws. For proving the laws of Geometry and gravitational laws one need not necessarily be a person free from defilements. Persons with defilements like anger, hatred and jealousy can make experiments and prove those laws in the laboratories, but they cannot experience how the laws of Dependent origination work. A Vipassana practitioner can experience how these laws work. He can see them working in his own fathom long body by developing insight and by remaining equanimous when pleasant and unpleasant sensations arise on the body.[305] For developing one's body and mind one purifies one's conduct and one's livelihood by following five moral precepts. Besides, one develops contentment, restraint of the sense faculties and *sati* and *sampajañña,* which internalize the process of purification and thereby bridge the transition from virtue to concentration. These two enable him to attain *paññā* so that he has what is called the knowledge and vision of reality, as it is—*yathābhūtañāṇa dassana.* Unless a person walks on the Noble Eightfold Path shown by the Buddha it is not possible for him to understand the truth of *paṭiccasamuppāda.*

It is on account of this that an intellectual understanding of this law will not bring the desired result. One may explain *paṭiccasamuppāda* very clearly from the intellectual point of view but unless he experiences it, unless he sees how each link of this chain is caused by the preceding link

305. M1 See *Mahāsaccaka Sutta* where development of body means insight according to the commentary, because a Vipassana practitioner is not overwhelmed by the experience of pleasant feelings through his development of insight and when unpleasant feeling arises one is not overwhelmed because one has developed concentration of mind and is able to escape from it.

and how it itself becomes a cause to produce another link, unless he sees at the experiential level that even pleasant sensations are ephemeral and do not give lasting pleasure, he cannot develop non-attachment and end suffering. There is another difference between the laws that apply to the physical world and those that apply to the moral-spiritual world. It is not possible for anyone to annihilate the gravitational force. A mango will fall down from a tree, it cannot go up; however, one can annihilate desires. One can even stop them from arising. Desires ordinarily overpower one but he can overpower them and root them out completely if he understands the working of this law.

Unlike Euclid's geometrical laws and Newton's gravitational laws, the laws of *paṭiccasamuppāda* are moral laws based on psychology, ethics and metaphysics. These laws, therefore, have great spiritual implication in the philosophy propounded by the Buddha. The second noble truth propounded by him says that *taṇhā* (desire) is the cause of suffering. It implies that suffering is not permanent. Remove the cause and the suffering will automatically come to an end. So the teachings of the Buddha are not pessimistic as they are made out to be by some but they hold out hopes for mankind. The fourth noble truth is the path leading to the cessation of suffering. This path is called the middle path because it avoids the two extremes of hedonism and asceticism. It has eight constituents that form the action-plan as to how to live the philosophy propounded by the Buddha. This Noble Eightfold Path consists of *sīla, samādhi* and *paññā. Sīla* means purity of physical and vocal actions, *samādhi* is the one-pointedness of wholesome mind. The mind can be wholesome when it is free from defilements. With this pure, undefiled and concentrated mind one can attain wisdom and will be able to see reality as it is. As the darkness of ignorance will be expelled by the light of wisdom one will be able to break the cycle of existence that causes endless suffering. *Papañca (sk.prapañca)* equivalent to Schopehauer's 'world' will cease. No world of suffering will come into being.[306]The Noble Eightfold Path happily and harmoniously combines psychology, ethics and metaphysics. *Sīla* is ethics. One can observe ethical precepts like abstinence from killing, lying etc. when he is not under the influence of craving, aversion and ignorance. *Samādhi* i.e. concentration of mind is not possible without understanding its fickle and unsteady nature and without purifying it from various defilements which is possible by observing *sīla* (moral precepts). This is psychology. When one attains *paññā* (insight, wisdom) one understands reality as it is. The realization of its impermanent nature makes him detached – this can be said to fall under metaphysics.

306. St Ph. p. 312

The Buddha's (in fact Siddhārth's) spiritual quest was primarily concerned with finding a way to end ubiquitous suffering. Suffering—physical and mental is experienced by all although not as sensitively as it was experienced by Siddhārth. He also discovered the root cause of the two kinds of suffering mentioned above. It is this root cause which causes one to be born again and again and suffer endlessly. Siddhārtha was concerned with eliminating the root cause of all kinds of suffering. And what is the root cause of all suffering? It is being born with five aggregates.

He left home seeking the noble (*nibbānā*), its opposite- the ignoble being the ubiquitous suffering mankind is subject to. Greatly sensitive as he was, he immediately learned that it was ridiculous to seek things that, like him, were subject to birth, old age, disease and death. Even a beautiful woman who inflames one's passion and desire is subject to old age, disease and death, let alone other material wealth like cow, goat, sheep, silver and gold - they do not last forever. How can things that are not permanent give one lasting happiness? How can one who is oneself subject to change enjoy lasting happiness?[307] To be infatuated with those impermanent things, to be attached to them when all are constantly changing is ignoble. This analytical thinking led him to see the danger in all things subject to birth, ageing, sickness, etc and to seek the ageless, deathless, sorrowless and undefiled supreme security from bondage of suffering-*nibbāna*.[308]

Ālārakālāma and Uddaka Rāmaputta to whom he went to learn how to end suffering and how to be free from the cycle of birth and death could not satisfy him. In fact, Uddaka Rāmaputta was not as efficient a teacher as his father Rama was, so in his *āśrama* he learnt the eighth *jhāna* all by himself. It is true that he learnt *samatha* type of meditation there, realized it and attained its knowledge and vision. As a consequence, this could ensure his happy life for thousands of aeons in the higher worlds. However, it could not show him the path to root out all defilements (*kilesas*) that cause suffering. *Samatha* type of meditation only helps one to keep out external objects impinging on one's senses causing sensations that give rise to desire and attachment. But how can one annihilate desires that keep on arising within all the time? The future Buddha could see two dangers. One was from outside when one's sense organs come in contact with their respective objects. One sees with one's eyes a visible object, contemplates upon its desirability and develops desire to have it. When this desire is not fulfilled, one suffers. The other danger was from within. There was a stock of *anusaya kilesas* (dormant mental impurities) deep within one's unconscious mind. They also come on the surface. This is a

307. M1(see *Ariyapariyesanā Sutta*)
308. ibid.

psychological fact that any thought arising in the mind manifests itself through sensations on the body. *Vedanāsamosaranā sabbe dhammā.*[309] They are either pleasant or unpleasant. One hankers after pleasant sensations and hates the unpleasant ones. Because even pleasant sensations do not last forever suffering is caused and suffering is caused also because some sensations are unpleasant.

The Bodhisatta was primarily concerned with discovering a way to end suffering. While looking for the way he had learned much about how suffering is caused.

So, when he went to Uruvela with a great resolve to practice austere penances to discover a way to end suffering, three similes that he had never heard before flashed across his mind.[310] The similes related to a wet sappy piece of wood lying in water, to another piece of wet sappy piece of wood lying on dry land away from water and to a third dry sapless piece of wood lying on dry land far away from the water. Howsoever one may try to produce fire by rubbing the first two pieces of wood with an upper fire-stick, one will be tired and disappointed but he will not be able to produce fire and heat. Why? Because those pieces of wood are wet and sappy. Only a dry piece of wood rubbed against another dry piece of wood can produce fire and heat.

This was a sort of 'eureka' for the Bodhisatta going to be the Buddha. He came to the conclusion that whether good samaṇas and Brahmaṇas feel or do not feel painful racking and piercing feelings due to exertion, they are incapable of knowledge and vision and supreme enlightenment because they do not live bodily and mentally withdrawn from sensual pleasures and their desire for sensual pleasures has not been abandoned or extirpated. Wet and sappy piece of wood stands for people who are filled with sensual desires. So long as sensual desires are there, it is impossible to attain peace and happiness let alone the highest good i. e. *nibbāna.*

With these three apt and relevant similes, he underlines the importance of becoming bodily and mentally free from sensual desire before he can end suffering and aspire for the greatest good i.e. *nibbāna*–a state of desirelessness.

Finding austere penances worthless, he did not lose heart. The million-dollar question before him was how to discover a path to end suffering. So, he once again concentrated his mind and applied it to look within. In other words, he started practicing Vipassana. This technique of meditation made it clear to him how desire--the cause of suffering arises and how it can be eradicated. In a flash, as it were, he saw how the mind works, how it reacts

309. A.3.158 *Mūlaka Sutta*,.

310. M see *Ariyapariyesanā Sutta*, *Bodhirājakumāra Sutta* and *Mahāsaccaka Sutta.*

under the old habit pattern and how it multiplies miseries. He saw that reversing the functions of mind could end suffering. It is here that the law of *paṭiccasamuppāda* became crystal clear to him.

One can say that this Law of Dependent Origination holds good in the spiritual world. It explains how *dukkha* comes into being and how it can be eradicated. It explains *papañca* (multiplication of *dukkha* or the coming into being of the cycle of birth and death). How one is to stop *papañca* and get rid of *dukkha* was the million dollar question before the would- be- Buddha.

He thought, unless he knew the real nature of desires and where they arise he could not end them. This made him look within. And while looking within, this Law of Dependent Origination became crystal clear. Looking within to see what happens there is Vipassana. *Samatha* type of meditation enables a meditator to attain concentration of mind and of course helps one to keep outside objects that come in contact with their sense organs and produce sensations at bay. But Vipassana helps one to see clearly how pleasant or unpleasant sensations arise in them which one either wishes to continue or discontinue. In both the cases there is a desire which when frustrated causes suffering. Pleasant sensations do not continue and are replaced by unpleasant ones giving rise to suffering.

Sensation is *vedanā* and it became clear to the would-be-Buddha that *vedanā* gives rise to *taṇhā*. How does it produce *taṇhā*? The Bodhisatta examined his own mind and saw that broadly speaking it consisted of four parts: *viññāṇa* (consciousness), *saññā* (perception), *vedanā* (sensation) and *saṅkhāra* (reaction). When any phenomenon occurs, say the eye comes in contact with any visible object, consciousness simply registers it. The second part, perception, recognizes it and evaluates it positively, negatively or neutrally in the light of the past experience. Perception, thus, gives rise to *vedanā* (sensation) which is either pleasant, unpleasant or neither pleasant nor unpleasant. It is here that *taṇhā* arises because the third part of mind wants to have more of the pleasant sensations and none of the unpleasant ones. One's reaction to have more of the pleasant and none of the unpleasant sensations (*saṅkhāras*) causes suffering because even pleasant sensations are not permanent. All sensations pleasant or unpleasant arise to pass away. The Bodhisatta saw this very clearly. Thus *aniccatā* (impermanence) became crystal clear to him. He realized it.

The future Buddha saw the process of the origin of suffering very clearly. Because of the five physical senses such as eye, ear etc and the mind, our contact with the countless phenomena viz. sights, sounds, odours, flavours, textures, various thoughts and emotions becomes inevitable. Contact gives rise to sensation—*phassa paccayā vedanā*. One likes to have more of pleasant sensations and hates to have the unpleasant ones. Thus desires are caused—*vedanā paccayā taṇhā*. *Taṇhā* becomes stronger and stronger producing *upādanaṃ--taṇhā paccayā upādānaṃ*. Strong desire (*upādanā*) produces *bhava* (becoming), which causes *jāti* (birth). *Upādāna paccayā bhava* and *bhava paccayā jāti.*

The future Buddha while looking within i.e. while practcing Vipassana must have made a beginning from here. Any serious meditator who concentrates his mind and develops *sati* (awareness) and *sampajañña* (thorough understanding) must make a beginning from here. Then he will very clearly and sharply see different kinds of sensations arising and passing away. The more he sees their impermanent nature the less he craves for them. He begins to develop detachment. Why be attached to even pleasant sensations that are only fleeting?

When the future Buddha came to see the process of how suffering arises, he went deeper to see how it can be ended.[311] He concluded that it could be ended by eliminating desires. This was a second 'eureka' for him, a 'eureka' with higher wisdom. Wisdom dawned upon him. He now knew that the things he desired are impermanent. Till now he was ignorant. He did not know their real nature. So he looked back and saw that till now what he did was because of ignorance. Thus, he came to know the first link, ignorance (*avijjā*), of the chain of causation.

How is one to eliminate suffering? Concentrating more on the process of origin of suffering, the Bodhisatta saw that the only way to eliminate desire - the cause of suffering is not to see sensations as pleasant or unpleasant but to remain equanimous. In other words, one should not react to them. If one remains equanimous, desires arise and pass away. When there is craving for pleasant sensations to continue and for unpleasant ones to stop one multiplies one's miseries. However, once one knows their real nature, one is on the way to develop non-attachment to them. One can do this by cultivating *sati* (awareness) and *sampajañña* (thorough understanding). *Sati* helps to see sensation every moment; moment after moment and *sampajañña* enables one to see it as impermanent. The two together help one develop *nirveda* (non-attachment). This is how suffering can be extirpated. How Vipassana can help one eliminate desires has been explained in my essay entitled 'Mechanism of Vipassana'.[312]There is no other effective way to end suffering. The only effective way is to practice Vipassana and cultivate equanimity. It is not possible to destroy the objects of the five physical senses and the objects of the mind. Nor is it possible to destroy the six bases of sensory organs. They will be there and the sensations which they produce, when they come in contact with their respective sense organs will also be there. The world is full of thorns.

---

311. D2 *Mahāsatipaṭṭhāna Sutta*

312. 'Mechanism of Vipassana' collected in this book

One cannot clear them all. The best way to protect oneself is to wear a pair of shoes. Similarly, the best way not to cause and multiply one's miseries is to not react to sensations and remain equanimous. And this is possible by understanding the impermanent nature of sensations. Continuous practice of Vipassana strengthens *bhāvanāmayā paññā* (wisdom developed from direct, personal experience), which enables one to see reality face to face and ultimately no trace of darkness remains.

How is one to practice Vipassana? This becomes clear if one remembers what the Buddha says about producing fire. The two pieces of dry wood should be continuously rubbed together to produce heat and fire. If they are rubbed off and on, fire cannot be produced. Vipassana should be continuously practiced to see *aniccatā* (impermanence) and develop *nirveda* (non attachment). Continuity of practice is the key to success.

One can know *aniccatā* by practicing *vedanānupassanā* - one of the four *anupassanās* described in detail in the *Mahāsatipaṭṭhāna Sutta*, the other three being *kāyānupassanā, cittānupassanā* and *dhammānupassanā.* These four *anupassanās*[313] are practised to establish oneself in mindfulness.

Vipassana led the Bodhisatta to see that if sensations are left unobserved, the desires caused by them grow stronger and stronger and cause more suffering. If sensations, which are the causes of desires are observed mindfully; their real nature is known. Once their impermanent nature is known at the experiential level, one is less likely to crave for them. This is how Vipassana is an effective means of eliminating desires.

Just as the Bodhisattva saw this process of the origin of suffering and how it can be ended very clearly and became the Buddha, any serious meditator of Vipassana can experience the truth of what the Buddha says about the origin of suffering and how it can be eliminated. He can realize the chain of causation and see its different links.

Vipassana meditation helps a meditator to experience the transitory nature of the body and mind. In the process of investigation of the ultimate reality of mind and matter, one discovers that whenever defilement arises in the mind - two types of changes take place at the physical level. When one is angry, his breath does not remain normal and smooth. It becomes rough. The other change is subtler in nature. It is bio-chemical. It is a sensation. A meditator is taught in a ten-day course to observe both respiration and sensation. Both can be made to act as warning signals if the meditator mindfully observes them. What happens is that most of the time one is not aware of the negativity arising in oneself and as a result reacts blindly and is overpowered by it. A meditator taught to observe one's breath and sensation has at least a few occasions when one clearly sees them and

313. For a detailed description of Vipassana see *Mahāsatipaṭṭhāna Sutta* in D2.

stops reacting blindly. This practice of mindful observation goes a long way in making two things clear to one. First, when any negativity arises in one his breath is not normal and he feels different kinds of sensations. The second thing one learns at the experiential level is that sensations are impermanent. This eventually leads one to develop detachment and remain equanimous. By remaining detached one cuts down one's desires and by remaining equanimous one does not multiply his miseries.

A Vipassana meditator trains himself in *sīla* before he is able to concentrate his mind. By observing *sīla* he promotes the purification of conduct and livelihood. Right speech, right action and right livelihood purify his conduct and livelihood. Then he begins to concentrate his mind by observing the incoming and outgoing breath. In this process, his mind wanders but with right effort he brings it back and developing right mindfulness he develops right concentration. This he does again and again. This is called right effort with *bhāvanāmayā paññā.* This makes his mind sharp and concentrated. With this mind, he begins to observe different sensations arising on his body. With the cultivation of two powerful tools—*sati* and *sampajañña*–he develops the knowledge of *aniccatā* (*aniccatā ñāṇa*). With this direct knowledge, he develops *nirveda* (non-attachment)

The link *vedanā*, therefore, is the most important in the chain of causation. Here one stands at a place where the road forks. If one react to sensations one multiplies his misery. But if one learns to observe the impermanent nature of sensations, does not react and remain equanimous he is on the path to develop wisdom. *Saññā* is gradually replaced by *paññā* (wisdom).

While practicing Vipassana meditation a meditator first begins to observe respiration. By being mindful one also observes the changes that it undergoes. One also sharply notices how changes are brought about. This observation helps him concentrate his mind. With this concentrated and focussed mind, he looks within and sees what sensations are produced when some negativity like anger, hatred etc. arises in the mind. He also experiences how he burns when negativities arise in him. This, he realizes, is undesirable. Who wants to burn? When pleasant sensations arise and he likes to have more of them, he is disappointed to see that they are also impermanent. This experience of *aniccatā* tears his veil of ignorance, and he begins to have a good understanding of this law.

Paṭiccasamuppāda can be explained in four ways. Either one begins from *avijjā* and goes up to *dukkha domanassa* etc. or one begins from *vedanā* and goes up to *dukkha* etc. or one begins from the end i.e. *dukkha domanassa* and traces it to *avijjā* or one begins from *vedanā* and goes up to *avijjā*.

While practicing Vipassana it is best to begin from *vedanā* and realize its different links. It has been explained here how *vedanā* gives rise to *taṇhā, taṇhā* causes *upādāna, upādāna* causes *bhava* and *bhava* causes *jāti, jarā dukkha, domanassa, soka* etc. So the chain from *vedanā to dukkha* becomes clear. But the question is why does one have *vedanā*? What causes *vedanā*? Going deep within, a meditator can see that *vedanā* is caused by *phassa* (contact), which means when a sense organ comes in contact with its respective object. Not only concrete objects like visible and audible cause contact but thoughts also produce contact. And contact is possible because of *nāma* and *rūpa*. The flow of *nāma* and *rūpa* is caused by consciousness i.e. *paṭisandhi viññāṇa*. Going deep one can see that consciousness is caused by a reaction called *saṅkhāra (skt saṃsakāra)*. What is *saṅkhāra*? It is the deed (*kamma*) that one does with volition. But one does these deeds in ignorance.[314] One's blind liking and disliking without understanding the real nature of things cause *saṅkhāra*. And why does one react? It is because one is ignorant of the nature of reality that one reacts to. So, one concludes that *avijjā* is the first link to set in motion this law of causation. One has been reacting blindly since time immemorial and it has become his habit pattern to do so, to react. A Vipassana meditator can come out of this habit pattern by observing respiration and sensation mindfully and having thorough understanding of the impermanent nature of what one desires and what one reacts to.

Practice of Vipassana, therefore, has a twofold function. It does not only make one mentally and bodily pure as one walks on the Noble Eightfold Path, observes *sīla* and practices *samādhi*, but also makes one fit to see how suffering is caused and how it can be ended by attaining *paññā*.

Thus, all the twelve links of *paṭiccasamuppāda*, which cause one to move in the cycle of birth and death, become clear. And this also becomes clear to one - how one can reverse this process and end suffering.

314. D2 (see *Mahānidāna Sutta*).

Buddha's Theory of Kamma and Rebirth

The theory of *kamma* and rebirth propounded by the Buddha is different from the same theory propounded by other Indian philosophical systems. The majority of Indian philosophical systems believe in a permanent soul. They regard this theory as the law of retribution.[315] They also regard it as inexorable. The sower is bound to reap what he has sown. If he has done unwholesome actions he is fated to suffer and if, on the other hand, he has done wholesome actions he is sure to enjoy their fruits. This is a kind of fatalism or determinism. Here the agent is not free. His hands are bound by his past *kammas.* According to the Buddha, on the other hand, it is neither a law of retribution nor it is inexorable. In other words, it is neither fatalism nor determinism. It is just a universal law of cause and effect. Nothing happens without a cause. One's birth is also conditioned by his *kammas.* But whether one will suffer in this life or not suffer or if one suffers the quantum of suffering depends upon what one does in the present life. One is not bound down by his past *kammas.* One is free to act and free to counteract the evil effects of his past *kammas.*[316]

It is true one is born to get the results of what he has done in the previous life, but he is not bound by their results. Had one not been free he would not be held responsible for what he does. If he is destined to be a murderer why expect him not to commit murders? Why hold him responsible for committing murders? If he is not free to choose his actions, he should not be held responsible for what he does.

To a question put by an American to Pandit Jawaharlal Nehru that if you believe in the theory of *kamma* and its fruits, how are you going to ameliorate your conditions since you are fated to reap all that you have sown, Pandit Nehru's reply was that, no doubt, the cards have been dealt out to us, we were not free to choose them but we are free to play them

---

315. What the Upanisads say makes clear that there is a permanent soul and one reaps what one sows. Those who do good deeds in former lives get desirable lives of Brāhmaṇas, Kṣatriyas or Vaiśyas. Those who do not do good deeds are born as Caṇḍālas, dogs or swine. (*Chāndogya Upaniṣad.*) The *Kausītakī Upaniṣad* holds more or less the same view(I.2) The *Bṛhadāraṇyaka Upaniṣad* (IV.4.5) says that one who does wholesome actions will become good and one who does unwholesome actions will become bad. The *Chāndogya Upaniṣad* also says that this law is operated by a superhuman agency. (ibid., V. 10.2).

316. See f.n.21.

the way we like. The huge wheel of *kamma* may come rolling to us, but we are free to dodge it, free to prevent it from harming us, free to make it take another course. The serpent is following us but we are free to protect us from it. In this sense we have freedom'of choice.

The Buddha was a humanist and he saw immense potentiality in man to ameliorate his condition. He saw in him the potentiality to transform his life of suffering to a life of happiness. But he did not believe in a permanent soul. When he was asked if there is no permanent soul, who reaps the fruit of *kamma* done by one, the Buddha's reply was it is neither the same person nor different as very ingeniously explained by Nagasena (*Na ca so na ca añño*).[317] There is rebirth, but the person born is not the same. If it were the same person, how can the results of his *kamma* bring about any change in them? When one did a particular *kamma* one had a certain volition but now one may have a different volition to do *kamma* and this *kamma* may be completely different from the previous one. Although one changes every moment, one does not change completely. The change can be understood as the change from childhood to youth, from youth to adulthood and from adulthood to old age. One does not remain the same but one does not become completely different either.

The law of *kamma* wrongly interpreted makes one a fatalist. One thinks one has to reap what one has sown. One is also made to think so by other people who have their vested interests to serve and who want to exploit a big section of poor and downtrodden people particularly in India with this weapon. According to them one is born poor because of his past *kammas*, one is born in a low caste because of his past *kammas*. This conclusion, according to the Buddha is ridiculous and untenable.

Kamma is the instrument of moral order. It is a *niyāma* just as *ṛtu, bīja, citta* and *dhamma niyāmas* are. There is an order in the physical world. Starry bodies move smoothly without colliding with one another, seasons change, seeds grow into trees and plants and they yield fruits and fruits again give seeds and seeds give bitter or sweet fruits according to their nature. One consciousness gives rise to another. As these *niyāmas* work without fail so does the law of *kamma* operate, but it operates to make one inferior or superior, ugly or beautiful, stupid or wise but not to make one a member of the artficially and unscientifically organised brahman caste or of śūdra caste. The Buddha does not believe in this. Buddha's world view is quite different from the brahmans'world view.

The law of *kamma* applies in the moral world. Dr. Ambedkar rightly says that "the law of *kamma* has to do only with the question of general moral order. It has got nothing to do with the fortunes or misfortunes of

317. See Mil, *Addhāna Vaggo*

an individual."[318] He further says "that the effect of the *kamma* recoils on the doer is not always true." Sometimes the actions of one affect others. The wrongs done by a king do harm to his subjects. His sins visit upon his subjects just as the sins of parents visit upon their children.

In the Brahman *weltanschauung* (world view) the ideal society has four classes which were based on graded inequality and each class engages in an occupation. It is binding on them that no class is to transgress. The soul of this theory is inequality. What was once based on Division of Labour according to one's capacity and ability became one's occupation in virtue of his being born in a particular caste. One's father's occupation began to determine the caste of one's children. Even though the sons of a brahman were not educated and were not able to recite and teach the Vedas they began to call themselves brahmans and others who were able to do that were not allowed to call themselves brahmans and were condemned to remain at the station where their fathers were. With the passage of time brahmans propounded the theory of their origin from the mouth of Brahmā and began to wield the weapon of superiority over others. The law of *kamma* was used as a very effective weapon to condemn those who were looked down upon by them. They were inferior because of their unwholesome actions and the brahmans were superior because of their wholesome actions. The result was that ability and capacity being neglected by the brahmans became the first casualties. What was a changing concept in the beginning became frozen and the society was cursed to be divided into castes and sub castes, which have no scientific basis. The law of *kamma* which operates in the moral realm was made to operate in the social realm and birth in a particular caste was made to depend upon one's action.

The Buddha put forward several scientific, biological, common sense arguments to prove that all people have the same characteristics and are equally capable of attaining spiritual height. The difference found in them is caused by his wholesome or unwholesome actions. Birth in brahmin caste does not make one superior and birth in śūdra caste does not make one inferior. It is one's *kamma* that makes the difference. The concept of caste is not universal but it is India made as said above and made particularly by the clever priests who conceived the idea of exploiting others for their own interest.[319]

The Buddha had a few things in his mind when he propounded the theory of *kamma* and rebirth. He was born in an ethical milieu in which religious leaders like Puraṇa Kassapa and Makkhali Gosāla propounded the

318. B&HD p. 245.

319. See my essay entitled 'Buddha's Law of Kamma and Rebirth vis-à-vis Social Order' collected in this book.

theory of non-action and the theory of fatalism respectively. According to Pūraṇa whatever one does one is not tainted. One is neither defiled by doing unwholesome actions nor one is purified by doing wholesome actions. There is no sin. There is no merit either. Whatever one does, whether one kills or steals or commits adultery or tells a lie one does not do any evil. One does not earn any merit either by giving *dāna* or performing sacrifice. "In giving, self-control, abstinence and telling the truth, there is no merit, and no merit accrues[320].

According to Makkhali Gosala 'there is no cause or condition for the defilement of beings, they are defiled without cause or condition. There is no cause or condition for the purification of beings, they are purified without cause or condition. There is no self-power or other-power, there is no power in humans, no strength or force, no vigour or exertion. All beings, all living things, all creatures, all that lives is without control, without power or strength, they experience the fixed course of pleasure or pain through the six kinds of rebirth.... Both fools and wise have to run on and circle round eight million four hundred thousand aeons till they make an end of suffering[321].'

Ajita Kesakambalī propounded the doctrine of annihilation. "There is nothing given, bestowed, offered in sacrifice, there is no fruit or result of good or bad deeds, there is not this world or the next, there is no mother or father, there are no spontaneously arisen beings... human being is composed of the four great elements, and when one dies the earth part reverts to earth, the water part to water, the fire part to fire, the air part to air, and the faculties pass away into space...Fools and wise, at the breaking-up of the body, are destroyed and perish, they do not exist after death[322].'

Pakudha Kaccāyana said, 'whoever cuts off a man's head with a sharp sword does not deprive any one of life, he just inserts the blade in the intervening space between these seven bodies (*paṭhavī, āpo, tejo, vāyo, sukkha, dukkha* and *jīvitindriya*)[323]

Thus, there was a chaos in society. The masses were confused. 'Why do wholesome actions when we do not earn any merit? Why not do unwholesome ones when they do not harm us? Why not take a loan and enjoy life with dainty dishes as long as we live?'

Yāvajjivet sukhaṃ jīveta, ṛṇaṃ kṛtvā ghṛtaṃ pīvet/
Bhasmībhūtasya dehasya punarāgamanaṃ kutah//

---

320. LDB, p. 94, (see from the translation of *Sāmaññaphala Sutta*)
321. ibid.
322. ibid. p. 96.
323. ibid.

The masses were not inspired by what Pūraṇa Kassapa said. As it is easy to go down the sloping path they did so and did not think it incumbent upon them to live an ethical life and observe moral precepts. To live an ethical life requires exercising control over one's sense organs, requires thinking of others' good and welfare and not of one's own good and welfare. So whether there is rebirth or no rebirth observation of ethical precepts is meaningless as it has no effect.

Ajita Kesakambalī propounded annihilationism. There is no rebirth according to him. And if there is no rebirth, why fear to reap the results of unwholesome actions? 'You do whatever you like to do when you die that is the end of it.' There is no question of suffering as a consequence of doing unwholesome actions.[324]

In Makkhali Gosāla's view man is helpless. He has no strength, no vigour to do something to come out of his suffering. He has been allotted a measure of suffering which he has to experience. Whatever he may do and he cannot do much he will end his suffering only after he passes through the six kinds of rebirth.[325] "Just as a ball of string when thrown runs till it is all unravelled, so fools and wise run on and circle round till they make an end of suffering."[326]

The Buddha was convinced of two things. There is rebirth. People are born again and again so long as the energy produced by their *kammas* is not exhausted. And they do have to reap the fruit in this life or in the next life of what they sow in a certain way unless they counteract it. When they are reborn and it is the energy released by their actions that they are reborn, they have to reap their consequences but not in the mechanical way in which some philosophers interpret. It is true a person is born because of his desire and the results of his actions in one life follow him in the next, but he is not bound to experience their consequences. He is free to make a choice and prevent their consequences from necessarily visiting him.

There are two things to be noted here. Whatever actions one does, their results will follow him and they will follow him in his rebirth because the energy produced by his *kammas* causes one's rebirth. The Buddha's assertion that people are free to choose their actions holds out great hope for humanity. One has freedom to counteract his past *kammas*. Buddha's 'Theory of *Kamma* and Rebirth' does not only say why one should live an ethical life and perform wholesome actions but also avers that one has great potentiality to not only end his suffering as a result of unwholesome actions but to break the cycle of birth and death and attain *nibbāna.*

324. ibid.

325. See *Sāmaññaphala Sutta.*

326. LDB p. 95

In many passages of the Tipiṭaka he says that whatever one does that makes his personality. Whatever he does that shapes his personality. *Taṃ hi tassa sakaṃ hot, taṃ ca ādāya gacchati.*[327] He is what he has done and he will be what he does. It is very clear, therefore, that one is free to choose his action in the present life. If Yama[328] says to somebody, 'since you have done the unwholesome action you alone will have to reap its consequences', it does not mean that he is fated to do so. There is no fatalism in Buddhism. What it implies is that one is responsible for what he does. Nobody else is responsible for it.

Thus, the Buddha propounds the theory of *kamma* and rebirth in such a way that makes one responsible for what he does but gives him freedom to choose his action in the present life to counteract what he did in the past. Whereas other religious teachers do not make one responsible for what he does and yet propound that he will have to reap what he does, the Buddha says that he is responsible for his work no doubt, but he is free to make up the loss that he has incurred in past lives.

That is why the Buddha says in the *Dhammapada* that one does evil by oneself and one defiles oneself. But the story does not end there. It is also as true that one can purify oneself by not doing unwholesome work and by doing wholesome work.

Attanā va kataṃ pāpaṃ, attanā saṃkilissati/
Attanā akataṃ pāpaṃ, attanā va visujjhati/
Suddhī asuddhi paccataṃ, n'āñño aññaṃ visodhaye//[329]

It is very clear from this that a person has freedom to choose his actions. He is not 'cribbed, cabined and confined' by his actions. Well, he is responsible for his actions no doubt, but he is also free to play the cards dealt out to him in the way he likes.

The Buddha asserts that a person is what he does. *Kammassakā, māṇāvā, sattā, kammadāyādā, kammayoni, kammabandhu, kammapaṭisaraṇā, kammā satte vibhajati yadidaṃ hīṇappaṇītatāyāti.* (Student, beings are owners of their actions, heirs of their actions; they originate from their actions, are bound to their actions, have their actions as their refuge. It is action that distinguishes beings as inferior and superior).[330]

---

327. S1 87, *Piya Sutta*

328. A1.163.*Atha kho tayāvetaṃ pāpakammaṃ kataṃ tvaññevetassa vipākaṃ paṭisaṃvedissasī ti.*

329. Dh 165.

330. *Cūḷakammavibhaṅga Sutta* The Shorter Exposition of Action p. 1053 The Middle Length Discourses of the Buddha by Bhikkhu Ñāṇamoli and Bhikkhu Bodhi, Wisdom Publications, Boston, 1995).

One cannot understand the full meaning and implication of this theory unless he tries to understand it in the light of the Law of Dependent Origination. This law says that neither cause nor effect is permanent or stable. Both change every moment. Cause gives rise to effect which in turn becomes cause and in this way the cycle goes on until it stops when the energy moving the cycle is exhausted completely. And this happens when all desires are extirpated.

The Buddha had seen it at the experiential level that sensations produce desire which grows stronger and stronger till there is becoming (*bhava*) followed by birth, old age, disease and sorrow, lamentation etc. Mainly there are three kinds of desire, *kāma taṇhā, bhava taṇhā* and *vibhava taṇhā.*

It is *taṇhā* which is the source of energy to move the cycle of birth and death. This accounts for one's rebirth. All volitional actions are desire producing. So long as one performs his actions impelled by his desires, his actions will produce results which will follow him like his own shadow. But the actions of one who has annihilated all desires are like fried seeds incapable of germination. Arahants also do wholesome actions but such actions are not tainted. They do such actions without desiring any fruit in return.

Now the most important question is if the results of one's actions are so powerful that they can influence and shape the present life of the doer, where do they live? This question has been very ingeniously answered by Nāgasena—one of the finest minds that came after the Buddha. He made it very clear by giving an apt illustration. Can any one say where the fruits that have not yet been produced by the tree live? They come year after year. When they are produced by the tree one sees where they are. But one cannot exactly point out where they live unless they become manifest. Similarly, one cannot exactly point out where the *vipākas* of the actions done by one live. But the actions done by one name and form do follow it like a shadow[331].

There are two questions inseparably connected with the theory of *kamma* and rebirth. The first is if nothing is permanent, if there is no permanent soul who is born and the second question is how rebirth takes place. These two questions also have been as ingeniously answered by Nāgasena. How rebirth takes place can be understood with the help of a few illustrations. When a lamp is lighted by another lamp does one say that the former migrated to the latter? Or when a disciple learns a verse from his teacher does one say that the verse migrated from the teacher to the pupil? This is how rebirth takes place[332].

331. *Milindapañho, Buddhavaggo*

332. ibid., *Buddha Vaggo*

There is another point connected with rebirth. King Milinda asks if there is no being then who is reborn and whether he will be free from all the results of the wholesome and unwholesome actions done by him in the past. Nagasena answers this question brilliantly. He says that what is reborn is because of his actions in the past. A thief who steals mango from a mango tree when caught cannot make a plea and escape from punishment by saying that the mango he stole is not the same mango planted long back in the earth. Can one ever imagine a mango in the absence of a mango tree and can he ever imagine a mango tree without sowing a mango seed in the soil? The mango the thief stole is because of the mango planted in the soil. Therefore, he cannot escape punishment. As a mango fruit comes into being because of the mango tree so one *nāma* and *rūpa* is born because of the actions done in the past. The past actions do influence the rebirth. Nagasena explains how *kamma* influences rebirth by bringing in the process philosophy. This philosophy says that things continue to exist and change at the same time. One cannot imagine curd without milk nor can he ever imagine butter without curd and he cannot imagine the latter two without the former. Here is another example. A fire is burning throughout the night. The fire at 10 o'clock in the night is different from the fire at 8 o'clock in the evening but the latter fire cannot be imagined without the former. A person who made fire at 8 o'clock to warm himself up cannot excuse himself for the loss caused by the spark of that fire at 2 o'clock in the morning saying the fire which caused damage was different from the fire he made.

A girl married early to a man cannot be married to another man and claimed by him as his wife on the ground that she as a grown up woman is different from the girl who was married to the first man.

If a pot of milk turns sour will the milk man not claim the price of the milk given earlier? Will the man be justified in refusing to pay the price to the milk man because the milk has turned sour?

Another important question connected with the theory of *kamma* and rebirth is, "Does he, who is born, remain the same or become another?" Nagasena replies that he is neither the same nor different. Just as a person who commits a crime is the same who gets punishment so what is reborn is not completely different from one who grows up. A child is born, he grows up, he goes to school, he learns from a teacher and when he grows to manhood he may look different but, as a matter of fact, all these states are included in one growing process. Just as in a burning lamp continuity is maintained through change, so continuity in one *nāma* and *rūpa* is maintained through changes. To make it more clear just as continuity is maintained through changes when milk turns into curd, curd into butter, butter into ghee, similarly the continuity of a person or a thing is maintained. One phase or state comes into being, another passes away and the rebirth is as it were simultaneous.[333]

The theory of *kamma* and rebirth underlines two points. First, all actions that one does with defiled mind and he can do even wholesome actions also with defiled mind will have their effects like the third law of Newton which says that every action has equal and opposite reaction. As a result, one is reborn again and again till all his desires (*taṇhā*) are exhausted. Second, the effects of the *kammas* are not inexorable because all *kammas* are not of the same nature. By analysing the function of *kammas* the Buddha proves that out of the four types of *kammas* such as *Janaka kamma* (reproductive), *Upatthambhaka kamma* (supportive), *Upapīdaka kamma* (counteractive) and *Upaghātaka kamma*[334] (destructive) the last two can counteract and destroy other *kammas* which are likely to produce serious *vipākas* (results). *Upapīḍaka kamma* destroys the results (*vipāka*) of other *kammas* and *upaghātaka kamma* destroys weak results and produces its own. How can the result of a *kamma* be destroyed is proved by a beautiful example? A pinch of salt added to a cup of water can make it salty and undrinkable but if it is thrown in a river, the river water will still be drinkable.[335] What it means is this. Unwholesome effects of *kamma* can be more than made good by doing wholesome actions in the present life. One is free to play the cards that he gets from the past life. The message is that one is free to ameliorate his conditions in the present life by walking on the path of *sīla, samādhi* and *paññā.*

333. ibid., *Addhāna Vaggo*

334. See my essay entitled 'The Problem of Kamma and Rebirth as Discussed in the *Milindapañho*' included in my book entitled Essays on Buddhism and Pali Literature, Eastern Book Linkers, Delhi,1994.

335. A1.282 *Loṇakapalla Sutta.*

Ethicisation—an Important Constituent Element of the Buddha-Dhamma

Early Buddhism or Theravāda as a religion is quite different from other religions of the world. Here there is no belief in a superhuman controlling power, nor is there an exhortation or prescription to worship such power whether it is a personal God or gods. As a consequence, there are no rites and rituals that necessarily go with the act of worshipping.

If one reads the history of the religions of the world it becomes clear to them that the origin of many religions is in 'fear'. In the beginning of civilizations when people saw the forces of nature they were terribly afraid of their furies and the havoc they created. The howling wind blowing at a great speed and the flash flood causing enormous destruction and devastation, the rain god pouring incessantly for a number of days struck terror and horror in mankind. They had intuitively learnt that a stronger and more powerful person had to be appeased so that he does not create trouble for others and let them live in peace. They knew how to appease them. By the same token they thought to appease the forces of Nature by supplicating to them, by praying to them and even by offering sacrifices to them. When these forces appeared before them they immediately saw through their great might and realized that they had only little might and strength in comparison to their gigantic and superhuman might and strength. They felt helpless and weak. And it is in this situation that they thought of praying to them. As a consequence, hymns were composed and rites and rituals were performed to placate these furious forces of Nature.

Religion is also said to have originated because people wanted favours from gods or God in whom they believed. Somehow or other they considered themselves lacking in some power because things did not happen the way they wanted them to happen. And so they thought to pray to such gods or God to receive their/His favours who they believed were so powerful that they could, if they wanted, change the course of events in the lives of those people who worshipped to propitiate them. They also prayed to them for wealth and progeny.[336]

On account, perhaps of these causes Sir James George Frazer--the author of the famous 'The Golden Bough' says that, "By religion, then, I understand a propitiation or conciliation of powers superior to man which are believed to direct and control the course of nature or of human life. Thus defined, religion consists of two elements, a theoretical and a practical namely a belief in powers higher than man and an attempt to please them.

336. 357 See the hymns to god of fire, god of wind and Indra etc. in the *Ṛgveda*.

Of the two, belief clearly comes first, since we must believe in the existence of a divine being before we can attempt to please him. But unless the belief leads to a corresponding practice, it is not a religion but merely a theology. In the words of Sir James George Frazer, 'faith, if it hath not works, is dead being alone.' In other words, no man is religious who does not govern his conduct in some measure by the fear or love of God. On the other hand, mere practice, divested of all religious belief, is also not religion."[337]

The author also goes on to make a distinction between religion and morality. How is religion different from morality? He says that "Two people may behave in exactly the same way, and yet one of them may be religious and the other not. If the one acts from the love or fear of God, he is religious, if the other acts from the love or fear of man he is moral or immoral according as his behaviour comports or conflicts with the general good. Hence belief and practice, in theological language, faith and works are equally essential to religion which cannot exist without both of them. But it is not necessary that religious practice should always take the form of a ritual, that is, it need not consist in the offering of sacrifice, the recitation of prayers, and other outward ceremonies. Its aim is to please the deity and if the deity is one who delights in charity and mercy and purity more than in oblations of blood, the chanting of hymns and the fumes of incense, his worshippers will best please him not by prostrating themselves before him, by intoning his praises and by filling his temples with costly gifts but by being pure and merciful and charitable towards people for in so doing they will imitate so far as human infirmity allows the perfection of the divine nature. It was this ethical side of religion which the Hebrew prophets inspired with a noble ideal of God's goodness and holiness were never weary of inculcating. Micah says, 'He hath showed thee, o man, what is good and what doth the Lord require of thee, but to do justly and to love mercy and to walk humbly with thy God?'"[338]

The author further goes on to say, "But if religion involves, first a belief in superhuman beings who rule the world and second an attempt to win their favour, it clearly assumes that the course of nature is to some extent elastic or variable and that we can persuade and induce the mighty beings who control it to deflect for our benefit the current of events from the channel in which they would otherwise flow. Now this implied elasticity or variability of nature is directly opposed to the principles of magic as well as of science both of which assume that the processes of nature are rigid and invariable in their operation."[339]

337. Sir James George Frazer, The Golden Bough 1922.

338. ibid.

339. ibid.

As far as early Buddhism is concerned, we find that the Buddha does not believe in the gods and God with a capital "G" who control the course of nature. He also does not believe that the course of nature is elastic or variable. He believes in universal laws which operate without fail. These laws are the laws of Nature. If there were gales and hurricanes, if there were dark clouds pouring incessantly, if there were lightning in the sky, if there were scorching rays of the sun, if there were great floods in the rivers, it was because they followed certain laws of Nature. They were not caused by angry gods. He also pointed out that as such phenomena happen in the outside world because of the laws of Nature operating inexorably so many things that happen within us also follow the laws of Nature as inexorably. Just as the nature of fire is to burn, so is the nature of enmity. One who has enmity is sure to burn. Enmity cannot be ended by enmity as fire cannot be put out by fire.[340] He said that a mind which is not controlled can do us greater harm than an enemy can do to us. Similarly a mind which is controlled can do us greater good than our parents can do to us.[341] because mind is the spring of all actions good or bad. These are laws of Nature, eternal laws of Nature (*Dhammo sanantano*). Just as some physical laws operate unfailingly in the physical world so some laws operate as unfailingly in the spiritual world. By giving such examples he was able to disabuse one's minds of believing in the furies of Nature calculated to do him harms and also of the superstitious belief in worshipping and placating them to be kind to him and save him from destruction and death. He was also able to drive out fear from one's minds. Why does fear arise in one? It arises because of one's ignorance. If one understands that whatever happens in Nature happens because of certain laws he will be reconciled to them and learn to take things in their true light. When one is able to understand the laws that operate within him he is sure to learn how to get rid of unpleasant things that happen to one.

What is religion? What is the function of religion? Why do people live a religious life? Religion, as one understands it, is philosophy and ethics put into practice. In other words, when philosophy becomes one's 'conduct in life' it is religion. The function of religion, according to the Buddha is to make one inculcate those values that people live by and make one's life happy and peaceful. If one lives in peace and harmony and lets others also live in peace and harmony he is religious. Another function of religion is to make one spiritually richer and more sublime. He must be able to cultivate and practice the four *Brahmavihāras* such as loving kindness (*mettā*),

340. Dh.5 Na hi verena verāni, sammantīdha kudācanaṃ.

341. Dh 43 Na taṃ mātā pitā kayirā, aññe vā pi ca ñātakā/Sammāpaṇihitaṃ cittaṃ, seyyaso naṃ tato kare//

compassion (*karuṇā*), sympathetic joy (*muditā*) and equanimity (*upekkhā*). Yet other function of religion is to end all kinds of suffering such as physical, and mental which one is subject to. Suffering is an existential problem of all beings because it is a ubiquitous fact of life. The Buddha said that suffering is caused by craving. This he explained with the help of the Law of Dependent Origination. Nothing is uncaused. Therefore if the cause is removed the effect will cease to be. But how to get rid of craving? How to eliminate and extirpate craving? For eliminating craving he said that by walking on the Noble Eightfold Path one can destroy his cravings and put an end to his suffering. Cravings cause one's bondage. They bind him to the wheel of life and death. Walking on the Noble Eightfold Path is a sure means of ending one's suffering and attaining liberation. Therefore, walking on the Noble Eightfold Path is religion.

The philosophy of the Buddha has an in-built action-plan. This may be contested by scholars who will say that every Indian philosophy has an in-built action-plan to execute it. But there is a difference. The Buddha's philosophy, as we know, grew not out of his intellectual quest for reality but from his realization, from his wisdom attained at the experiential level. This he called absolute knowledge (*yathābhūtañāṇadassana*) which was possible by practicing Vipassana meditation. If other systems of philosophy had some kind of technique of meditation to put them into practice we do not know much about them. Besides, even if they had some kind of technique it was coloured by their belief in theism. But we know how the Buddha attained wisdom by practicing Vipassana meditation. He has also left the details of the technique for us to learn, practice and develop. When we see the truth as it is with the knowledge gained at the experiential level, we grow wise, purge our minds of different kinds of defilements like greed, aversion, anger, jealousy and so on and then we live a religious life. So long as these defilements are there in our minds we are bound to work under their influence. And so long as we work under their influence we cannot live in peace. We will keep on burning with the fires of these defilements. A truly religious person will make an attempt to put them out. They will not allow them to have their way and burn them. If the purpose of religion is to make one 'cool and quenched', happy and peaceful and free one from all kinds of troubles, then these fires will have to be extinguished. How to put out these fires? How to extinguish them is the question of all questions which the Buddha is primarily concerned to answer. In other words, the function of religion, according to the Buddha, is to enable one to live a virtuous life which will be possible only when the fires of defilements are put out.

There are many fires which burn mankind. Each mental defilement is a fire but the main fire is craving which is at the root of all our sufferings. Therefore, without wasting time to find out the answers to metaphysical questions such as whether the world is eternal or not eternal, whether the life principle is the same as the body and whether the Tathāgata is or is not or both or neither after dying. He calls these questions indeterminate and finds them useless and not at all profitable for putting an end to suffering and attaining *nibbāna* He explained it at length in the *Cūlamālunkya Sutta* in the *Majjhima Nikāya*. He, like a pragmatic philosopher, exhorts people to walk on the Noble Eightfold Path to achieve the *summum bonum* of life. Liberation from the cycle of birth and death as also freedom from suffering are the supreme goals of life. These goals can be achieved by practicing religion. He was convinced that practicing religion alone can enable one to end suffering and attain Arhatship. Therefore, in the words of T.W. Rhys Davids he 'not only ignored the whole of the soul theory, but even held all discussions as to the ultimate soul problems with which the Vedānta and the other philosophies were chiefly concerned, as not only childish and useless but as actually inimical to the only ideal worth striving after—the ideal of a perfect life, here and now, in the present world, in Arahatship.'[342]

But which religion? As I said earlier, the Buddha's view of religion is quite different. In order to understand his view of religion one has to take into account the social milieu and religious atmosphere that prevailed during his time. If one looks at the social milieu and religious atmosphere he will find that there was a veritable chaos at that time. There were religious leaders like Pūraṇa Kassapa, Makkhali Gosāla, Ajita Kesakambalī, Pakudha Kaccāyana and Sañjaya Vallaṭṭhaputta who did not believe in ethical values. Pūraṇa Kassapa propounded the theory of non-action and said that if one kills, steals and commits adultery, no evil is done by him. 'If with a razor-sharp wheel one were to make of this earth one single mass and heap of flesh, there would be no evil as a result of that. No evil would accrue... In giving, self- control, abstinence and telling the truth, there is no merit, and no merit accrues.'[343] According to Makkhali Gosāla 'there is no cause or condition for the defilement of beings, they are defiled without cause or condition. There is no cause or condition for the purification of beings, they are purified without cause or condition. There is no self-power or other power, there is no power in humans, no strength or force or vigour or exertion... Just as a ball of string when thrown runs till it is all unravelled, so fools and wise run on and circle round till they make an end of suffering.'[344] Thus one finds that Makkhali Gosāla was a fatalist or a determinist. Ajita Kesakambali was an annihilationist. He said,' there is nothing given, bestowed, offered in sacrifice, there is no fruit or result of

342. BHL p. 39
343. LDB, p. 94
344. ibid. pp. 94-95

good or bad deeds, there is not this world or the next, there is no mother or father... Fools and wise, at the breaking-up of the body, are destroyed and perish, they do not exist after death.'[345] Pakudha Kaccāyana believed that 'there are seven things which are not made. They are uncreated, unproductive, barren and false ... thus there is neither slain nor slayer, neither hearer nor proclaimer, neither knower nor causer of knowing.'[346] Sañjaya Velaṭṭhaputta evaded all questions that were put to him and did not commit himself to any view.[347]

None of them believed in the theory of *kamma* and rebirth, none of them gave importance to purity of conduct, none of them put a premium on ethical values and none of them believed that one can attain his salvation by making efforts. They believed that salvation is possible not with human effort but it happens when the time comes. They did not believe in living an ethical life. One may commit several murders but will not reap any evil consequence. In short, the atmosphere prevailing at that time was most chaotic, unethical and unreligious.

The Buddha saw through all these perceptively. He wondered how people could live in peace and harmony in society if there are no ethical rules to follow. If killing, stealing and indulging in adultery are not checked, if they are allowed to become the order of the day there will be chaos in human society. There will be no peace and harmony. Besides, one will not exercise restraint on mental defilements like greed, aversion, anger etc. and instead of one getting over them they will control one and cause their ruin. And so long as these defilements are allowed to have their way, how can one be able to control his mind which is so fickle that it leads one by the nose. And if one does not control his unsteady mind, how can he put it to good use. Therefore, the first thing the Buddha wanted one to do is to make his mind pure, In other words, he wanted one to free his mind from defilements that make one indulge in many wrongful acts. His exhortation to observe at least five precepts is a great step forward to enable one to lead an ethical and religious life. It is by observing these precepts that one will be able to lessen his defilements like craving and aversion and finally drive them out of his mind.

When the Buddha explained the cause of suffering through the Law of Dependent Origination he made it crystal clear that if the cause of suffering is removed, suffering will end. And craving which is the cause of one's suffering can be rooted out only when one understands the impermanent nature of worldly reality and develops non-attachment to

345. ibid. pp. 95-96
346. ibid. p. 96
347. ibid. p. 97.

it. To develop this, it is incumbent on one to realize at the experiential level the true nature of reality with which one interfaces. To realize this, controlling of mind is the first requisite and mind can be controlled when efforts are made and defilements like greed and aversion that agitate one are eliminated. Observing precepts, therefore, is a necessary condition of controlling one's mind which will enable him to see reality clearly. In short, observing ethical precepts will enable one to control his mind which, in turn, will enable him to see reality as it is. As he had realized that all things of the world are in a constant state of flux i.e. whatever arises passes away he was sure people will realize the same at the experiential level if they practice Vipassana meditation. On realizing the transitoriness of things they will develop non-attachment to worldly things that cause cravings and will become free from them. In other words, they will end their suffering. This precisely is the goal of religion.

That is why he ethicized the concept of religion. Not that the idea of observing ethical precepts was not there in other religions. It was very much there in all theocentric religions. But it did not get as much importance as devotion to God did. Somehow or other observing precepts was subordinated. Like Lord Mahāvira the Buddha made ethics supremely important. He said human beings must observe ethical precepts to live a religious life. *Sīla* (virtue) is the foundation on which the edifice of religion can be built. One cannot think of being religious without observing precepts though one can be religious without believing in God. One cannot think of cultivating qualities which can ennoble one, can fill their hearts with the milk of human kindness and softness without observing ethical precepts. How can one kill, steal, commit adultery, tell a lie, take intoxicants and be religious? In theocentric religions kind God had to take the responsibility of absolving people committing wrongful acts of sins if they came to his refuge. But in the Buddha-Dhamma there was no scope of being absolved of sins by some higher power. The Buddha-Dhamma is homocentric. One has to act oneself to be rid of unwholesome acts. How can one have defilements like greed, anger and yet be religious? How can one become religious without his having qualities like kindness, generosity, sympathy and truthfulness? Therefore, observing moral precepts was very necessary. In a homocentric religion like the Buddha-Dhamma Ethics was seated on a high pedestal. But this is not all. This, according to him, is only the first step. There are other equally important steps to take before one becomes truly religious and achieves the highest goal of religion. But to observe ethical precepts is the first and most important step. When it is said that the Buddha ethicised the concept of religion what precisely is meant is that in order to practice religion one should walk on the Noble Eightfold Path which consists of not only *sīla* (precepts) but also *samādhi* (concentration of mind) and *paññā* (insight wisdom). An in-depth analysis of Buddha-Dhamma makes it clear that the Buddha has great faith in the spiritual potentiality of man, sees him not as a fly, helpless and weak but as the maker of his own destiny. Man, according to him is supremely capable of going deep into the causes of his suffering. One understands what is good for him and without passing the buck on to some invisible forces for his suffering he accepts full responsibility for it and makes effort to walk on the Noble Eightfold Path to lead a good ethical life to end it. He makes effort to control his fickle and unsteady mind and sees for himself with his *paññā* (wisdom), which he develops by seeing the impermanent nature of things, however beautiful and attractive they seem to be, at the experiential level, develops non-attachment (*nirveda*) to them, cuts down or extirpates his cravings for them and proportionately becomes free from suffering. What one finds here is the Buddha's unshakeable faith in humans and this is his humanism. This has been analyzed in one of my essays.[348]

The goal of religion, according to the Buddha, is to be free from burning with craving and aversion which are at the root of all one's sufferings and experience coolness and happiness. Now what is happiness? In the words of George Grimm, "it is but the dissolution of a tormenting *thirst* or craving through its satisfaction. We consider the attainment of any possession or goal as happiness only when we had *striven* for them formerly, i.e. when we had a craving for them. This happiness will be the greater, the stronger the craving now stilled had been whereas it will be absolute when the craving has been annihilated forever."[349].

Schopenhauer sees in 'will' the cause of suffering. His concept of 'will' is almost the same as the Buddha's concept of craving (*taṇhā*). "Who so has uprooted craving, what should he strive for any more?"[350] the Buddha says in one of his dialogues.

According to the Buddha, craving (*taṇhā* or *tṛṣṇā*) as has been said above, is at the root of all one's suffering and when this craving is annihilated one is free from suffering.

Schopenhauer says almost the same thing when he says, "That we feel so unspeakably happy if set free for a moment from the grim urgency of willing, leaves us to conjecture how blissful must be the life of a man whose will is wholly stilled; freed from the torments of desire and fear he observes smilingly the illusory phantasms of this world which had beset and tormented him, like chessmen scattered about the board after the

348. Angraj Chaudhary, An In-Depth Analysis of Early Buddha-Dhamma, Somaiya Publications Pvt Ltd, Mumbai, 2003.

349. Buddh Wisd, p. 47

350. ibid., p. 48. This question of the Buddha is quoted here.

game is ended. If we picture to ourselves the heavenly peace of such a life we shall hunger for it from the depths of our own misery and despair, since willing (in the guise of greed, fear, envy, anger) binds us fast, pulling us hither and thither with a thousand cords."[351]

Interpreting this Grimm goes on to say, "Just consider a man who has *no* further will, who has caused this 'deepest, darkest, most mysterious force of nature' to disappear, who thus no longer is compelled to use his cognizing-apparatus for satisfying any thirst or desire! Could there be anything more sublime, more peaceful than this absolute willlessness?"[352]

Although Schopenhauer speaks of genius-like viewing of things so that the cognition of things should be perfect, he cannot view things perfectly. He finds himself swallowed by the 'immeasurable ocean of will'[353] and he finds no means to escape it. As far as understanding at the intellectual level is concerned one may not find any difference between the Buddha and Schopenhauer. Both talk of different degrees of cognition when they say that a peculiar mode of looking at things must be developed so that things are seen with genius-like cognition. What does this cognition consist in? It 'consists in an extraordinary deepening of the normal manner of looking at things.'[354]

What Schopenhauer calls 'genius-like cognition' I would like to call 'saint-like or *arhat*-like cognition.'

But how to develop it? Schopenhauer, like Heraclites, did not know. Heraclites also propounded the philosophy of flux. Things are constantly changing. Nothing is permanent. Every thing is in a constant state of flux. One cannot take bath in the same river twice. The Buddha says the same thing. But why is it that Heraclites and Schopenhauer could not become the Buddha? To my mind the answer lies in the fact that the Buddha talks of a *paññā* (wisdom) which is known as *bhāvanāmayī paññā* i.e. the wisdom that develops at the experiential level. There is a world of difference between knowledge gained through intellect and one gained through experience. The latter enables one to see things more clearly than the former. One is able to see things not with a 'dull gaze' but with a 'genius-like' or 'arhat-like' gaze. When one sees at the experiential level that all things of the world are not permanent but are constantly changing one develops non-attachment and does not have craving for it. This realization goes a long way in making him extirpate desires and becoming willless which is the precondition for annihilating suffering. Neither Heraclites nor Schopenhauer could discover

351. WWR, Vol.. I
352. Buddh Wisd, p. 49.
353. DBRR, p. 53.
354. ibid. p. 50.

and map out any path by walking on which one can develop that 'genius-like' or 'arhat-like' vision to see the real nature of things, develop non-attachment to them, destroy the desires caused by them, thereby root out the cause of suffering and ultimately put an end to it. The Buddha does this magnificently. He does not only know but also he sees. In the *Mūlapariyāya Sutta* the Buddha has shown that only he can have real knowledge who has become free from craving, aversion and ignorance i.e. who has become a *khīṇāsava* and it is he alone who can know the true nature of reality. It means that only an arhat can have correct cognition of things and one who has correct cognition of things can be an arhat in the true sense of the term. An arhat is the embodiment of real knowledge and non-attachment that follows from real knowledge.[355]

The difference between Schopenhauer and the Buddha has been clearly brought out by George Grimm. "That these two, Schopenhauer and the Buddha, did not see quite the same from the mountain of knowledge, is explained first by the fact that Schopenhauer, so to say, had only climbed the first slopes of the mountain, while the Buddha from the summit 'looked down into this world of pain.' Schopenhauer, the man of will, convinced as he was of the impossibility of influencing his will, was incapable of making any attempt to develop within himself the genius' mode of contemplation, but had to wait in patience till a lucky hour of itself should bring a cognition more or less free from willing, the depth and duration of which he was unable in any way to determine. The Buddha, on the other hand, who by the extreme purity of his entire mode of life, in advance had cleansed his cognition from all the perturbations of willing, had thus acquired the power of transporting himself, at will and for as long as he liked, into the deepest contemplation, to remain in a state of pure cognition, wherein the whole truth of the world then revealed itself to him." [356]

There is a second difference between the two. Whereas Schopenhauer applied himself to explaining 'the primary phenomena in the individual and in the whole as the world' and saw the "ideas" as the form of these primary phenomena and as their content the immeasurable ocean of will, the Buddha, without caring at all for explaining the phenomena, wanted to find the end of suffering. 'Strait gate' to that realm where there is no suffering disclosed itself to him. He entered this realm.[357]

Religion, according to the Buddha, is purity of conduct, purity of mind. A truly religious one is free from all defilements of mind and all his actions

---

355. See my article entitled '*The Mūlapariyāya Sutta*—a Treatise of Buddhist Epistemology and Ontology' collected in E BP L.

356. ibid., pp. 52-53.

357. DBRRM p. 53.

mental, vocal and physical are wholesome actions—actions that have wholesome roots like non-greed, non-hatred and wisdom. To purify mind from all defiling factors such as craving, aversion etc is the quintessence of the Buddha's teachings. With his deep experience and profound insight, he arrived at the conclusion that to get rid of suffering, craving (*taṇhā*) has got to be rooted out. But how to annihilate it? By bringing about a spiritual change in oneself. And what is this spiritual change? It consists in understanding the real nature of things, attaining wisdom and developing *nirveda* (non-attachment) at the experiential level.

This is possible by walking on the Noble Eightfold Path. *Sīla* is one of the constituents of this path. The Buddha said emphatically that concentration of mind and attainment of wisdom to see things clearly are not possible without observing five basic moral precepts. If one does not kill, steal, commit adultery, tell a lie and take intoxicants one will be able to control his mind which, in turn, will enable him to see the real nature of things. When one does this, he realizes that things are not permanent. They arise to pass away. This realization enables him to develop non -attachment to things which previously were the causes of craving.

Like the Hebrew prophets the Buddha concerned himself with the ethical side of religion which is more or less the same in the two religions. However, there is one basic difference. Whereas the Hebrew prophets and people practice ethical codes out of fear of or reverence to God the Buddha wanted one to observe five precepts not out of fear of any god but out of conviction gained by his own reasonable thinking. He should practice them to drive out various defilements from his mind, make it pure, be merciful and kind and compassionate, and 'walk humbly and do justly.' As far as eliminating defilements from the mind is concerned 'Early Buddhism' lays great emphasis on walking on the Noble Eightfold Path and working out one's own salvation. As far as kindness and compassion are concerned one finds great concern for them in Mahāyāna Buddhism. The concept of Bodhisattva that developed in Mahāyāna Buddhism has this sublime aim, "I will not enter into *nibbāna* so long as there is even one suffering being in the world." What a great concern for the well-being of all beings! What great and sublime altruism!

The philosophy of the Buddha is homocentric as said above. He regards humans as the centre and circumference of his philosophy which does not mean that he cares less for other beings. It also does not mean that man is regarded as superior so that he can exploit other beings and nature for his own comfort. But he regards man as having immense potentiality to ameliorate his conditions. He has arrived at the conclusion that man is responsible for his miseries and it is he who can, by his efforts, come out of them. The Buddha could see with his wisdom (*paññā*) that it is one's mind that binds him to the wheel of existence and as a consequence causes his suffering but it is his mind once again which can liberate him from this inexorable bondage. The Buddha's understanding of the psychology of one's mind is very deep. "The mental natures are the results of what we have thought, are created by our thoughts, are made up of our thoughts. If one speaks or acts with an evil thought, sorrow follows them as a consequence even as the wheels follow the foot of the drawer i.e. the ox which draws the cart."[358] And happiness follows if one acts with a wholesome or pure thought.

One's mind is the spring of all his actions, good or bad. So, sorrow and happiness proceed from his mind. But the nature of mind is very fickle and unsteady. This has got to be controlled and it can be controlled by walking on the Noble Eightfold Path. One's mind is not steady because it works under the influence of desires. If one wants to eliminate or reduce one's desires he himself can do so by walking on the Noble Eightfold Path. The Buddha says that 'self is the lord of self, what higher self could there be?[359] Purity and impurity depend on one's own self. No one can purify another. A person can purify oneself. One can be an island to his own self. The Buddha's assertion that one can put an end to his suffering appeals to all. Even confirmed atheists also have a lot of hope to achieve the highest good without believing in and depending on God or gods.

Lord Buddha was the wisest and most rational and pragmatic philosopher of all philosophers of the world. Like Plato he was shorn of all kinds of emotionalism. Swami Vivekananda says about the Buddha, "And consider his marvellous brain. No emotionalism. That great brain was never superstitious."[360] He further says "See the sanity of the man. No gods, no angels, no demons, nobody. Nothing of the kind. Stern, sane, every brain cell perfect and complete, even at the moment of death."[361] He was so sane and perfect that he always advised his disciples not to follow him blindly nor to take for granted what he said without weighing the pros and cons of his words but he wanted their faith (*sraddhā*) in him to be illumined by *prajñā* (wisdom). In the *Kesamutti Sutta* what he says is that one do only that which he finds for his benefit and good and for other's benefit and good and not blindly follow others however logical and great they may appear to be.

---

358. Dh 1&2 *Manopubbaṅgamā dhammā, mano seṭṭhā manomayā/Manasā ce paduṭṭhena, bhāsati vā karoti vā/Tato naṃ dukkhamanveti, cakkaṃ va vahato padaṃ//*

....

Tato naṃ sukhamanveti, chāyā'va anapāyinī//

359. Dh160 *Attā hi attano nātho, ko hi nātho paro siyā.*

360. Prabuddha Bhārata, Vol. 88, quoted from an article entitled 'The Marvellous Brain Buddha' p. 187.

361. ibid.

The Dhamma that he taught produces results in this very life here and now. He says, "come and see" and if one practices his teachings one reaps fruits here and now and not in distant future as other religions promise.

Whereas ethicization, on the one hand, results in not necessarily believing in God or other super powers for one's salvation, on the other hand, it results in a belief in the results of *kamma* and rebirth. Wholesome actions guarantee entry into heaven and unwholesome actions result in torture and punishment in hell if one believes in heaven and hell. If one does not believe in them wholesome actions will do one good here and now. Compared to the philosophical and ethical theories propounded by the Buddha's contemporary thinkers like Pūraṇa Kassapa, Makkhaligosāla, Ajita Kesakambalī and Pakudha Kaccāyana who did not believe in *kamma* and rebirth according to one's actions and consequently denied their importance and who believed in what is called the helpless nature of man and in fatalism, his ethical theory for people's pollution and purification is logical and holds out a hope for humankind to ameliorate their condition because they have the capacity and freedom of choice to extricate themselves from the bondage of suffering. His theory is really *par excellence.*

In one of my essays entitled 'Buddhism: Where Philosophy and Religion Converge'[362] I have shown that the Buddha did not only propound a philosophy like most of the philosophers of the world but in his philosophy there is a built-in action plan which when executed becomes religion. His explanation of the causes of suffering through the Law of Dependent Origination is philosophy which is based on one's sound psychology but his exhortation to walk on the Noble Eightfold Path and live a *brahmacariya* life to extirpate the cause of suffering and experience *nibbānic* bliss is religion. For attaining *paññā vimutti* (release by knowledge) seven limbs of wisdom (*bojjhaṅgas*) have to be developed, they depend for their perfection on the four arisings of mindfulness (*sati paṭṭhāna*) which in turn depend upon three wholesome actions, physical (*kāyika*), vocal (*vācika*) and mental (*mānasika*). For these actions to be good and wholesome a perfect control of the sense-faculties is needed which is developed by mindfulness and comprehension. These are perfected by wise consideration (*yonisomanasikāra*) which is possible only when there is faith which in turn grows from listening to true Dhamma and this is possible by 'following after the worthy man (*sappurisa sevana*)'

In order to live a *brahmacariya* life one has to work hard and walk on the Noble Eightfold Path observing precepts and practicing meditation.

362. See my essay entitled 'Buddhism: Where Philosophy and Religion Converge' in 'Buddhism in India and Abroad' Somaiya publication, Mumbai,1999.

Tumhehi kiccamātappaṃ akkhātāro tathāgatā.[363] The Tathāgatas only show the path. One has to work out one's own salvation by walking on the Noble Eightfold Path as said by the Buddha in the *Gaṇaka Moggallana Sutta* in the *Majjhima Nikaya.*

I have also shown in the essay referred to above that the Buddha says it clearly that unless one undertakes the journey and sets one's foot one cannot reach the goal. That is why the Buddha's teachings contain a large number of active action-words like *āsevati* (practice), *bhāveti* (to increase), *ghaṭati* (to exert oneself), *vāyamati* (to strive) and *uṭṭhahati* (to arise to exert oneself). It is clear from the tone and tenor of the teachings of the Buddha that religion is not passive thinking but active doing. Walking on the Noble Eightfold Path requires tremendous strength and great exertion. One walks on the path, lives an ethically pure life, drives out defilements from his mind and thus makes his conduct pure. This is religion. Vipassana form of meditation, if practiced sincerely, can make one really religious because this goes a long way in purifying his mind and achieving a calm state of it which is the goal of religion. Observing precepts (virtue) is an integral part of practicing Vipassana. The Buddha himself said in answer to a question that

> *"When a wise one, established well in virtue,*
> *Develops consciousness and understanding,*
> *Then as a bhikkhu ardent and sagacious,*
> *One succeeds in disentangling the tangles."*[364]

and underlined the importance of observing ethical precepts in living a religious life and extirpating cravings.

363. Dh276.

364. Vism 2 *Sīle patiṭṭhāya naro sapañño, cittaṃ paññañca bhāvayaṃ/Ātāpī nipako bhikkhu, so imaṃ vijaṭaye jaṭanti//*

Buddha's Concept of Mind and World Peace

How can peace be promoted in the world? Who can promote it? What role does mind have to play in planting peace in the world? What is the Buddha's concept of mind? Unless one knows the answers to these questions one will not be able to show the role of the Buddha's concept of mind for promoting world peace.

The *Citta Vagga* of the *Dhammapada* describes the nature of mind, particularly of the realm of desire (*kāmāvacara Bhūmi*). According to the Buddha there are four planes of consciousness. A consciousness of the *kāmāvacara* plane is very fickle. It is also very difficult to guard and control. But as a man undertakes his spiritual journey from *Kāmāvacara* plane to *Lokuttara* plane the difficult-to-guard and control mind becomes very well- guarded and very well -controlled because one making his spiritual journey drives out all the disturbing factors called *nīvaraṇas* like *kāmacchanda, byāpāda* etc.and becomes wiser and wiser as he progresses from *Kāmāvacara* to *Rūpāvacara* to *Arūpāvacara and* finally to *Lokuttara plane.* This journey is undertaken on the path of *sādhanā* and the purpose of it is, among other things, to control the mind as well as to purify it from different defilements.

Buddha's concept of mind, therefore, is psycho-ethical. The nature of mind described here is not only based on psychology but also on ethics. This concept, therefore, is a happy union of 'what is' and 'what ought to be'. The *Cittavagga* of the *Dhammapada* describes mind as unsteady (*phandanaṃ*) fickle (*capalaṃ*), difficult to guard (*durakkhaṃ*), difficult to control (*dunnivārayaṃ*), hard to check (*duniggaha*) swift (*lahuno*) and goes wherever it likes to go (*yatthakāmanipātino*). Another set of characteristics of mind is that it is difficult to perceive (*sududdasaṃ*), very subtle (*sunipuṇaṃ*), faring far (*duraṅgamaṃ*), wandering alone (*ekacaraṃ*), bodyless (*asariraṃ*) and lying in a cave (*guhāsayaṃ*). The last two characteristics make it clear that the mind is imperceptible, immaterial and colourless. Although the Buddha never said where consciousness resides it has been said by later scholars like Buddhaghosa that *hadayavatthu* is the seat of consciousness.

So this mind is the spring (*Gangotrī*) of all actions good or bad. The *Yamaka Vagga* of the *Dhammapada* underlines the importance of mind when it says that mind is the forerunner of all states, good or evil (*Manopubbaṅgamā Dhammā*). Mind is the chief (*manoseṭṭhā*) and all states good or evil are made of mind (*manomayā*). That mind is the spring of all actions is the psychology of mind but actions are categorized as wholesome and unwholesome. Therefore, it has been simultaneously studied here how mind works and what it is influenced by. It has been said that there are six roots of actions. Greed (*lobha*) aversion (*dosa*) and ignorance (*moha*) are the unwholesome roots of actions and under their influence actions done are unwholesome. The wholesome roots of actions are non-greed (*alobha*) non-aversion (*adosa*) and non-ignorance (*amoha*). Actions performed under the influence of these roots of actions are wholesome. This study of mind brings one to the domain of ethics.

If one wants to make progress on the spiritual path he is required to get rid of all defilements which are negative and harmful. In other words, he has to be free from all that drag him from the path of *sādhanā* and all such negative forces have to be supplanted by positive forces—the forces that enable him to smoothly make progress on this path.

The Buddha says epigrammatically—'I declare that volition is *kamma.*'[365] So, if one's volition is bad his actions will be bad. If his volition is good his actions will be good. To plant peace and not to wage a war in the world is a positive outlook on life. It has been said by Dr. Radhakrishnan that war actually begins in the mind of man which implies that peace also begins in the mind of man. Unless one's mind is purged of all negative forces there can be no peace in one's mind and consequently there can be no peace in the world.

We have seen that mind is the fountainhead of all actions. Therefore, going to war and fighting are all prompted by our mind. This mind must be evil because it works under the influence of defilements like pride, superiority complex, greed and aversion. Why does one go to war? Either because he hates the people for some reason or other and tries to subjugate them or he has an eye on their wealth or he likes to expand his kingdom or territory or influence. Or he might have his eyes on some rare important minerals of that country. Hitler made a holocaust of the Jews because he hated them and considered his race superior to all the races of the world. He considered himself a pure Aryan. In recent times Americans have their eyes on Iraq's oil. So they want to invade Iraq on one pretext or the other. Individuals fight among themselves on account of these defilements because they also have greed and aversion and other negativities in them.

So unless one purges his mind of these defilements he cannot fill his heart with love and compassion which are necessary conditions for planting peace in the world. So long as one burns with the fires of jealousy, pride and superiority complex there is no chance of his being able to promote and plant peace in the world.

---

365. A2.120: DhsA133 *Cetanāhaṃ, bhikkhave, kammaṃ vadāmi, cetayitvā kammaṃ karoti kāyena vācāya manasā*

We know that *rāga*, *dosa* and *moha* are the roots of unwholesome actions. Out of these *moha* (ignorance) is the greatest of all because *rāga* and *dosa* are caused by *moha*. If *moha* is replaced by *paññā*, *rāga* and *dosa* will cease to be or at least will be considerably reduced.

The question is how to go about developing our wisdom or attaining knowledge so that primary defilements like *rāga* and *dosa* and secondary defilements like pride, superiority complex hatred and others will be eliminated. In Buddhist Literature there is a book called *Visuddhimaggo* or The Path of Purification where it has been described in detail as to how to go about purging our mind of defilements and making it pure. All steps of walking on the Noble Eightfold Path have been set forth very lucidly and scientifically here. Because individuals make a nation, therefore, it is the primary duty of individuals to practice meditation in such a way that their minds are purified. Only a pure mind with roots of *kusala kamma* can think of love, compassion and peace. Only such an ennobled mind can enable one's heart to be filled with the milk of human kindness and if all people experience this divine feeling within themselves there can be no war. Therefore, some thinkers have gone to the length of saying that the Heads of States must practice the four *Brahmavihāras* like *mettā, karuṇā, muditā and upekkhā* in order that they may not ever feel inclined to go to war with any other nation in the world. These sublime feelings will also enable them to think of the Comity of Nations where all nations will have equal rights, where no nation, howsoever small, will be browbeaten by other big and powerful nations and where all of them will lay their heads together to think only of the weal and welfare of humanity as a whole. It is precisely for this reason that Plato brings in the concept of the Philosopher king. The king has to be a philosopher not like Leibnitz but like a real religious man. He should be a religious man not in the sense of observing rites and rituals but a man who should think of doing good to others, who dispenses justice tempered with mercy. He should always be concerned with the welfare of the people. It is clear from the *Kūṭadanta Sutta*[366] that material well-being can be established by attending to the needs of farmers, businessmen and other unemployed persons of the kingdom. And there has to be a king who can look into their needs and take care of them

But all that has been said above is concerned with the theoretical aspect of planting peace in the world. The practical side of it is purifying one's mind of defilements. How can one do so? It is a million-dollar question. It is a great task. Not so easy. Practising Vipassana which teaches one to be aware of all actions, great or small, good or bad that one does is the only way by which people can get rid of *rāga* (craving)

366. D1 *Kūṭadanta Sutta*

and *dosa* (aversion), attain wisdom (*paññā*) and learn to live a pure life. The awareness and the equanimity that go with Vipassana enable a person to examine and evaluate whether what he thinks and does is good or bad and as a consequence enables him not to react to pleasant and unpleasant sensations and multiply his misery. If one practices Vipassana and becomes fully aware of all that he does or thinks then he will be able to know the nature of reality, attain wisdom (*paññā*) understand the futility of becoming greedy and jealous and finally think of experiencing peace in one's life and not to keep on burning with jealousy and hatred. Slowly and steadily this process of realization will help him experience peace not only within himself but also will enable him to work for peace in the world.

Because peace can be realized within oneself so unless a sizeable number of people or at least a few of them who matter most in the society or who really believe in planting peace in the world walk on the Noble Eightfold Path or practice Vipassana as taught by the Buddha peace cannot be promoted in the world. If political organizations like the UNO and the Security Council are manned by such people world peace can be promoted because only such persons will have a clear understanding of the defilements that burn one and do not allow him to realize peace.

But this is not possible without having a clear understanding of the concept of one's mind. If one has understood his mind clearly and if he has supplanted all unwholesome roots of actions by the wholesome roots then whatever he speaks and does will be pure and happiness will accompany him just as his shadow does. It is by understanding the nature of one's mind and walking on the Noble Eightfold Path to purify it from defilements that one can promote peace within and without. Practicing Vipassana is the most practical and efficacious method for achieving this end.

Mechanism of Vipassana

What is Vipassana? It is a technique of meditation. By practising it one learns to look within. Why does one look within and what does he see there? When he tries to be aware most of the time he is aware of the conscious mind called *paritta citta* which is a very small part of the mind. A great part of the mind is unconscious or subconscious. After Siddhārtha Guatama learned the two higher (seventh and eighth) stages of *arūpāvacara dhyāna* (formless meditation) he came to the conclusion that he was not free from the cycle of birth and death. He realized that he was far away from getting rid of suffering. Why? Because although he could control his conscious mind, the unconscious mind was not under his control. Much activity takes place there of which one is hardly aware. He discovered that it is one's mind, both conscious and unconscious, which creates desires and desires cause suffering. So far he had learned to control his conscious mind but how to be aware of the subconscious mind and how not to allow it to create desires in ignorance was the problem before him. So he discovered the technique of Vipassana meditation.

How does it work? Before one understands its mechanism he should bear in mind a few things. First, desire (*taṇhā*) is at the root of all one's suffering and second, one creates desire in ignorance. Because he does not know the real nature of things he falls for them. If he knew with *bhāvanāmayā paññā* that everything, howsoever beautiful it may look, is impermanent he would not hanker after it. In order to know the real nature of things he has to live in the present and living in the present means being mindful and realize impermanence i.e. he has to develop *sati* and *sampajañña.*

Creation of desires is a twofold process. When one likes something he likes to have more of it and when he does not like a thing he likes to get rid of it. Both are desires all the same. Therefore creation of desires is a continuous process. Not only when one is awake he creates and multiplies them but also when he is asleep he does so. One's unconscious mind or *antarmana* goes on multiplying them endlessly. How one's conscious mind creates desires is easy to understand but how his unconscious or subconscious mind does it is difficult to understand.

One comes in contact with the outside world with the six sense organs he is endowed with. Each sense organ has its object in the outside world. The eye has *rūpa* (visible object), the ear has *sadda* (sound) and so on. When a sense organ comes in contact with its object, consciousness (*viññāna*) arises. One just knows that something has happened. This consciousness is neutral. Then perception (*saññā*)- the second part of the mind knows it and evaluates it. Then *vedanā* or *saṃvedanā* arises which gives rise to *taṇhā* (desire). If it is something he likes, he has pleasant sensations (*sukhada saṃvedanā*) and if he does not like it, he has unpleasant ones (*duhkhada saṃvedanā*). This is the third part of the mind. He wants more of pleasant sensations and wants to get rid of unpleasant ones. In both the cases he begins to desire, desire to have more of pleasant sensations or desire to get rid of unpleasant ones. This is *saṅkhāra*—the fourth part of the mind. Thus he begins to produce misery. From this it is clear that it is sensations, pleasant or unpleasant, which cause desire. *Vedanā paccayā taṇhā.* This is one of the twelve links of the Law of Dependent Origination (*paṭiccasamuppāda*) propounded by the Buddha. This law explains the mechanism of how one creates one's misery and how he can end it. Vipassana helps one end it because it helps him understand the true nature of things i.e. impermanence and also helps him keep cravings and aversions away by knowing their nature.

The Buddha explained through the Law of Dependent Origination that desire (*taṇhā*) is the cause of suffering because all desires cannot be fulfilled. *Taṇhā paccayā upādanaṃ* (desires cause deep attachment or clinging) and *upādāna paccayā bhava* (clinging causes becoming). He also showed in many of the *suttas* that sensations (*vedanā*) have both mental and physical aspects. Therefore *vedanā* is like a bridge between mind and body. Thoughts arise in one's mind but sensations caused by them are felt on his body. *Vedanā samosaranā sabbe dhammā.* If he learns to see *vedanā* objectively i.e. without making any reaction he can stop his miseries from arising and multiplying. A time will come when all latent desires will be rooted out and he will put an end to his suffering.

The practice of *samatha* meditation can help one control one's conscious mind and not allow it to come in contact with the outside objects. As a result, there will be no sensation, no desire and no suffering. But how to stop unconscious or subconscious mind from reacting to sensations that are constantly caused by various *dhammas* arising deep within one without his being aware of them?

In ancient India the *samatha* type of meditation was taught and practised to control and concentrate mind so that the fickle and unsteady mind was controlled and not allowed to hanker after various objects of the world. Thus the process of the creation of desire was stopped. Siddhārtha Gautama learned this technique of meditation from Ālāra Kālāma in his hermitage and learned a higher form of it all by himself in the hermitage of Uddaka Rāmaputta (Uddaka Ramaputta was not his teacher like Ālāra Kālāma) and learned to control his mind. But as said above he realized that although with this technique he could control his conscious mind he could not control his unconscious mind where continuous reactions take place and desires are multiplied. He also realized that so long as he did not get rid of the *anusaya kilesas* that lie deep in his unconscious mind and so long as he was not able to keep a guard on its working, he would not be rid of suffering. This led him to think a little more deeply about the working of his unconscious mind. This also led him to discover the technique of Vipassana. Vipassana is to look within and see all sensations that arise there equanimously. This process of looking within enables one to realize the impermanent nature of all things at the experiential level which, in turn, makes one come out of ignorance and develop non-attachment to all objects of the world. Observing sensations and realizing their impermanent nature make one wise. *Vedanā*, instead of producing *taṇhā*, begins to produce *paññā* (wisdom).

Vipassana enables one not to create new *saṅkhāras* by observing sensations equanimously. When new ones are not produced then the old *saṅkhāras* come up on the surface from one's *antarmana* and die out because one does not react to them. One can understand this with the help of a simile. Imagine a fire. It will keep on burning till the fuel is added to it. If the fuel is stopped being added, then it will burn till the old stock is there. It will extinguish as soon as the old stock is exhausted. This is the law of nature. When one reacts to sensations he adds fuel to fire i.e. he keeps oil and wick ready for the sparks of reactions to catch. Old *saṅkhāras* come up on the surface like leaping sparks. But when one learns not to react he allows them to die out and not become fire. That is why it is said that old *saṅkharas* die out and new ones are not produced. *Khīnaṃ purāṇaṃ navaṃ natthi saṃbhavam.* This, in short, is the mechanism of Vipassana.

Let us understand this mechanism in detail. For practising Vipassana it is necessary to control one's monkey mind. One has also to train it.

Although the practice of observing precepts helps one in restraining one's words and deeds, this restraint is not so useful unless the mind is restrained. Because the mind is the spring of all actions, wholesome or unwholesome, mind has got to be purified.

For purifying mind it is necessary to control it. While practising Vipassana one learns to concentrate it by being aware of the incoming and outgoing breath. This subject of meditation is universal inasmuch as it transcends all castes and creeds and it is common to all. Besides, this is not outside of anyone but it is always with him.

In a ten-day course one learns to observe the incoming and outgoing breath and thus sharpens one's mind. One develops mindfulness more than ever. With this sharp and concentrated mind one begins to observe the sensations that arise on his body more clearly. Thus observing sensations he learns their impermanent nature at the experiential level. Vipassana *bhāvanā* makes one clearly see that whatever the nature of sensations, pleasant, unpleasant or neutral they do not last forever. Even though one has pleasant sensations and wants them to continue, that never happens. They do change. So is the case with the other two kinds of sensations. This realization at the experiential level which one has over and over again leaves not an iota of doubt in him that sensations are in a constant state of flux. From such experiences he learns *aniccatā*. He sees it as a phenomenon. Practising vipassana he develops *nirveda* i.e. non attachment.

One is attached to things of the world particularly to the beautiful things he likes in ignorance. He clings to them and wants to have more of them and wants them to continue because he does not know their real nature. Intellectually he knows that all the objects of the world are impermanent. But Vipassana enables him to see their real nature at the experiential level. This repeated experience makes the scales of his eyes fall. Thus, realizing the impermanent nature of things in the world he does not feel like being attached to any thing.

How does he realize the impermanent nature of things?

Vipassana makes one mindful. Mindfulness enables him to see sensations. Seeing sensations he begins to see their impermanent nature at the experiential level. Thus he is able to see the impermanent nature of the things of the world. He develops attachment to the objects of the world because he does not know their real nature. Once their real nature is seen directly he gradually develops non attachment. He now does not crave for them. Once his craving ceases, desires do not multiply and consequently suffering also does not multiply. At least he comes to a stage where he does not create new *saṅkhārās.*

But it is not so easy to achieve mindfulness and begin to realize *aniccatā*. One's mind is very fickle and unsteady. Unless this monkey mind is controlled and restrained he will not be able to see the impermanent nature of things. Mind needs to be trained to achieve concentration.

The first part of the training of mind in a ten-day course is to practise *ānāpānasati* i.e development of mindfulness of the incoming and outgoing breath. Respiration is a subject of meditation. It is a universal subject because it is with all meditators belonging to any caste, race or creed. It is also universal because it remains readily available to every one. So it is a non-controversial subject of meditation.To begin the practice of *ānāpāna sati* i.e. awareness of respiration a meditator sits comfortably in an upright posture. He keeps his back and head straight and closes his eyes. There should be no distraction in the room where he sits to meditate. With his closed eyes he begins to turn his attention from the outer world to the world within. He keeps his attention fixed on the breath going in and coming out of the nostrils. He keeps his attention fixed on the natural breath. It has been rightly said that, "This is not a breathing exercise; it is an exercise in awareness. The effort is not to control the breath but instead to remain conscious of it as it naturally is: long or short, heavy or light, rough or subtle. For as long as possible one fixes the attention on the breath, without allowing any distractions to break the chain of awareness."[367]

Very soon he realizes the difficulty of keeping his attention fixed on respiration. He finds it very difficult to remain aware of his respiration for a long time. Very soon he tries to be aware of his respiration he is distracted either by a pain in the legs or somewhere else or distracted by some thoughts and memories of the past or some plans to be executed in the future. The more he tries to suppress these distracting thoughts and memories, the more they catch his attention. He pays attention to a thousand things but his respiration. It is so because of the habit pattern of mind which is ingrained since time immemorial. This habit pattern of mind has got to be changed. He sits with renewed determination to give attention to the incoming and outgoing breath, but a thousand things jump into his mind.

It does not take long for a meditator to discover that it is very difficult to control his mind. Like a spoiled child it wants this toy now and that toy again after some time. This is how a meditator learns to discover his true nature. Although he finds it very difficult to live with reality he sincerely tries to do so and again in his attempt he fixes his attention on his respiration. His mind runs away again but he tries to bring it back on his respiration. He is instructed not to be annoyed at this because if he is annoyed he reacts. He is instructed not to lose his temper. So he does not lose his temper nor does he lose heart but he tries again and again to bring it back on his respiration. His attempt to do it over and over again calms his wandering mind and he learns to repeat this exercise without tension and without discouragement. He has to repeat this exercise and continue his practice with patience and calmness. This is right effort. In short, to bring his mind back to respiration and to continue his attention on respiration is right effort.

Right effort (*sammā vāyāmo*) leads to right awareness (*sammā sati*). If a meditator makes effort to keep his mind fixed on his incoming and outgoing breath, the first thing he does is he learns to live in the present. He also learns to detach himself from the past as also learns to keep himself from the future. Thinking either of the past or of the future makes him unrealistic. But if he keeps his mind fixed on his respiration he learns to live in the present. He learns what he is doing in the present. Being aware of the present he does not do any thing in ignorance. He is aware of what is happening now. When he lives in the past memories or when he plans for the future he either remembers his past which is gone or plans for the

367. William Hart, The Art of Living, p. 73

future which is not yet come. In both the cases he is not with reality. He can live with reality only in the present. This practice of fixing his attention on respiration makes it possible for him to live in the present. It also enables him to be fully aware of what he does in the present. He does not do any thing now in ignorance.

The technique of *ānāpāna sati* is a method to develop one's ability to be aware of the present moment. If one develops this ability, one is less likely to do anything in ignorance. There is another reason for developing awareness of respiration. It can enable a meditator experience ultimate reality.

'Focusing on breathing can help us explore whatever is unknown about ourselves, to bring into consciousness whatever has been unconscious. It acts as a bridge between the conscious and unconscious mind, because the breath functions both consciously and unconsciously. We can decide to breathe in a particular way, to control the respiration. We can stop breathing for a time. And yet when we cease trying to control respiration, it continues without any prompting.'[368]

When one's mind begins to wander and he can no longer fix his attention on respiration it is good to breathe intentionally and breathe slightly hard in order to fix the attention more easily. As soon as the awareness of respiration becomes clear and steady he then allows his respiration to be natural whether it is hard or soft, deep or shallow, long or short, or fast or slow. His whole purpose is to observe the present reality, *yathābhūtañāṇadassana.* When he breathed intentionally he did observe a particular kind of reality. From this he comes to see a subtler reality when his breath becomes natural. Thus he makes progress in being aware of a subtler reality.

One's breath is a great signal of what goes on in his mind. So long as the mind is peaceful and not disturbed by any negativity like anger, aversion, fear or passion, his breath is regular and gentle but as soon as any defilement arises in mind his breath becomes irregular, more rough, heavy and rapid. Such respiration acts as signal and alerts one to the defilement that arises in his mind. If he observes his respirations attentively and mindfully he can know of the negativity that arises in his mind. Thus he gets to know a reality. The reality is that whenever any defilement arises in one's mind his breath becomes unnatural. Thus he begins to see reality as it is.

There is another good reason for practising awareness of breathing in and breathing out. We know that our goal is to free our mind from negativity. So every step we take towards that goal must be pure. It must be wholesome also. Therefore the object that we take recourse to for

368. AL p. 75

achieving the concentration of mind must be wholesome. Breath is such an object. It has a reality. We cannot have craving or aversion toward breath. It is, therefore, an appropriate object of attention. Bill Hart sums up Sri S.N. Goenka's view in these words, "In the moment when the mind is fully focussed on respiration, it is free from craving, free of aversion, and free of ignorance. However brief that moment of purity may be, it is very powerful, for it challenges all one's past conditioning. All the accumulated reactions are stirred up and begin to appear as various difficulties, physical as well as mental, which hinder one's efforts to develop awareness."[369]

When we feel that we are not making progress or we are slow to do so we become impatient and angry. Sometimes sloth and torpor get over us. We begin to doze off as soon as we begin to meditate. We feel like having so many excuses not to continue with the observation of respiration. We tend to become impatient and sad. But it is at this stage that we practise right effort. If awareness deludes us we must pursue it time and again. A time is bound to come when we will attain concentration of mind and begin to be clearly aware of our respiration. We may at times be assailed by doubts about the teacher or the teaching or by doubts about our own ability to meditate. But a sincere effort to develop awareness of mind will clear all our doubts.

These hindrances arise only in reaction to our success, however, little it may be. Our perseverance will make them disappear. Continuity of this practice will go a long way in our achieving concentration of mind and our being aware of breath whether hard or soft, deep or shallow, long or short, fast or slow.

After practising *ānāpāna* for three days and a half, meditators begin to practise Vipassana. Vipassana means to look within in a special manner. What do they do when they practise it? With their minds concentrated by practising *ānāpāna* they are now more sensitive to see what is happening within. They are now better able to observe them. What used to pass unnoticed is now mindfully observed by them. This observation enables them to live in the present time and with the present reality. Neither there is remembering the past nor there is thinking of the future. Meditators are 'anchored to the present.' They come to observe different kinds of sensations on their bodies. These sensations arise because of the interaction between mind and body. Whenever there is interaction between the two, and there is always their interaction, sensations either pleasant or unpleasant or neutral arise. The Buddha experienced that even thoughts cause sensations let alone gross sensual objects coming in contact with their respective sense organs. *Vedanā samosaraṇā sabbe dhammā.* As our respirations make us aware

369. AL p. 76

of the kind of defilement that arises in our mind so our sensations on the body make us aware of different kinds of defilements arising in our mind. Just as an angry man's breaths are fast so he experiences hot sensations on his body. These sensations are caused by his anger and they can make his life miserable. But if he learns to observe them equanimously without reacting to them, the strength of these sensations will become less and less and he will be far from being miserable, This is the benefit of Vipassana. One is taught to sharpen one's mind with the help of *ānāpāna* and Vipassana and see things equanimously. Being equanimous means being free from craving and aversion. And being mindful means to see the impermanent nature of pleasant or unpleasant sensations. They arise to pass away. And so is the case with neutral sensations. They also do not remain neutral for a long time. They also change. This realization on the part of the meditator is a tremendous realization. He begins to understand that if even pleasant sensations are not permanent why hanker after them? Thus, he develops non-attachment to things. With the practice of Vipassana he always lives in the present time, sees the impermanent nature of not only sensations but of all phenomena and thus develops wisdom not to crave for the things of the world and finally develops non-attachment which leads him to *nibbāna.*

Vipassana enables one to see clearly where and why *taṇhā* (craving) arises. It arises wherever there is anything agreeable and pleasurable (*Yaṃ loke piyarūpaṃ sātarūpaṃ, etthesā taṇhā uppajjamānā uppajjati, ettha nivisamānā nivisati*).[370] Sights, sounds, smells, tastes, tangibles and mind-objects in the world are agreeable and pleasurable. When they come into contact with their respective sense organs sensations arise. If they are pleasant, craving arises and if they are unpleasant aversion arises. The former speaks of a desire to have more of the pleasant sensations and the latter speaks of a desire to get rid of unpleasant ones soon. In both the cases there is desire all the same. *Vedanā paccayā taṇhā* and *taṇhā paccayā upādānaṃ. Taṇhā,* therefore, is responsible for our misery. The Buddha discovered from his own experience that between the object and the reaction there is a missing link of *vedanā.* What we want are not the objects of the world as such but we want to have more of the pleasant sensations and less of the unpleasant ones. Therefore he taught us the technique of Vipassana to observe *vedanā* without making any reaction. Thus we do not multiply our miseries. We do so also because we have the knowledge of reality as it is. We also know at the experiential level that things are not permanent. If they are not permanent why hanker after them and suffer?

When a vipassana meditator sees this clearly and also sees that sensations, pleasant or unpleasant are impermanent, he develops non-

370. D.2 *Mahāsatipaṭṭhāna Sutta*

attachment to them. This non-attachment that he develops is based on his wisdom (*paññā*), on his *yathābhūtañāṇadassana*, on his knowledge and vision of reality as it is.

Understanding the mechanism of Vipassana is to understand the process of one's creating misery as also the process of coming out of it.

It has been said in the *Satipaṭṭhāna Sutta* that establishing of awareness is the only way for the purification of beings, for the overcoming of sorrow and lamentation, for the ending of suffering and grief, for the gaining of right path and for the realisation of *nibbāna*. *Ekāyano maggo sattānaṃ visuddhiyā, sokaparidevānaṃ samatikkamāya, dukkhadomanassānam atthaṇgamāya, ñāyassa adhigamāya, nibbānassa sacchikiriyāya.*[371] The same can be said about Vipassana.

371. ibid.

Bhāvanāmayā Paññā-An Invaluable Contribution to World Culture

Of the three *paññās, sutamayā, cintāmayā* and *bhāvanāmayā*, the Buddha gives more importance to the last one than the first two, because it is this *paññā* which when developed enables one to be non-attached to worldly things that produce desire—the cause of suffering. It also enables him to break the cycle of birth and death and become liberated. It is by virtue of the cultivation of this *paññā* that one really comes to know why and where *taṇhā* arises and how and where it can be ended. What is necessary for developing this *paññā*?

For developing this *paññā* purity of mind is a *sine qua non* and this purity of mind cannot be attained without observing moral precepts. Only when five moral precepts like abstaining from killing, stealing, committing adultery, telling lies etc and from taking intoxicants are observed, defilements like aversion, greed, sensuality, pride etc. can be rooted out. Under the influence of these defilements man violates precepts.

Abstaining from intoxicants is the most important condition for mind to work properly. How can it work properly under the influence of intoxicating things? Concentration of mind cannot be achieved if it is under the influence of pollutants like greed, aversion jealousy etc. They are powerful distracting agents. Observation of precepts enables one to get rid of them.

Once the concentration of mind is attained it is easy to see the nature of things clearly at the experiential level. Experience keeps a dear school. Even fools can learn in the school of experience. What does it do? It enables one to see things happening the same way over and over again, Sensation, which is an important object of meditation when one practices Vipassana, arises on his body and passes away. Whatever its nature is, pleasant, unpleasant, or neutral, it keeps on changing, does not last forever. He experiences this again and again. Thus, his *bhāvanāmayā paññā* develops and he realizes with its help that nothing in this world is permanent. Thus, the veil of the darkness of ignorance is rent and he develops non-attachment to things of the world to which he used to be attached when he did not know their true nature.

The beauty of this *paññā* is that like the first two it cannot be developed by a man whose mind is full of defilements like craving and aversion. Freedom from defilements is the necessary condition for developing this *paññā*. Because physical and vocal actions follow one's volition, wholesome or unwholesome, so only freedom from defilements will keep both these actions pure.

With this *paññā* developed one can prove the veracity of the Law of Dependent Origination and the Law of Impermanence, profound laws taught by the Buddha. With the help of the Law of Dependent Origination he proved how suffering is caused and how it can be ended. With the help of the Law of Impermanence he showed why should one give up attachment to worldly objects, attachment which causes desire—the root cause of suffering.

But persons who are not pure, in other words, who do not observe *sīla* and whose physical and vocal actions are not pure are not spiritually fit to develop this *paññā* let alone understand it. The laboratory where the experiment of whether the Law of Impermanence and the Law of Dependent Origination are true or not can be made only in this fathom long body by a person who has a pure mind and whose conduct is good and pure.

Thus, it becomes clear that whereas the first two *paññās* can be understood by anybody whether his mind is pure or not, *bhāvanāmaya paññā* can be developed and understood by persons who have cultivated mental purity. It can only be understood by those who have cultivated mindfulness (*sati*) and who with its help understand the impermanent nature of reality i.e. who have developed *sampajañña* and these two qualities cannot be expected in a person who does not observe virtue (*sīla*). The concept of *bhāvanāmayā paññā* and how to develop it, therefore, is an invaluable contribution by the Buddha to world culture.

As far as I know, the word *'prajñā'* is found in Indian Sanskrit Literature such as *Ṛg Veda, Upaniṣadas,* the *Rāmāyaṇa,* the *Mahābhārata and* the *Gītā* but it has been used not in the sense of '*bhāvanāmayā paññā*' which means direct knowledge i.e. knowledge gained at the experiential level. I have not come across any literature except early Buddhist literature where it is mentioned how this is cultivated and developed and how it becomes direct knowledge. It is the Buddha who talks about this *pañña* and shows how it can be developed and cultivated. The technique by which it can be developed and cultivated is Vipassana and for practicing this technique of meditation it is incumbent upon one to observe *sīla* and practice *samādhi* so that all defilements from mind can be driven away. Thus, the understanding developed by practicing Vipassana is pure as it is based on direct experience and not on reason. Such understanding drives out all darkness of ignorance. One sees reality in a constant state of flux, develops *nirveda* (non-attachment to worldly things), ends one's misery and becomes fully liberated.

Culture is a very complex concept. It has been defined by many persons in different ways and their definitions depend upon what they considered important. Matthew Arnold[372] in his book *Culture and Anarchy* has said that

---

372. CA

culture is 'a pursuit of our total perfection by means of getting to know, on all the matters which most concern us, the best which has been thought and said in the world.'

I would like to add here that not only knowing 'the best that has been thought and said' can be said to be the best element of culture because only knowing cannot lead to perfection but when it is practiced in life it leads to perfection. Attainment of this perfection is exalting, sublime and beautiful element of culture. It is not only thinking the best, knowing the best and saying the best that makes one perfect but that which is put into practice, that which is lived in life and that which brings about a transformation for the better in life that makes culture worth aspiring after.

In this context I would like to say that the Buddha has not only thought and said what is the best but has pointed out the way to attain it. To attain the best is to walk on the Noble Eightfold Path.

The Path to Attain Bhāvanāmayā Paññā

The Buddha has explained in many of the *suttas* the training that one has to undergo in order to develop this *paññā.* This training is gradual and there are several steps leading to its culmination. With the help of a beautiful simile he has shown how this training is given to produce the right type of effect. In the *Gaṇakamoggallāna Sutta* he says that "when a clever horse trainer obtains a fine thoroughbred colt, he first makes him get used to wearing the bit, and afterwards trains him further."[373] In the same way when the Tathāgata obtains a person to be tamed he first disciplines him by asking him to be 'virtuous, restrained with the restraint of the Pātimokkha' and asks him to be 'perfect in conduct and resort, and seeing fear in the slightest fault, train by undertaking the training precepts.'[374]

After he gets into the habit of observing precepts he is further asked to guard the doors of his sense faculties. Why? Because unless the doors are guarded well he will, because of the ingrained habit of mind, see a beautiful form or hear a melodious sound or smell a sweet perfume and so on and will go on desiring them and create more miseries for him. When the sense faculties are unguarded 'unwholesome states of covetousness and grief' are likely to invade him. So, the Buddha expressly asks him not to grasp at the sign of an object nor at its features. (*Nānunimittagāhī hohi, nānu vyañjanagāhī hohi.*) *Nimitta* means the object such as a woman and *vyañjana* means detailed description of her features such as green eyes, the eye like that of a doe or lotus and so on. The same thing applies to all

373. MLD, p. 874

374. ibid.

the objects of other sense faculties if they are left unguarded. Therefore, restraint of all sense faculties should be practiced.

After observing precepts and practicing restraint of the sense faculties the Buddha teaches him to become moderate in eating. Why? Because if one is not moderate in eating[375] he will fall a prey to sloth and laziness. Food should be taken not for amusement nor for intoxication nor for the sake of physical beauty and attractiveness. It should be taken only for the continuance of body so that a holy life can be lived. It should also be taken for developing endurance so that one can terminate old feelings without arousing new feelings and be healthy and blameless.

The next quality, which the Buddha asks him to develop is wakefulness. Only when one is awake one will be able to purify one's mind of 'obstructive states'.[376] The next step of the training is to develop mindfulness (*sati*) and full awareness (*sampajañña*) which should be cultivated in all situations of life.[377]

After he develops mindfulness and full awareness he is disciplined further. He is asked to 'resort to a secluded resting place: the forest, the root of a tree, a mountain, a ravine, a hillside cave, a charnel ground, a jungle thicket, an open space, a heap of straw' after returning from his almsround and having his meal he sits down cross-legged, keeping his body erect and establishing mindfulness before him. He then purifies his mind of five hindrances such as *kāmacchanda* (covetousness, sensuality), *vyāpāda* (ill-will), *thīnamiddha* (sloth and torpor), *uddhaccakukkucca* (restlessness and remorse) and *vicikicchā* (doubt). After he has got rid of the five hindrances he is fit to practice meditation (*jhāna*). He enters into first *rūpāvacara jhāna* which 'is accompanied by applied and sustained thought, with rapture and pleasure born of seclusion. With the stilling of applied and sustained thought, he enters upon and abides in the second *jhāna*, which has self confidence and singleness of mind without applied and sustained thought, with rapture and pleasure born of concentration. With the fading away as well of rapture he abides in equanimity, and mindful and fully aware, still feeling pleasure with the body, he enters upon and abides in the third *jhāna*, on account of which noble ones announce: He has a pleasant abiding who has equanimity and is mindful'. With the abandoning of pleasure and pain, and with the previous disappearance of joy and grief, he enters upon and abides in the fourth *jhāna*, which has neither-pain-nor-pleasure and purity of mindfulness due to equanimity."[378]

375. ibid. p. 875
376. ibid.
377. ibid.
378. ibid. p. 877

Anyone who trains himself like this purifies his mind of all defilements. He does not further create them by guarding the doors of his sense faculties perfectly. What is needed for guarding the doors of sense faculties is wakefulness, which can be cultivated by being moderate in eating food. Wakefulness leads him to develop mindfulness (*sati*) and full awareness (*sampajaññā*). When these qualities are developed he becomes fit for practicing *jhāna* to attain concentration of mind and with this concentrated mind he sees reality as it is. Knowing the impermanent nature of all the objects of the world he develops non-attachment (*nirveda*) to them and thus stops creating desires—the root cause of suffering. All this is done by having knowledge at the experiential level. Thus, *bhāvanāmayā paññā* goes a long way in ending his suffering. This *paññā* also enables him to see how and where suffering is caused and also enables him to know how and where it can be ended. The philosophy of the Buddha has an action-plan. What he propounds can be practiced in life and its fruit can be tasted here and now.

Nature of Pāli Literature

What is the nature of Pāli literature? Is it only ethico-religious or psycho-philosophical in nature? Isn't it a combination of "*darśana*"(vision) and "*varṇana*" (expression of vision)--the two characteristics necessary for a poet according to Bhaṭṭatauta[379]? If this literature expresses the experiences of the Buddha and his disciples in poetic speech, can it then not be called literature and compared with English, French, German and Italian literature of the west and Sanskrit, Hindi or other literature of the east? Because there is no Homer here, no Dante, no Shakespeare, no Tolstoy, Dostoevsky and Gorki, no Kālidasa, Rabindranath Thakur, Premchanda and Nirala, will it not be called literature? Even though it has the poetic utterances of the *theras* like Mahākassapa, Raṭṭhapāla, Tālapuṭa and Vaṅgīsa and therīs like Ambapāli and Sumedhā, the Telakaṭāhagāthā by Bhikkhu Kalyāniya, the Jinacarita by Medhaṅkara, the Pajjamadhu by Buddhappiya, and above all the poetic utterances of the Buddha himself, does it not come under the category of literature? After all, what is that which one calls literature? What are its distinguishing features?

In the first chapter of my book entitled 'Comparative Aesthetics: East and West'[380] I have analyzed the distinguishing features of literature. Although the emotive use of language as against its scientific use, similes and metaphors and above all imagination are found in literature, they cannot be said to be its exclusive distinguishing features, for similes and metaphors are found in history and philosophy and an element of imagination is there in didactic stories, say in the stories of Pañcatantra by Viṣṇu Sharma and Gulistān by Shekha Sadi. Sometimes the emotive use of language is found in history and there can be great poetry without the element of imagination as will be shown here. So, what distinguishes literature from history and philosophy is its capacity to delineate different kinds of sentiments such as love, laughter, compassion, heroism, wonder, loathsomeness and quietude. Unless a literary work does this, it cannot be called literature in the comprehensive sense of *Kāvya*, which in Greece is called 'Poeisis' and in German called 'Dichtung'. The other distinguishing feature is that literature delights us in so far as it describes our own sentiments and feelings, our own joys and sorrows, love and hatred, and our own victory and defeat. It seems to be the description of our own self

379. Bhaṭṭatauta: *Darśanādvarṇanādaccātha rūḍhā loke kaviśrutih* (Quoted in Kāvyānuśāsanam, p. 379)

380. Chaudhary, Angraj: Comparative Aesthetics: East and West, Eastern Book Linkers,Delhi,1991, p. 3.3 ibid., p .1

in a way in which history and philosophy are not. They do not describe us as intimately as poetry, novels, dramas and stories do.

Poets and writers have the sensitivity to experience as deeply the pains and pleasures, love and hatred and victory and defeat of the characters they create as they have the capacity to communicate effectively their feelings in a poetic mode of speech. The two necessary characteristics that make a poet are vision (*darśana*) i.e. capacity to feel and (*varṇana*) i.e. the ability to express. Croce's[381] impression and expression are nothing but Bhaṭṭatauta's 'vision' and 'expression of vision." Another distinguishing feature of literature is the element of imitation, which made Plato expel poets from his Republic.[382] He looks down upon poetry because it is an imitation of an imitation of the Ideas and so thrice removed from reality. But in spite of Plato, a great mass of literature with the element of imitation does exist and gives us not only pleasure but inspires us to espouse important causes in society.

Pāli literature, particularly canonical literature, does not create characters as imaginatively as other literatures do. In other literature of the world, the author's imagination plays a great role. Kālidāsa created Śakuntalā imaginatively. So did Shakespeare create Hamlet, Ophelia and Desdemona. So do other writers create their characters imaginatively. Although these characters are created imaginatively, they are so life-like that they resemble us as they throb with the same kinds of emotions and passions as we do. When we read about them, we get great pleasure. Why do we get pleasure has been very convincingly explained by Coleridge. The characters created by artists are so life-like, are so like us that we identify with them by 'willingly suspending our disbelief.' We know Hamlet is not real, Ophelia, Desdemona and Śakuntala are not real, Horī is not real, yet they are so life-like that they seem to be one of us. We avidly read about them, about their pains and pleasures, joys and sorrows and victory and defeat. We laugh and weep with them. But although we shed tears when they meet their tragedy, still we enjoy the literature that depicts their tragedy.

In Pāli literature, at least in Canonical literature, imagination does not play any role. Here the Buddha is real and so are his disciples--both monks and nuns. It is they who record their sweet and bitter experiences of their lives. Therefore this literature may be called autobiographical but, of course, in a limited sense. So while reading this literature one does not have to resort to what Coleridge calls 'willing suspension of disbelief' as

381. ibid. p. 1

[4] Aes.

382. Plato: Republic, Book X

one has to do when reading the literature of imagination and imitation. When I say that both imagination and imitation are absent from Pāli literature I do not want to detract from their value but I want to show the superiority of Pāli literature over other literature where they play their role. In fact, there is a great mass of literature all over the world where both elements are found. Poets and artists gifted with imagination and skilled in imitation have produced literature which has in the words of Horace[383] both 'dulce' and 'utile' and which has inspired and entertained mankind since time immemorial. Coleridge[384] regards imagination as a synthesizing faculty; a faculty, which brings about organization, and harmonization and enables one to see the real nature of things. Aristotle[385] regards imitation as a creative act and not as bare copying.

I do not undermine, as I said, the importance of imagination and imitation. What I want to say is that Pāli literature is indeed literature--and great literature at that--without these elements.

Mammaṭa, one of the great aestheticians defines *kāvya* or literature in these words.

> *"Niyatikṛtaniyamarahitām hlādaikmayīmananyaparatantrām/*
> *Navarasarucirām nirmitimādadhatī bhāratī kaverjayati"//*[386]

Poetry or literature is not governed by the laws of Nature, its characteristic is to produce delight; it is not dependent on others, it delights inasmuch as it delineates nine sentiments.

Poetry, according to Mammaṭa, transcends the laws of Nature. It is a law of nature that the lotus blossoms during the day when the sun shines. The moon shines in the night, both the sun and the moon are never together, the smell of a lotus can come only from a lotus but in the world created by the poet such laws do not operate. The moon-like face of the beloved can shine in the dark night and the lotus perfume can come from the breath of one's beloved. Therefore it is said that in this vast world of poetry, a poet is the only creator. He fashions the poetic world as he likes it.

> *"Apāre kāvyasaṃsāre, kavireve prajāpatih/*
> *Yathāsme rocate viśvaṃ, tathāsme kurute idaṃ"//* [387]

Whatever sentiment a poet wants to depict—the sentiment of love, laughter, compassion or the feeling of dispassion, he delineates that

383. LCIR p. 47
384. BL Chapter XIV, CAEW, p. 18
385. ATP&FAS. p. 123
386. Mammaṭa, *Kâvya Prakâśa,Ullāsa* 1, Kârikâ 1.
387. *Agni Purāṇa*

sentiment. But the world he creates always delights us. Even if a work of art is tragic, it produces delight and only delight. It is true when one wistnesses a tragedy he sheds tears but after he comes out of the theatre, he feels light. He is not sad but he feels delighted. Due to its cathartic effects, his excessive emotions of pity and fear that weigh upon his heart are drained away and he feels light and enjoys this state. What are the reasons for it? The reasons, to my mind, are two. First, the tragedy that he witnesses played out in the theatre on the stage is not his tragedy yet it looks like his own. He identifies himself with the character that meets his tragedy but in his heart of hearts he knows that he is not caught in the web of tragedy.

Second, although he feels tragic emotions, he remains unaffected because of a phenomenon called 'psychic distance'[388] between the tragic character to whom tragedy happens and him who only witnesseses it. The tragic feelings and emotions are described in such an effective and powerful poetic speech that the sentiments lying deep within one are aroused. One finds the hero expressing his own feelings and then he takes his (hero's) suffering to be his own. Abhinavagupta[389] has explained how language plays an important role in arousing one's sentiments. Language is a social activity, with the power to depict the thoughts and feelings which people commonly share. When a poet or a writer depicts the feelings and sentiments of a character imaginatively created by him, the readers willingly suspend their disbelief, identify themselves with him and laugh and weep with him as the case may be.

Although Śakuntalā, Ophelia and Desdemona seem to be life-like, throbbing with real human sentiments and passions, they are not as real as Khemā and Uppalavaṇṇā. Whereas in other literature the characters are made out to be what they are by artists, and they speak the language put into their mouths by them, in Pāli literature the Buddha and the *theras* and *therīs* utter verses expressing their own experiences of life. They are historically real persons expressing their experiences of life i.e. they are themselves poets and poetesses in whom one finds both vision and expression of that vision, together.

Pāli literature is different from other literatures in other respects also. Although the Buddha has been described here as the sun shining in the night, which seems to be against the law of nature, it is actually a

---

388. Edward Bullough says that psychic distance 'has a negative, inhibitory aspect, the cutting out of the practical sides of things and of our practical attitude to them and a positive side...the elaboration of the experience on the new basis created by the inhibitory action of distance.

389. Abhinavagupta's *Abhinavabhāratī*, See my Comparative Aesthetics, pp. 105 to 107

metaphorical and poetic expression. But as far as its content is concerned there is no element of creative imagination in Pāli literature. Whatever the Buddha and his disciples say is what they have experienced directly. All they say is based on *yathābhūtajñāna* i.e. the knowledge of reality as it is, not as it is imagined to be. While reading Pāli literature one does not have to suspend one's disbelief as one has to do while reading poetry, dramas, novels and other genres, because no character is created in Pāli canonical literature from imagination. The feelings and sentiments of all personalities are real, born out of their own experiences. They suffer and express. T.S. Eliot[390] says in 'Tradition and the Individual Talent' that in order to achieve objectivity the creator should not be the sufferer, otherwise there will be cheap sentimentality only. But in Pāli literature the man who suffers and the artist who creates are one and the same. This is not the case with the characters found in the novels and dramas of other literature. Hamlet, Ophelia and Desdemona need a Shakespeare to create them, Tess of the D'urbervilles needs a Hardy to create her and Śakuntalā needs a Kālidāsa to create her. But Ambapāli does not need anybody else to give vent to her experiences of impermanence, which she feels when she sees her beauty wasted by old age. She herself experiences disenchantment and expresses it. She also expresses how she made a strong determination to practice Vipassana and realize arahanthood. Uppalavaṇṇā herself fights with Māra, puts him to rout and expresses her joy of victory. She has developed that spiritual power which stands her in good stead and enables her to attain the *summum bonum* of life.

However, the case of non-canonical literature is different. Here there are stories, which are about persons who may not be historically real but who are created by monk artists. It is the works of the Pāli canon--chiefly the verses of the Elders--which are being referred to here.

So what has been said by the Buddha and the *theras* and *therīs* is what they actually discovered at the experiential level. There is nothing here which is imagined nor is there anything here which is imitated. Everything that is described and expressed is based on the infallible laws of nature, on the *ṛta.* Therefore Pāli literature expresses the universal, what it expresses is true for all time and for all people of all countries.

If it is said here that enmity cannot be put out by enmity, it can be put out by non-enmity only, this is a statement about an important law of nature. The nature of fire is to burn and burn others. It can be put out by water, which is cool and makes others cool and quenched. "*Nahi verene verāni, sammantīdha kudācanaṃ, Averena sammanti, esa dhammo sanantano.*"[391]

390. SE

391. Dh 5

In Pāli literature if *rāga* (craving) *dveṣa* (aversion) and *moha* (ignorance) are called fire, it cannot be called a metaphorical statement as in other literatures, it is based on one's experience, on one's realization at the experiential level. The more one satisfies desires, the more they grow demanding satisfaction. The more he has desires, the more he burns. So if the Buddha has said that there is no fire like craving ("*Natthi rāga samo aggi*"[392]), there is no imagination here. It is the experienced truth. It may be a metaphorical expression in other types of literature where imagination has its role, but here it is real, grown out of one's experience. Whereas in other literature craving, aversion and ignorance are said to be fires, it is possible that they are not actually experienced by the artists but they are imagined to be so. There are many writers who describe a sea without ever seeing it. They just imagine it. It is a mental construct. So it is second hand. To know the truth at the experiential level is one thing and to imagine it as the poets do is quite another. As Shakespeare[393] said: -

"The poet's eye, in a fine frenzy rolling,
Doth glance from heaven to earth, from earth to heaven
And, as imagination bodies forth
The forms of things unknown,
The poet's pen turns them to shapes, and gives to airy nothing
A local habitation and a name."

The poet creates seemingly real entities, however fantastic, letting his imagination run riot, and creates equally realistic surroundings in which he places his characters--all this out of airy nothing. He does all this in the 'fine frenzy' of the creative process.

This applies *mutatis mutandis* to all artists who write different genres of literature. But this is not the case with Pāli Canonical literature. The Buddha uttered the *gāthā*[394], where he says that he has destroyed the house made by cravings and seen the builder so well that he (the builder) can make a house for him no more. He has annihilated all cravings and clingings. He now burns no more and feels *nibbānic* happiness. This calmness and tranquillity is communicated to others most effectively through graphic language, using an extended metaphor. But this is no fanciful metaphor

392. ibid. 202

393. Shakespeare: A Midsummer Night's Dream

394. *Anekajāti saṃsāraṃ, sandhāvissaṃ anibbisaṃ/Gahakārakaṃ gavesanto, dukkhā jāti punappunaṃ//*

Gahakāraka diṭṭhosi, puna gehaṃ na kāhasi/
Sabbā te phāsukā bhaggā, gahakūṭaṃ visaṇkhataṃ/
Visaṅkhāragataṃ cittaṃ, taṇhânaṃ khayamajjhagâ//

used purely to excite the emotions--it is a metaphor born out of his own experience and used to awaken in others their own faith, inspiration and desire to work for liberation. According to the Buddha it is our cravings which make us suffer and go round the wheel of life and death. So he extirpated them. He made this clear by saying that he witnessed the builder, i.e. cravings (*gahakāraka diṭṭhosi*) and ended the cravings so completely that he felt *nibbānic* happiness—a happiness like no other, that one feels after all his cravings are rooted out.

The Buddha was a philosopher unlike other philosophers. His philosophy was born out of his own experience. It was not based on his reasoning and intellectual thought like the philosophy, say, of Heraclites and Leibnitz. Heraclites did talk of everything being in a state of flux as the Buddha said, but he had perhaps not experienced this flux. And what have Leibnitz's monads got to do with our getting rid of misery? We can get rid of misery only by eradicating cravings and we can eradicate them by practicing *sīla samādhi* and *paññā*-in short, by walking on the Noble Eightfold Path as the Buddha did. Then he propounded the philosophy of the Four Noble Truths, describing what he had discovered by his own rigorous practical investigation. The fourth Noble Truth is an action-plan of how to put the philosophy he propounded into practice.

From the universal Law of Dependent Origination the Buddha knew that cravings give rise to clingings which, in their turn, cause *bhava* (the state of existence) and *jāti.* (birth) followed by suffering, sorrow, tribulation etc. The language the Buddha uses to express the misery-multiplying nature of cravings is graphic and powerful. And he is emphatic when he says that one's misery can be ended by the complete destruction of his desires.

But how do one'sdesires arise? They arise because of one's ignorance. Because he does not know the real nature of things he is attracted towards them. He develops cravings for them. However beautiful the things of the world may be they are always in a constant state of flux. If one realizes this at the experiential level, he will not be attached to them and he will have no craving for them. He will develop non-attachment and dispassion. The Buddha has taught us to develop this kind of non-attachment by practising Vipassana. When one realizes the real nature of things at the experiential level, this realization itself gives him divine joy.

> *"Suññāgāra paviṭṭhassa, santacittassa bhikkhuno/*
> *Amānusī ratī hoti, sammā dhammaṃ vipassato"//*[395]

As one sees the arising and passing away of all *khandhas* (aggregates i.e. *rūpa, vedanā, saññā, saṅkhāra* and *viññāṇa*) he begins to realize that all

395. Dh 373

things of the world that he craves for are burning. In this way real non-attachment develops and his fire of craving is put out. He feels 'cool and quenched.'

All such experiences form the warp and woof of Pāli literature, particularly of the *Theragāthā* and the *Therīgātha*. The *theras* and *therīs* poetically describe under what compelling circumstances they left home and took to ordination, how some of them were tormented by desires, and what *nibbānic* happiness they felt when they extirpated them by walking on the Noble Eightfold Path as shown them by the Buddha and as they experienced directly the impermanent nature of all things that give rise to cravings.

The themes of other literature of the world are victory and defeat, happiness and suffering, union and separation--all mundane subjects. Thomas Hardy has shown in his novels that life is full of suffering and if there is happiness it is but 'an occasional episode in the general drama of pain.'[396] Hamlet poignantly expresses the existential problem of life. 'To be or not to be, that is the question.'[397] Macbeth suffers so much after murdering Duncan that he says, "No, this my hand will rather the multitudinous seas incarnadine, making the green one red."[398] All these are sufferings or the causes of sufferings. The cessation of suffering and the divine happiness that follows from it are not described here. The theme of Pāli literature is the supreme peace that is experienced after extirpating desires and after ceasing to burn from their fire. The subject here is supramundane.

Of the four *puruṣārthas* in life *mokṣa* or *nirvāṇa* (or supreme peace) is the highest one. This forms the central theme of Pāli literature. How man can cease to burn from the fire of desires and what this extinction of fire is like, how peaceful it is, is another great theme of Pāli literature. In short, the main topic is the supreme peace far away from the fever and fret of life. The poet of the great epic *Mahābhārata* comes to realize at the end, after a great battle is fought and many lives are lost, that what is most important and valuable in life is peace, not war; quenching, not burning. Yudhiṣṭhir comes to realize the futility of war. Who was there to celebrate the victory and who survived to enjoy it? His attitude at the end of the battle is that of resignation. The great epic ends with an expression of a desire for quietude and peace, which are most valuable in life.[399]

In Pāli literature one finds the Buddha and his disciples discussing again and again how desires (the root cause of suffering) can be extirpated

396. Thomas Hardy, Tess of the D'urbervilles.

397. Shakespeare, Hamlet, Act III, scene I

398. ibid., Macbeth, Act II, scene II

399. *Mahābhārata*

by walking on the Noble Eightfold Path—observing precepts, practicing meditation and developing wisdom with which one can see the impermanent nature of things and consequently develop non-attachment (*nirveda*). The Buddha and his disciples--both monks and nuns--have experienced impermanence and developed *nirveda* and in the verses they utter they express the joy and happiness they have attained after annihilating desires.

What Dr. Ramachandra Shukla[400] said about the *Siddha* literature does not apply to the *udānas* of the Buddha and the utterances of the *theras* and therīs. Dr. Shukla did not find any evidence of personal experience in what the *Siddhas* said; he found only enumeration of *dharmas* but who will deny that the utterances of the *theras* and therīs do not have their sweet and bitter experiences? They describe them in a language, which arouses in one the same kinds of feelings and experiences, the same kinds of suffering and joy, which they felt. They describe the conflict that goes on in their minds. Conflict is a great element of poetry. They struggle to vanquish craving, aversion and ignorance—the three unwholesome roots of actions and when they get over them they describe the great joy and sense of victory they experience. They also describe their strong resolve to put out the fire of craving, aversion and ignorance and also their unquenchable thirst to cease to burn and experience supreme peace. The *theras* and *therīs* describe their experiences of life. One *therī*, Muttā by name, says that she is rid of three crooked things, mortar and pestle and her crooked husband:-

"Sumuttā sādhumuttāmhi, tīhi khujjehi muttiyā/
Udukkhalena musalena, patinā khujjakena ca"//

How woman-like are her experiences! And, like the other *theras* and *therīs* she also describes the supramundane joy that she feels after attaining arahanthood:-

"Muttamhi jātimaraṇā, bhavanetti samūhatāti"

That is why I say that Pāli literature takes off from where other literatures land. It rises above the eight worldly states such as loss and gain; victory and defeat; praise and blame and happiness and misery. These invariably disturb one. This literature describes them no doubt but rises above them and either describes the *nibbānic* experiences of the *theras* and *therīs* or describes their efforts to realize it. Even the poorest of them does not have a desire to earn wealth but he wants to be free from the burning caused by suffering. The *theras* and *therīs* are not slaves to their desires, they transcend them by understanding the impermanent nature

400. Ramachandra Shukla: *Hindi Sāhitya kā Itihāsa, Nāgarī Pracāriṇl Sabhā*, Varaṇasī, Samvat 2057 pp. 11-12

of things they have a desire for and speak of the peace they experience by the beat of their drum as also by unfurling their flag of victory.

It is in this respect also that Pāli literature differs from other literatures of the world. One does not find any description of love or war here. Nor does he find it describing poverty and the suffering caused by it, nor does he find it describing the insult that one suffers from the caste system. All these are pushed to the background. What forms the main concern of the *theras* and *therīs* is how to end cravings and attain *nibbāna* and break the cycle of birth and death. They are not as much concerned with *artha* (wealth) and *kāma* (sex) as they are with *dharma* (living an ethical life) and *mokṣa* (liberation)—the *summum bonum* of life.

Mammaṭa while pointing out the special characteristic of poetry (literature) says that the six tastes (*rasas*) of the world such as sweet, salty, bitter etc are not always liked by all persons nor always by the same person. But the *rasas* created by poets and artists are always liked by all persons. In real life a man falls in love or fights a battle or meets his tragedy but when he dies it is all over with him. But when an artist describes him falling in love or fighting a battle or meeting his tragedy, he creates works of art, which is eternal. All the actions of a character such as falling in love or fighting a battle and meeting his tragedy do not remain confined only to him but they become universal. They become true of all people. All people are affected by his sentiments and feelings because all of us have latent in us the permanent dispositions such as love, laughter, compassion, and heroic sentiment etc. as explained very clearly by Abhinavagupta.[401] If a person is an ascetic he may not have the sentiment of worldly love but he will have other sentiment—for instance, the sentiment of quietude, which arises after he develops non-attachment to all worldly things by understanding their impermanent nature.

Pāli literature also like other literatures of the world gives us the highest pleasure. But it delineates mostly the sentiment of quietude. The *rasa* delineated here is *śānta rasa*. This is certainly true in the case of Canonical Literature.

In all the literatures of the world where imagination plays a role love is a theme which has been described in all its permutations and combinations. Romeo wishes to be the gloves on the hands of his beloved so that he could kiss her cheeks.

"O, that I were a glove upon that hand, That I might touch that cheek."[402]

Here Romeo expresses his passionate love for Juliet. But howsoever

---

401. Abhinavagupta: *Abhinavabhāratī*, See Comparative Aesthetics: East and West, p. 102

402. Shakespeare, Romeo and Juliet, Act II, sceneII

passionate and sincere this love may appear to be it is a desire all the same. And desire is at the root of suffering, and sensuous love is very terrible as the verses and prose of Pāli literature show with the help of many similes. The fire of sensuous love keeps on burning, bringing nothing but misery, and it is very difficult to put it out.

In Pāli literature the misery-producing, terrible nature of sensuous desire and how it keeps on burning and burning has been brought home to us with a number of apt similes, such as those used by Sumedhā in her verses:-

> "Like the sharp blades of swords are sense desires,
> Like the poised heads of snakes prepared to dart,
> Like blazing torches and like bare known bones,
> Transient, unstable are desires of sense,
> ....
> A pestilence, a boil, and bane and bale,
> A furnace of live coals, the root of bane,
> Murderous and the source of harrowing dread."[403]

Sumedhā understood the impermanent nature of sensuous desires. She also understood the truth that they cannot be satisfied. Even if the seven jewels were to rain down in all the ten directions, there would be no satisfaction with sensual pleasures. So she turned to that 'that groweth never old.'

In other great literature of the world there is an attitude of resignation towards life and suffering. Edgar in King Lear gives vent to the inevitable attitude of resignation, which characterizes King Lear.

> Men must endure
> Their going hence, even as their coming hither.
> Ripeness is all.[404]

In comparison to this, the attitude of Sumedhā, Ambapālī and other therīs, who had all kinds of terrible experiences, is not that of resignation or defeatism. 'Ripeness is not all' for them. They realized the great truth

---

403. *Asisūnūpamā kāmā, kāmā sappasiropamā/Ukkopamā anudahanti. aṭṭhikaṅkala sannibhā//*

Aniccā addhuvā kāmā, bahudukkhā mahāvisā/
Ayoguḷova santatto, aghamūlā dukhapphalā//
....
Sattisūlūpamā kāmā, rogo gaṇḍo aghaṃ nigham
Aṅgārakāsusadisā, aghamūlaṃ bhayaṃ vadho//

404. Shakespeare: King Lear,Act V, scene II

of the Buddha's words that all things are impermanent and cravings are at the root of all suffering. So they felt inspired to walk on the path shown by the Buddha and work out their salvation. Their experiences of the spiritual journey they undertook form the theme of a literature where the sentiment of quietude (*śānta rasa*) born out of *nirveda* (non-attachment) pervades. Ambapālī contemplates her wasted charms in her *gāthās* which do not only epitomize her beauty, grace and charm but also powerfully express her painful realization of their transitory nature.

"Glossy and black as the down of the bee my curls once clustered,
They with the waste of the years are like unto hempen or bark cloth,
Fragrant as casket of perfumes, as full of sweet blossoms the hair of me,
All with the waste of the years now rank as odour of hare's fur..."[405]

The *theras* also like the *therīs* understood the importance of walking on the Noble Path and practising Vipassana in solitude.

Tālpuṭa's pious wish to live within the woods and practice meditation after his poignant realization of impermanence is expressed in the following words:-

"O when shall I, who see and know that this
My person, nest of dying and disease,
Oppressed by age and death,
Is all impermanent,
Dwell free from fear lonely within the woods
Yea, when shall these things be?"[406]

He admonishes his own self who after inspiring him to lead an ordained life now drags him to live in this world in these words, 'how come, you are

405. *Kāḷakā bhamaravaṇṇasadisā, vellitaggā mama muddhajā ahuṃ/*
Te jarāya sāṇavākasadisā, saccavādivacanaṃ anaññathā//
Vāsitova surabhī karaṇḍako, pupphapūra mama uttamaṅgajo/
Taṃ jarāyatha salomagandhikaṃ, saccavādivacanaṃ anaññathā//
....
Cittakārasukatāva lekhikā, sobhare su bhamukā pure mama/
Tā jarāya valibhippalambitā, saccavādivacanaṃ anaññathā//
Bhassarā surucirā yathā maṇī, nettahesumabhinīlamāyatā/
Te jarāya abhihatā na sobhare.....................
....
Pīnavaṭṭasahituggatā ubho, sobhare su thanakā pure mama/
Thevikīva lambanti nodakā,....................

406. *Kadā aniccaṃ vadharoganīḷaṃ, kāyaṃ imaṃ maccujarāupaddutaṃ/*
Vipassamāno vītabhayo vihassaṃ, eko vane taṃ nu kadā bhavissati//

cutting the roots of the tree which is about to bear fruits.'[407] This is a very good example of Dr. Jekyll admonishing Mr Hyde.[408]

These are sublime verses, which delineate *śānta rasa*. To my mind this is a great contribution made by Pāli literature to the field of delineating aesthetic sentiments. Bharata in his *Nāṭya Śāstra* could not elaborately describe this *'rasa'* as there was not much literature dealing with it. It was Pali literature and epics such as the Buddhacaritaṃ and dramas such as Sāriputra Prakaraṇaṃ written in Sanskrit by Aśvaghoṣa which delineated *śānta rasa* and made it occupy a prominent place in literature.

Almost all the works of Pāli and Sanskrit Literature with Buddhist themes are great works of literature inasmuch as they do not have only aesthetic elements such as similes and metaphors but they have extra-aesthetic elements also. As T.S. Eliot says, "the 'greatness' of literature cannot be determined solely by literary standards, though we must remember that whether it is literature or not can be determined solely by literary standards."[409]

Pāli literature has all the hallmarks of great literature and moreover carries the sublime message of the Buddha to walk on the Noble Eightfold Path, experience the impermanence of all things, develop *nirveda* and put an end to suffering. Besides, it also deals with the four sublime states of *mettā* (loving kindness), *karuṇā* (compassion) *muditā* (sympathetic joy) and *upekkhā* (equanimity).

To attain *preyas*[410] (objects of desire like a lover, a beloved, or mundane things) is not the objective of this literature. Therefore there is no erotic sentiment here, no heroic sentiment, which one feels when one fights a battle for the object of love or for achieving one's ambition. There is no sentiment of laughter because it does not go well with pursuing high spiritual ideals. There is certainly *jugupsā* (disgust) but its express purpose is to drive out attachment.

It is a literature which pulsates with the philosophy of spiritual pragmatism, with humanism and humanitarianism. It is a literature with a supramundane theme. It is a literature, which embodies an effort to purify one's mind of all negativities like craving and attain supramundane bliss. In short, it is a literature where literary, philosophical, ethical and religious elements are inextricably welded together.

407. *Ropetva rukkhāni yathā phalesī, mūle taruṃ chettu tameva icchasi/Tathūpamaṃ cittamidaṃ karosi, yaṃ maṃ aniccamhi cale niyuñjasi//*

408. Robert Louis Stevenson, Dr. Jekyll and Mr. Hyde.

409. EAM p. 93

410. CAEW, p. 224

This literature uses similes and metaphors to achieve quite a different objective from that of other literatures. For arousing erotic sentiments the moon is very dear to the Romantics because it inflames the passions of lovers, particularly of those enduring separation. But in the *Theragāthā* the moon has been put to a different use. The *theras* have closely observed the waxing and waning of the moon. To them, therefore, a person free from lust, ill-will and other negativities is like the moon that shines on the full moon day in a cloudless sky. Not only the moon but also the other objects of nature such as the sailing clouds in the sky, the verdurous woods and the graceful peacock have been used not to arouse passions but to help the *theras* sit in meditation and attain *nibbāna*. Such objects of nature are not used to excite passions in the *theras* but they are used to inspire them to progress on the path of *sādhanā*.

The spring season, which is very suitable for arousing erotic passions in most of the world literature, is put to a sublime use here.

"Now crimson glow the trees, dear Lord, and cast
Their ancient foliage in quest of fruit" [411]

This is a beautiful description of the spring season. The trees casting their old leaves in quest of fruit is a visual image original enough to be compared with such description in any other world literature. The *theras* feel inspired to make a quest for the Great Fruit (*nibbāna*). To know more about how nature is described in Pāli literature one is referred to my essay on Nature in the Theragāthā.[412]

Pāli literature is rich in similes, metaphors and parables, which are born out of inner experiences either of the Buddha or of his disciples. A man full of sensual desires is like a wet piece of wood in water; one who is partly rid of them is like a wet piece of wood out of water but one who is completely rid of them is like a dry piece of wood on land and away from water. How can one produce fire by rubbing together the first two kinds of pieces of wood? But by rubbing together the two pieces of wood of the third kind fire can immediately be produced.[413] The Buddha says, with the help of these apt similes, that so long as there is sensual desire in one, one is far away from *nibbāna*.

---

411. *Aṅgārinodāni dumā bhadante, phalesino chadanaṃ vippahāya/Te accimantova pabhāsayanti, samayo mahāvira bhāgī rasānam//*

Dumāni phullāni manoramāni, samantato sabbadisā pavanti/...

Pattaṃ pahāya phalamāsasānā, kālo ito pakkamanāya vīra//...

412. Angraj Chaudhary, Essays on Buddhism and Pali Literature, Eastern Book Linkers, Delhi,1994,pp. 136-153

413. M2 (See *Bodhirājakumāra Sutta*).

The complete destruction of desires is compared to a palm tree, which has been rendered baseless, which cannot sprout again.

Man asking metaphysical questions such as whether the world is eternal or not eternal, finite or not finite is compared to a man struck with an arrow who will not let the doctor take out the arrow unless he answers all sorts of irrelevant questions which have no bearing on relieving him from pain. [414]

According to Kumārakassapa's mother, who took ordination after delivering Kumārakassapa, this body is full of filth and dirt. So if what is inside were to come outside we would always have to protect it from crows and dogs.

"Sace imassa kāyassa, anto bāhirako siyā/
Daṇḍaṃ nūna gahetvāna, kāke soṇe nivāraye"//[415]

What is there in this body, which one can call beautiful? Ambapālī uses apt similes to describe the great change that has been brought about by her old age. What were beautiful once are now loathsome and ugly.[416]

That man's life is very rare has been aptly illustrated by giving the example of a one-eyed tortoise[417] that lives in the sea and comes out once every hundred years. A yoke with one hole in it floats on the water from north to south and from east to west as the wind blows. Is it possible for the tortoise to put its neck in the hole of the yoke? It is almost impossible. Similar is the case of one to be born as a man. Man's life is indeed very rare.

This rare life should not be wasted. How this rare life is wasted has been explained by the parable of a person wounded by an arrow, the metaphor mentioned above. A kind doctor is called in to pull out the arrow from his body and relieve him from pain but he says to the doctor that unless he answers questions put to him he will not allow him to pull out the arrow. The questions that he asks are not relevant.[418]

In short, Pāli literature is great literature not only because it conveys the great and sublime message of the Buddha, which he gave out of his own experiences but also because of the similes, metaphors and parables that he and his disciples used to clearly and powerfully describe their feelings and experiences. The Buddha showed the path and his disciples walked on it and liberated themselves from the bondage, fever and fret of life. If one walks on the Noble Eightfold Path one cannot only observe social ethics to

414. M2 *Cūlamālunkya Sutta*

415. ApA2.228

416. Thi See the *gāthās* of Ambapālī

417. M3.207

418. M2 (See *Cūlamālunkya Sutta*).

live happily and peacefully but also cultivate values like loving kindness and compassion that can go a long way in ennobling and chastening one's life. It can also help one to, at least, minimize his suffering, if not completely eliminate it.

Mammaṭa says that *kāvya* is written for fame, wealth, practical instructions and for achieving good.[419] The Buddha and his disciples had no such materialistic ends in view. The exclusive aim of Pāli literature is to enable one to realize peace and happiness, which is the highest good.

Pāli literature can go a long way in giving a new definition of *kāvya* as 'Death of a Salesman' by Arthur Miller changed the definition of tragedy.[420] Mammaṭa's definition is not comprehensive. Because Pāli literature chiefly delineates the sentiment of quietude (*ṣānta rasa*), deals with the universal laws of nature and depicts reality as it is (*yathābhūtajñāna*), so it can be defined as '*niyatikṛtaniyamasahitāṃ*. Its concern is only to depict and describe the universal law of nature in action, firmly rooted in reality, but the language used and similes employed are certainly vivid--engaging the reader's imagination like the best of poetry.

T.S. Eliot in his essay on 'Goethe as the Sage[421] says that "the true sage is rarer than true poets, and when the two gifts, that of wisdom and that of poetic speech, are found in the same man, you have the great poet. It is poets of this kind, who belong not merely to their own people but to the world." The Buddha and his disciples–the *theras* and *therīs*–have both the gifts of wisdom and poetic speech and therefore Pāli literature belongs to the whole world.

---

419. *Mammaṭa, Kāvyaprakāśa, Kāvyaṃ yaśase arthakṛte, vyavahāravide śivetarakṣataye/*

420. AMIMTVol. 40 no. 3, Fall 1960, pp. 329-340

421. OPP, p. 207

Ethicization of the Concept of Beauty: A Great Contribution by the Buddha

If one looks at the concept of beauty according to the Buddha, it will not take him long to see that his concept of beauty is not physical. What he says about physical beauty can be summarized in the following *gāthā*:

> *"Na chaviyā sundaro hoti, na chaviyā hoti asundaro/*
> *Kammunā sundaro hoti, kammunā hoti asundaro"//*

It is true that physical beauty is what attracts one first. But why is it that the Buddha does not put a premium on it? He expressly says, "Beauty is nothing to me, neither the beauty of the body nor that that comes of dress."[422] It is clear from this that he does not give any importance to physical beauty. If the physical beauty that one is endowed with is not valued by him, how can he value the beauty gained by beautifying things such as clothes, jewellery, garlands and sandalwood powder? He would certainly not give any importance to beauty acquired even by such means as plastic surgery.

Beauty is a quality that gives us pleasure. 'Symmetry, order and proportion'[423] constitute beauty, says Aristotle, as they appeal aesthetically to our sense of seeing. When all limbs of a person are symmetrical and proportionate, when he has a certain magnitude, he looks beautiful. But because this beauty does not last and is in a constant state of flux, how can it be valued highly? Symmetry, order and proportion may be the prerequisites for architectural beauty, but as far as human beauty is concerned, they are not the essential characteristics. Human beauty, unlike architectural beauty, is constantly changing as it is influenced by human emotions. In the first place it is very short-lived and changes with time, and secondly it is every moment influenced by emotions such as anger, jealousy, etc. quite unlike the beauty of a non-living thing. Keeping this in mind, the judges who select Miss Universe or Miss India take into consideration not only the physical beauty but also the qualities of the head and heart of those who take part in the Beauty Contest. Of what use is the physical beauty of a girl if she has no grey matter in her head and no generosity and compassion in her heart?

The Buddha realized with his three kinds of *pariññā* the transitory nature of physical beauty.[424] He also knew well that as it is the first thing

422. BGB, p. 324.
423. Aristotle, Metaphysics
424. MA 1. p. 32

to attract people and cause passions in them to arise-- infatuating them; making them mad, proud and arrogant; hindering them from appreciating the noble values of life like love, sympathy and humility- it is not to be valued highly. Swayed by their passions, people go astray and commit many unwholesome actions. Ordinary mortals are sometimes so overpowered by physical beauty that they behave like animals and are a danger to society. How can there be peace and harmony in society if there are such persons in it? As physical beauty makes people proud, vain and glorious it is not to be trusted because one knows that these are not good qualities to be cultivated.

It is for these reasons that the Buddha does not give much importance to physical beauty. There are several instances in the *Tipiṭaka* where he reveals his attitude towards it. Abhirūpanandā was very proud of her perfect figure and would not go to the Buddha even when he wanted her to come to him for instruction. What the Buddha says to her about this body reveals once and for all his attitude towards physical beauty. It is 'diseased, impure and rotten.'[425] He asks her to develop the concentration of mind to meditate on the unpleasant. If she does so she will 'cast out the latent tendency to conceit', will not burn with the fire of sensual desires and will become cool and calm. Aḍḍhakāsī was a sex worker, very proud of her beautiful figure. Her pride grew more and more as many townspeople had fixed her price high and made her beyond the reach of ordinary people. But very soon she came to realize the ephemeral nature of her beauty and was disgusted with it:

> "But irksome now is all my loveliness;
> I weary of it disillusioned".[426]

Vimalā, a courtesan, was also proud of her perfect form and being conscious of 'the bloom of her beauty'[427] felt intoxicated.

'Intoxicated by my good complexion, my figure, beauty and fame'[428] she felt proud of her youth and despised other women. By ornamentation and decoration, she enhanced her beauty. But when she realized the true nature of physical beauty, which is subject to 'Time's scythe', she developed non-attachment (*nirveda*) and applied herself assiduously to attaining the ineffable *nibbāna.*

Khemā, the queen consort of Bimbisāra, was also very proud of her beauty and she would not visit the Buddha because he talked about beauty

425. EV, Thi 82
426. Psalms EB, verse 26
427. ibid., verse 52
428. EV, Thi 72

in disparaging terms. Once it so happened that she went to the Buddha and saw a celestial nymph waiting upon him. That nymph was far more beautiful than she. As soon as she saw her, her pride was gone and she became humbled. Not only this, the Buddha with his mystic power showed her that even celestial beauty also passes from youth to old age. As a result, the nymph came to have broken teeth, grey hair and a face full of wrinkles. Realization dawned upon Khemā that if celestial beauty were so transitory, what to speak of the worldly beauty like her? With this realization, she regarded her body as vile, a 'foul seat of disease and corruption.'[429]

Ambapālī—'this once famous Thais'[430] of India--was the embodiment of perfect beauty, nay the very personification of it. The description of her beauty from top to toe is very powerfully given by Ambapālī herself in her *gāthās*. Her hair was glossy and black. The curls of her hair looked like the down of the bee. It was very fragrant, as fragrant as a casket of perfumes. Her eyebrows looked as beautiful as the crescents nicely painted by artists, her eyes shone brilliantly like jewels--long and black, her nose was delicate and pointed, her teeth looked as beautiful as the colour of the plantain bud, her voice was sweet like that of a cuckoo, her neck was as polished as a conch-shell, her arms were round and cylindrical, her hands with golden rings in the fingers were beautiful, her breasts were beautiful--swelling, close together and lofty--her body was beautiful like a well-polished sheet of gold, her thighs were like the trunks of elephant and so on, but old age changed them altogether. With this great change, realization dawns on her. She is disenchanted and disillusioned by her wasted charms. So, leaving aside all her pride and conceit and thoroughly realizing the vanity of physical allure, she is convinced of the truth that the Buddha teaches, develops non-attachment (*nirveda*) and becomes 'cool and quenched.'

The Buddha finds nothing glorious in physical beauty. In most cases it is a snare which causes catastrophe; entraps men and women, taking them to their doom and destruction. What do men generally see in a woman's form? They see in it the five strands of sensual pleasure like sights, sounds, tastes, smells and things to touch. In one of the *suttas* of the *Aṅguttara Nikāya* the Buddha says: "Bhikkhus, I do not see even one other form that so obsesses the mind of a man as the form of a woman."[431] A man's heart is enslaved by the sound (voice), scent, savour and touch of a woman. In the same way: "Bhikkhus, I do not see even one other form that so obsesses the mind of a woman as the form of a man." In the same way there is no sound, no odor, no taste and no touch that so obsesses the mind

429. Psalm EB Thi 139

430. Psalms EB, Introduction p xl.

431. NDB, p. 89

of a woman as those of a man.[432] From this observation of the Buddha, it is clear that attraction to a man's or a woman's body is fraught with danger. These five strands of sensual pleasure arouse great passion and this is what physical beauty leads to. Although one does not find women saying that a man while going, standing, sitting or lying down, laughing, talking, or singing etc. will stop to ensnare the heart of a woman, it is clearly said that "Monks, a woman, even when going along, will stop to ensnare the heart of a man; whether standing, sitting or lying down, laughing, talking or singing, weeping, stricken or dying, a woman will stop to ensnare the heart of a man."[433]

Woman has been regarded as a veritable snare of Māra. Her physical beauty arouses only passion. Khema's is no exception. Māra in the form of a young man says to her, "you are young and beautiful, I also am young and in my prime. Come, Khemā, let us delight ourselves with the five-fold music."[434] Māra also tries to tempt Upacālā with these words:

"Why do you not approve of birth? One who is born enjoys sensuous pleasures. Enjoy the delights of sensuous pleasures."[435]

That physical beauty prompts one to commit rape is clear from what Māra says to Uppalavaṇṇā: " Going up to a tree with a well-flowered top, you stand alone at the foot of the tree; you have not even any companion; O, Child, are you not afraid of rogues?"[436]

Subhā Jīvakambavanikā's eyes were so beautiful that they increased more and more the craving for sensual pleasure of the rogue who stopped her while she was going to the delightful Jīvakamba wood. He asked her to take delight in carnal pleasures with him. On being asked what he found beautiful in her body which is 'full of corpses, filling the cemetery, of a breaking nature' he replied that "your eyes are, indeed like those of Turī, like those of a kinnari inside a mountain; having seen your eyes my delight in sensual pleasures increases more.'[437] He further said that her eyes were "like the bud of a blue lotus, spotless, like gold";[438] she had long eyelashes, she was of pure gaze. He said that he was captivated by her beautiful eyes.

Besides being a cause for rape, physical beauty is thought to be a very effective snare to entrap young men. This is clear from what the courtesan says to Sundarasamudda. She is very beautiful, attractive and charming.

---

432. ibid., p. 90
433. BGS part III, P.T.S., p. 56
434. EV Thi 139
435. ibid. 190
436. ibid. 230
437. ibid. 381
438. ibid. 382

Speaking softly and sweetly and with a smile, she says to him: "You are young to have gone forth. Abide in my teaching; enjoy human sensual pleasures."[439] But high-minded Sundarasamudda does not even reply to the courtesan's proposal.

It is clear from these examples that physical beauty arouses passion, persuades people to enjoy sensual and sensuous pleasures and makes them mad and burning to commit rape or other kinds of sexual misconduct. But those who see through this physical beauty with wisdom are not tempted by it. The Buddha says that this body is 'encased in skin and full of impurities, from the soles of the feet up and from the crowns of the head down. An account of what this body has inside makes one inclined to loathe it– the description has a nauseating effect on him.

Kumarakassapa's mother's description of the body is graphically terrifying and nauseating. If what is inside were to come out one would always have to guard oneself from crows and dogs.[440]

There is another point of view from which the Buddha describes physical beauty. Like all objects of the world, this body is in flames and every part of it also is in flames. They are burning and burning with the fires of craving, aversion and ignorance. When one comes to realize this with his higher wisdom and intuitive knowledge, all scales from his eyes fall and instead of being attracted by transitory objects, he develops non-attachment to them.

The Buddha, like Plato and other idealist philosophers, is not concerned with the transcendental concept of beauty. Plato believes in a world of 'Ideas'. Absolute beauty is also an Idea. All beautiful objects of the world partake of this Idea of beauty and all point to it. In the Phaedrus and in the Symposium, he proceeds from bodily beauty to ideal beauty and goes even beyond this to beautiful forms, beautiful practices and beautiful notions and ultimately, he contemplates 'the vast sea of beauty.' Plato's concept of beauty is metaphysical and ideal, but how can this concept be applied to human beings whom we want to judge as beautiful? No human being is the embodiment of the Idea of beauty as conceived by Plato. Whether a human being is beautiful should be judged not by his physical looks alone but also by his actions, by the human qualities he is endowed with. A human being may have a perfect figure, may have 'symmetry, order and proportion', but may be cruel and cantankerous. Instead of doing good to society, he may always think of doing harm to it and may even go as far as caring only for himself. The Buddha looks for beauty in human beings. He is not at all

439. K.R. Norman, The Elders' Verses P.T.S. 1971, Th 461

440. *Sace imassa kāyassa, anto bāhirako siyā/Daṇḍaṃ nūna gahetvāna, kāke soṇe nivaraye* verse by Kumārakassapamātā

concerned with the metaphysical beauty as Plato was. He does not conceive of beauty itself as a separate entity, different from a beautiful object or beautiful human being. And he does not consider him or her beautiful who has physical 'symmetry, order and proportion.' Beauty for him is an ethical concept, and one who is ethically good, one who has got rid of craving, aversion and ignorance and made his mind free from the different kinds of defilements that make him ugly is really beautiful.

One has seen why physical beauty is not held in high esteem by the Buddha. In the first place, it arouses passion. Secondly, it makes one proud, conceited and vain-- so much so that he belittles those who are not beautiful. It also makes him very selfish.

Physical beauty attracts people and makes them do more harm than good. "Bhikkhus, I do not see even one other thing on account of which unarisen sensual desire arises and arisen sensual desire increases and expands so much as the mark of the attractive (*Subha Nimitta*)."[441] Physical beauty has its limitations. One who is physically beautiful but who is devoid of intellect becomes boring; devoid of softness and good disposition becomes repulsive. If a physically beautiful person has anger and hatred as the ruling passion, he or she does not attract anybody. It is for these reasons that in beauty contests the parameters of who should be regarded as beautiful have changed over the years and the qualities of the head and the heart are taken into consideration.

Physical beauty is ephemeral. It is transitory. Therefore, it is not dependable. The Buddha has given so many examples to show how physical beauty is in a constant state of flux.

Physical beauty depends upon one's parentage and on the genes that one inherits from one's parents. It also depends on his past *kammas*–if one believes in the theory of *kamma* and rebirth. It is not in one's hands to become physically beautiful however much he tries and however much money he spends on beauty aids like massages, baths, creams, lotions, or even plastic surgery. Such aids to beauty have tremendous limitations.

His concept of beauty, like that of Thomas Aquinas, is no different from his ideal of the highest good. According to him, handsome is that that handsome does (as said by Socrates) and who can be more beautiful than one who attains the *summum bonum* of life? From this point of view, goodness (*śivaṃ*) is not different from beauty (*sundaraṃ*). Thus, the Buddha gives an ethical dimension to beauty. According to him, a man acting under the influence of craving, aversion and ignorance is not beautiful. He may look physically beautiful having symmetry, harmony and proportion',

441. NDB, p. 90

but if he has craving and aversion, he will be like a festering lily which smells 'far worse than weeds', as Shakespeare rightly says:

> "For sweetest things turn sourest by their deeds,
> Lilies that fester smell far worse than weeds."[442]

In many of the *suttas* the Buddha explains his view of beauty. In the *Mallikā Sutta,* he shows who is really beautiful. He says that even if one is physically beautiful, he will not be truly beautiful if he is susceptible to anger. He still has the negativities of mind. Unless he purifies his mind, he cannot be called beautiful. Anger will make him ugly.

In the *Cūlakammavibhaṅga Sutta*[443] he makes it clear that displaying anger, hatred and bitterness cannot make one beautiful. One will look ugly with all these negativities. But if one is not of angry and irritable character and does not display anger, hatred and bitterness, one is beautiful. In the *Ājānīya Sutta* of the *Aṅguttara Nikāya* the Buddha explains what constitutes real beauty and how a monk is blessed with it. If a monk is moral, if he 'dwells restrained by the *Pātimokkhas,* possessed of good conduct and resort, seeing danger in minute faults. Having taken the training rules, he trains in them. It is in this way that a bhikkhu possesses beauty."[444]

One modern philosopher interprets beauty and ugliness in exactly the same way as the Buddha. "The ugliest ugliness is not that which disgusts us in objects of nature, in the swamp, the distorted trees, in toads and reptiles, google-eyed fish monsters and massive pachyderms, in rats and monkeys. (I do not admit the view of real ugliness implied in this enumeration); it is the egoism which reveals its madness in malicious and frivolous gesture, in the furrows drawn by passion, in the shifty look of the eye and in crime."[445]

Aldous Huxley, in one of his essays says that 'real beauty is as much an affair of the inner as of the outer self'.[446] He goes on to point out that 'the beauty of a porcelain jar is a matter of shape, of colour, of surface texture. The jar may be empty or tenanted by spiders, full of honey or stinking slime—it makes no difference to its beauty or ugliness. But a woman is alive, and her beauty is, therefore, not skin deep. The surface of the human vessel is affected by the nature of its spiritual contents.'[447] He further says that he has seen women who are ravishingly lovely and may be called beautiful

442. Shakespeare Sonnet 94
443. M 1 *Cūlakammavibhaṅga Sutta*
444. NDB, p. 329
445. H Aes (Quoted on p. 402)
446. MANight, p. 152
447. ibid.

'by the standards of a connoisseur of porcelain. Their shape, their colour, their surface texture were perfect' yet they were not beautiful, because either they were empty or had some corruption. One could see through their spiritual emptiness or ugliness.

He goes on to say that 'There are numerous forms of psychological ugliness. There is an ugliness of stupidity, for example, of unawareness (distressingly common among pretty women). An ugliness also of greed, of lasciviousness, of avarice. All the deadly sins, indeed, have their own peculiar negation of beauty.'[448] How can they be called beautiful who commit deadly sins? Their physical beauty is bound to be affected, and it would be futile to look for some inner spiritual beauty in such people. So, he concludes that the beauty industry may be 'successful in prolonging the appearance of youth, of realizing or stimulating the symptoms of health, the campaign inspired by this cult remains fundamentally a failure. Its operations do not touch the deepest source of beauty—the experiencing soul.'

Although Huxley says almost the same thing about beauty as the Buddha said two thousand six hundred years ago, there is one basic difference between them. The Buddha says that beauty is not a matter of 'symmetry, harmony and proportion'—all yardsticks to judge somebody's external features, but beauty is a matter of what one contains within. Does one have qualities like love, compassion and sympathy? Is one free from anger, hatred and other defilements? If he has these qualities and if he is free from defilements he is really beautiful, although he may not have external symmetry, harmony and proportion. However, Huxley holds that 'for men and women to be beautiful, such social arrangements are necessary which give to every one of them an opportunity to live completely and harmoniously.' In other words, society is greatly responsible for the beauty of human beings. The Buddha, on the other hand, says that an individual is capable of attaining ethical and spiritual beauty by walking on the path of *sīla, samādhi* and *paññā.* He can extirpate all mental defilements that make him ugly. Achieving ethical beauty is in one's own hands, but for being physically beautiful one has to depend on parentage and on a conducive social atmosphere to live life fully and harmoniously.

This view of beauty as propounded by the Buddha can be regarded as a universal theory of beauty. No universal theory of physical beauty can be propounded inasmuch as perceptions differ from country to country and from region to region. There may be one type of look desirable to black people and another type of beauty desired by white people. The kinds of eyes, ears, nose, neck, arms, hips, waist, thighs, lips, teeth, face

448. ibid.

and hair regarded as beautiful in one country will not be regarded as such all over the world. A doe-eyed girl or a lotus-eyed girl or boy is regarded as beautiful only in India. It is not true of the girls and boys of black and Oriental races. Every race, or to be more precise every ethnic community, has its own concept of the physically beautiful. Fair complexion is an important criterion of physical beauty among the Aryan race but how can it be applied to Africans or Afro-Caribbeans?

By ethicizing the concept of beauty and making it more a matter of inside than of outside, the Buddha has given a theory of beauty which is universal, for who does not regard that human being as beautiful who lives a moral life, drives out all defilements--like anger, hatred and greed--and cultivates those exemplary qualities that the best of people live by.

ABOUT PARIYATTI

Pariyatti is dedicated to providing affordable access to authentic teachings of the Buddha about the Dhamma theory (*pariyatti*) and practice (*paṭipatti*) of Vipassana meditation. A 501(c)(3) nonprofit charitable organization since 2002, Pariyatti is sustained by contributions from individuals who appreciate and want to share the incalculable value of the Dhamma teachings. We invite you to visit www.pariyatti.org to learn about our programs, services, and ways to support publishing and other undertakings.

Pariyatti Publishing Imprints

Vipassana Research Publications (focus on Vipassana as taught by S.N. Goenka in the tradition of Sayagyi U Ba Khin)

BPS Pariyatti Editions (selected titles from the Buddhist Publication Society, copublished by Pariyatti in the Americas)

Pariyatti Digital Editions (audio and video titles, including discourses)

Pariyatti Press (classic titles returned to print and inspirational writing by contemporary authors)

Pariyatti enriches the world by

- disseminating the words of the Buddha,
- providing sustenance for the seeker's journey,
- illuminating the meditator's path.

www.ingramcontent.com/pod-product-compliance
Lightning Source LLC
Chambersburg PA
CBHW021048090426
42738CB00006B/243